AF339061

Keeping the Lights on

Paul Freund and Olav Kaarstad

Keeping the Lights on

Fossil Fuels in the Century of Climate Change

Universitetsforlaget

ISBN 978-82-15-01141-7

www.universitetsforlaget.no
Universitetsforlaget AS
P.O. Box 508 Sentrum
NO-0105 Oslo
Norway

Cover photo: NASA
Cover: Atle/Uniform
Design: Laboremus Prepress AS
Printed: PDC Tangen AS
Typeset: Sabon 11/16,5 pt.
Paper: 130 g Multiart Matt

Table of Contents

Table of Contents

Preface

This is a book about energy. Ten or twenty years ago such a book would most likely have been telling spectacular stories about the geopolitics of oil and natural gas, the less wonderful world of King Coal, and the birth and demise of nuclear energy. There is some of that in this book too but mainly it is a book about energy in a world increasingly affected by climate change. Since energy use is the main culprit in terms of human influences on the climate, taking a climate point of view makes the energy future look somewhat different from before.

Richard P. Feynman, one of the most influential physicists of the 20th century, said: "It is important to realize that, in physics today, we have no knowledge of what energy is. We only know that energy is conserved". In fact energy has many forms: motion, gravitational, heat, elastic, electrical, chemical, radiant, nuclear, and mass. It is something we can calculate but, so far, do not understand. So it is worth bearing Feynman's words in mind.

Not knowing what energy *is* may seem to be a slightly depressing starting point for a book such as this. We have, however, taken a practical approach, with the aim of sharing our understanding of where energy comes from, how it is used, and what could be done about tackling the problem of climate change. Our aim has been to write a book for a wide audience interested in such topics but not necessarily having much knowledge of them. With that in mind you will find only one equation (a very simple one in chapter 4), no tables and as few as possible specialised terms about energy.

We, the authors, met over a decade ago under the umbrella of the IEA Greenhouse Gas R&D Programme[1] (IEA GHG). At that time Olav Kaarstad had been the Norwegian representative on the executive committee since the start of the programme in 1991. Paul Freund came in as the new director of IEA GHG after many years of working with energy at BP. At an early stage we found that we shared many interests both within the fields of energy and climate and on other topics. The IEA GHG was (and still is) the global motor in analysing greenhouse gas emission abatement technologies on behalf of member countries and companies. Over the last few years, several people connected in various ways with IEA GHG have discussed writing a book together on the energy/climate topic. It all came to nothing, except for a few draft chapters at the bottom of various people's drawers. That is until Paul Freund ended his engagement with the IEA GHG and we decided to make the book happen.

For publishing we ended up in the good hands of Erik Juel of the Oslo University Press in Norway who shared our view on what this book should become.

Most books about energy topics have rather dull interiors, even if the text is well written. We had a goal of making this an interesting and thought-provoking book also in the visual sense; we wanted a lot of colourful illustrations to give more life to the energy and climate topics. Any author in contact with publishers can testify that this is a little like wishing for the moon. We were therefore happy to get the unconditional support of StatoilHydro – the employer of one of us (Kaarstad) – in the production of the graphs and drawings. This book represents, however, solely the views and opinions of the authors. Any blame - and we realise that there may be some - rests on the shoulders of the authors alone.

Elin Storsten has been responsible for making the illustrations. For this very demanding work, not made any easier by the authors, we would like to express our gratitude.

Our ambition has been to stimulate the reader to ask themselves good questions about energy and climate change. Answers are the easy part. It is the art of asking good questions that is difficult. To quote Aristotle: "The energy of the mind is the essence of life".

| Cheltenham, UK | June 2007 | Trondheim, Norway |
| *Paul Freund* | | *Olav Kaarstad* |

---

1   IEA Greenhouse Gas R&D Programme: http://www.ieagreen.org.uk/

Energy: the invisible commodity

Imagine you are driving a car. It suddenly runs out of fuel. You try calling for help using your mobile phone but the battery is flat. Common to both of these misfortunes is a lack of energy.

Energy is essential for modern society, but most forms of energy are invisible so their critical role in providing a vast range of services is easily overlooked. Nevertheless, we can recognise the effect energy has on us and on the world around us, even if we cannot always see it.

Fig. 1.1 Energy use permeates society but, mostly, energy is invisible

Energy comes in many forms

Sunshine provides heat and light, which are both forms of energy; burning fuel releases chemical energy; gravitational energy may be released in the form of running water, which itself has kinetic energy; sound is energy, as is radiation.

In our imaginary example, energy was not available to the car driver because of a lack of prior action, namely refuelling or recharging. Luckily, there are not many occasions in the modern world when we, as individuals, have to make a specific decision to obtain a supply of energy. More often, such supplies are provided under long-term contracts for fuel, such as electricity or gas, which require no action on our part other than throwing a switch or paying a bill.

When we burn fuel, we release chemical energy stored in the fuel which we can capture to boil water. We can harness the kinetic energy of moving water in a waterwheel which can turn an electrical generator. We capture sunlight in a solar panel which gets warm due to an increase in the amount of thermal energy it holds.

Although we talk about *producing* and *consuming* energy, to the scientist energy cannot be produced or used up. It can only be converted from one form to another. However, to a child in a darkened room wanting light, or a parent wanting to cook a meal, or a teenager wanting to listen to a CD, energy is just a

Useful energy

When energy is used, for example in a boiler, only some of it appears as useful output. The rest is described as being lost. In reality, this energy is discharged into the environment as low-grade heat. So the energy is not lost but it is no longer *useful*. A key aspect of the usefulness of energy is the temperature at which it is provided. Thus a power station may convert half of the energy in its fuel into electricity; the rest is ejected into the environment at a temperature of about 40°C, which is too low to be useful for any purpose. So it is described as lost. This is closely allied with the concept of energy efficiency, which is discussed below.

Fig. 1.2   Waste heat. A coal-fired power station such as this emits more than half of the energy in its fuel as waste heat from the cooling towers.

commodity, something which provides a service that they use much like any other. To the user, energy appears to be used once and then it is gone. Governments may exhort us to "save energy" but our use of energy is increasing each year, not because we want more energy but because we want more of the services that energy supplies.

Does it matter that the two pictures (popular and scientific) are so different? Can they be reconciled? Why is energy so important to modern society? Where does energy come from? Will it be so readily available in the future? Should we be concerned if it is not? In this book, we aim to explore these questions and provide some answers.

A brief history of energy supply and use

Stone-age men and women were happy if they had enough food and water, and somewhere safe to live. Meeting those basic needs would have required a modicum of energy, perhaps for cooking and for some warmth in winter, which they achieved by burning wood. As humans became more familiar with the use of fire, they found they could smelt metal ores to produce implements. The development of charcoal, made from wood, provided a more effective means of supplying energy for metal-working. Charcoal was the first example of an *energy carrier* – where one means of supplying energy, in this case wood, was converted into a different form that was more convenient or more effective for the user. Various types of energy carrier play a major role in supplying the modern world with energy. However, the conversion of the original fuel into an energy carrier necessarily "loses" some energy during the process. This is part of the price to be paid for the convenience of energy carriers.

For a Roman patrician, being able to harness fuel for heating provided the comfort of bath houses and warm buildings, despite the inclement weather of the northern European colonies. However, wealthy Roman families did not concern themselves with the actual process of heating since the fuelling of their under-floor heating systems, the hypocaust, would have been done for them by others. Thus the consumption of a service, in this case heating, was separated from the supply of energy – the start of a trend which has continued to this day.

It was not until many years after the collapse of the Roman Empire that the energy consumed by an individual again approached that of a patrician. Up until the Industrial Revolution, energy was used for basic functions (heat and light)

Slavery as an energy source

Slavery was often essential to the economy, an accepted feature of all ancient civilizations. The philosophers of Greece did not consider the institution of slavery as morally objectionable. Classical Greeks often referred to their slaves in terms which placed them on a level with working animals. Both domesticated animals and slaves were used as sources of energy, practices which may have developed with the introduction of agriculture ten thousand years ago.

Fig. 1.3 Slavery has long been seen as a source of energy.

With few exceptions, slaves in ancient Greece were treated humanely but slavery in the Roman Empire differed in several important aspects from that of ancient Greece. In Rome, the masters had more power over the slaves, including that of life and death. Little is known about the everyday lives of slaves but, in general, it was much worse to be a field slave than a domestic slave. The field hands, or *familia rustica,* were the largest section of the slave population. On one estate alone, as many as 40,000 slaves worked as ploughmen, ditchers and foresters. Slaves like these, having a life expectancy of about ten years in the field, provided Rome with its greatest source of economic wealth.

A single slave could produce between 60 and 100 watts, the equivalent of the power used by a light bulb. This meant that the highest concentration of power under human control – thousands of slaves at a construction site – reached no more than 100 kilowatts (kW) in sustained effort. One hundred kilowatts is similar to the maximum power of the motor of a modern family car.

Since Roman times, the institution of slavery has taken many forms, ranging from those captured in war, to those born of a slave mother, to various forms of serfs or tenants working on farms owned by the aristocracy. Even today, there are forms of servitude similar to slavery affecting large numbers of people in a few areas of the world.

The slavery in North and South America has probably been the best documented. Through the slave trade with Africa, 10 to 15 million Africans were sold as slaves. Of those that survived the journey, 38% went to Brazil, 17% to the Spanish speaking countries of South America, 40% to the West Indies, and 6% to the USA. This trade mainly took place in the 18th century. Denmark was the first country to abolish it in 1792, followed by Britain in 1807, and the United States in 1808. In Brazil, slavery was not abolished until 1888.

Chapter 1 | Energy: the invisible commodity

Fig. 1.4 A hypocaust or caldarium at the Roman Baths in Bath, England. The floor has been removed to reveal the space through which the hot air flowed tc heat the floor tiles.

similar to how it had been used since prehistoric times. The Industrial Revolution was marked by the development of industrial machinery which was critically dependent on reliable supplies of energy from coal and water. So, from that time onwards, there was a considerable expansion of the range of uses of energy.

After the Industrial Revolution, the growth of cities to house workers meant that new energy carriers had to be developed to provide lighting in factories and heat for cooking in homes. Town gas, manufactured from coal, could be burnt in a mantle to produce a clear light. This was later replaced by electricity, also made using coal or water power.

Energy in the 21st century

Energy is the unseen lifeblood of modern society. In an industrialised country in the 21st century, we use energy to alter the environment in which we live – we make buildings more comfortable by heating or by air-conditioning. We use ligh-

Energy efficiency

The concept of energy efficiency reflects how much useful service is provided in relation to the energy consumed. Thus, an electric motor may convert 95% of the electricity it consumes into the mechanical work of turning the shaft. It would be said to be 95% efficient. On the other hand, an internal combustion engine may be only 10% to 30% efficient in converting the energy in its fuel into mechanical work, but there may be other reasons why it is more attractive for some applications than an electric motor.

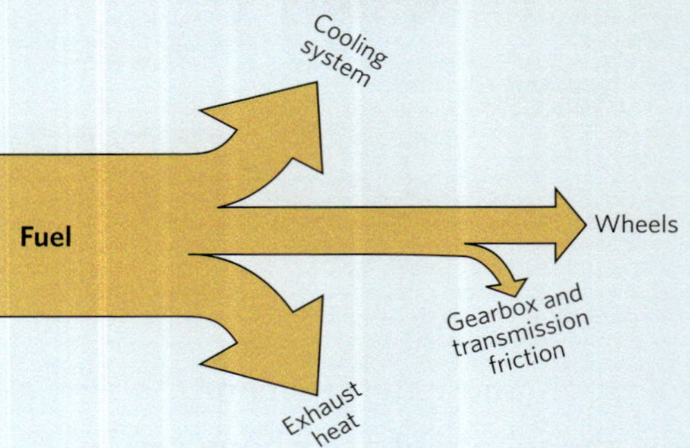

Fig. 1.5 Energy flows into and out of a car engine.

The efficiency of a car engine depends on the temperature difference between the highest temperature in the engine and the temperature of its waste heat (e.g. the exhaust or the cooling water). Thus, the higher the temperature at which energy is available, the more useful it will be, and the more efficient will be the engine.

The term "energy efficiency" can also be used to describe the performance of a system, for example the energy used in heating a building. In that case, the energy efficiency of the building not only reflects the efficiency of the heating appliance, but also the standard of insulation and the level of ventilation, as well as heat gains from appliances and sunshine. All these determine the amount of energy needed to achieve the desired level of comfort.

The concept of energy efficiency is also used in an even broader sense – someone may make a phone call instead of travelling to a meeting; a builder may use wood instead of concrete to build a house. Both of these result in less energy being used for very similar outcomes, which may be described as energy efficient. However, it is difficult for the individual to measure this change in energy use – it is something which can only really be done at the national level.

This indicates that the concept of energy efficiency must be considered carefully, to ensure that the appropriate context is understood.

ting so we can see better, especially after sunset or in places away from natural light. By refrigerating our food, using energy, we can keeper it longer before we cook it, another use of energy.

We use energy to travel and to move goods. Whether it is a family car which covers 300 km in 3 hours, or a passenger aeroplane which uses a similar amount of fuel in 30 seconds and can travel a similar distance in 30 minutes carrying 200 people, most forms of transport rely on a convenient (and relatively inexpensive) supply of energy to move us faster than we could do on our own.

Chapter 1 | Energy: the invisible commodity

Natural gas is widely used for heating and cooking in industrialised countries whilst biofuels are widely used in developing countries

Electricity is used for lighting and mass transport. It is mostly generated by coal

Road and air transport rely on oil-based fuels

Fig. 1.6   Some uses of the main energy carriers and fuels

Energy is essential for modern communication and entertainment. As well as recharging the battery in the mobile phone, the whole of the phone system depends on energy – electricity for the transmitters on the masts, for the control system which locates the phone, and for the computer which calculates a bill for using the system.

Similarly, entertainment depends on energy for lighting the theatre, for sending signals to the television, for putting a communications satellite in orbit or for operating a DVD player.

More dramatic are some of the industrial uses of energy. The energy used in melting iron or rolling steel or casting glass makes a striking visual spectacle. Around one third of all primary energy is used for industrial purposes[1]. However, much of it is hidden from view – energy is used for making plastics and other chemicals, for making fertilisers and cement, and for refining aluminium, amongst other things. Energy is key to these processes and industry goes to great lengths to use it as efficiently as possible, with minimum waste, which is why most of these industries do not make a spectacle out of using energy.

Today's list of energy uses is much longer than a similar list would have been during the Roman Empire. Modern industrialised societies have long since passed the stage at which energy is simply used to provide the necessities of life. The demand

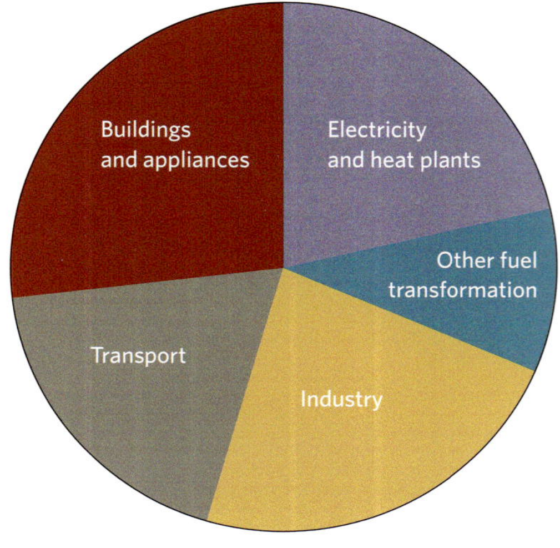

Fig. 1.7 How the world used energy in 2003 (Based on data from Energy Technology Perspectives, 2006, OECD/IEA, Paris).

for energy has risen as new activities have been developed; the cost of supplying energy has fallen over the years; the efficiency with which energy is used has improved, which has also reduced the cost of using it. Not surprisingly, this has increased the demand for energy – not because we want to use energy but because we want to enjoy the opportunities that using energy brings.

Making use of energy

The single-family car is a good example of the sort of opportunities which modern technology offers for increasing the use of energy. Major improvements in vehicle technology have happened in living memory – the internal combustion engine, burning petrol as its fuel, has powered the family car for a century but its leading role was not always so clear. At the start of the 20th century, there were as many electric vehicles as there were oil- or steam-powered ones. A clue about the future came from the first 48-hour endurance race organised by the Automobile Club de France in 1895 which was convincingly won by a car using an internal combustion engine. One of the factors which helped was the limited space occupied by fuel storage (in today's compact family car, fuel only occupies about 2% of the space provided for the passengers). Although the 1895 race may have given an indication of the eventual winner, it actually took many years to see off

Fig. 1.8 Growth in UK energy use per capita over 100 years showing the differences between the various uses.

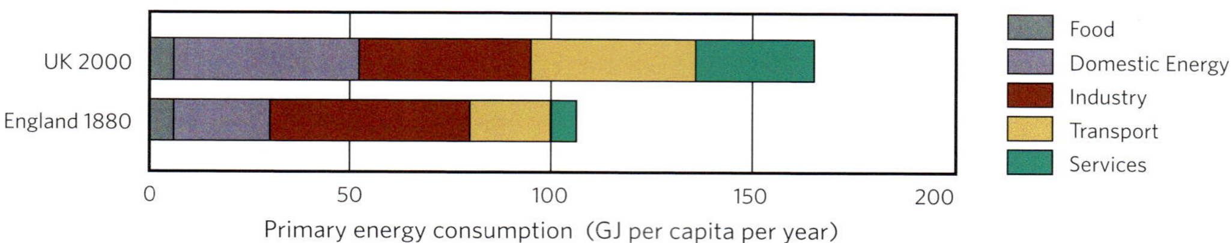

the competition – even the model-T Ford, the first mass-produced car, could run on either alcohol or petrol.

A long period of improvement followed during which engine efficiency, amongst other things, improved. Burning the fuel more efficiently helped reduce emissions of partly-combusted fuel. The development of tetra-ethyl lead as a fuel additive enabled higher engine performance. However, some decades later, environmental concerns about lead meant it had to be removed again (once alternatives were available).

The increase in the number of vehicles on the road led to pressure for further emissions control, which was achieved by the introduction of 3-way catalysts to deal with any non-combusted fuel as well as oxides of nitrogen (the use of catalysts was not feasible until lead additives had been removed from the fuel). However, the introduction of catalysts reduced the efficiency of engine systems, leading to an increase in fuel consumption.

Increasing fuel prices and the stricter regulation of emissions have been met by the refinement of engine management systems and improvements in engine design. A new option, the hybrid vehicle, avoids running the engine except when this can be done at maximum efficiency. Many alternatives to the internal combustion engine have been recognised, but it is not yet clear whether any of them will come to dominate the vehicle market, and it is certainly not clear which one that might be.

So improvements in technology have led to more efficient vehicles, with lower emissions and lower running costs. In turn this has led to greater numbers and increasing vehicle sizes. Coupled with measures to control emissions, fuel consumption in the transport sector has risen, a trend which is continuing with no end in sight.

Another good example of developments in end-use technology is lighting. The first lighting appliances were candles or lamps using animal fat. Mineral oil gained attention because it provided cleaner lighting – this was before it was used as a vehicle fuel. Town gas (made from coal) improved the quality of the light but, when electricity (also made from coal) became available, the light this produced was much more attractive so it quickly took over the role of lighting buildings. Since then the efficiency and controllability of electric lighting has steadily improved. Even so, the original version of the technology (i.e. filament lamps) still serves a large proportion of the general lighting market whilst newer technologies, such as fluorescent lamps, halogen lamps and light emitting diodes, have gained market share only in particular niches, even though they are more efficient.

Thus, the means of using energy, as with other technologies, passes from a phase of initial competition amongst many types to a smaller number of technologies which dominate the industry. Mass production enables costs to be reduced whilst broader requirements are introduced into the design, e.g. emission control and size or speed. Eventually alternatives develop but the established technology is so dominant that it can fend off many competitors, adapting all the while by improving fuel economy and reducing emissions until finally it reaches a limit. This limit may be forced on the industry by external concerns such as environmental protection, or for some other reason. As a new technology comes to dominate the market, the whole cycle may start again.

Delivering energy to the user

As individuals, we place the greatest value on the energy carriers which are convenient, clean, safe and easily deliverable. Major users of energy, such as steel mills or chemical plants, are concerned more than anything else about the reliability and the price of energy. Where we have a choice, we select the energy carrier which best suits our particular needs. For example, consider the fan motors which are an integral part of many pieces of equipment at home and in the office. Motors could be run on other energy carriers, e.g. oil or gas, but electric motors are quiet to run, reliable and can be controlled easily. In addition, they are efficient ways of using energy at the point of application. For these reasons, electricity is used in buildings to power motors for air conditioning, to operate lifts (essential technology for tall buildings), and to power the pumps which carry water to every floor of the building.

Fig. 1.9 Skyscrapers in Hong Kong.

Chapter 1 | Energy: the invisible commodity

Increasing use of electricity

Electricity is convenient and easy to use. A turn of the switch and it is on. Such convenience determines its popularity. This is despite the price of electricity being quite high, for each unit of energy delivered, compared with the alternatives. Global electricity consumption has been rising and is set to at least double by 2030, according to most published projections. This growth surpasses the growth rate of any of the sources of primary energy, e.g. coal, oil, or natural gas. The trend of rapidly growing electricity use seems set to continue as consumers in the developing countries acquire the appliances that make life easier for their counterparts in the industrialised countries. Developing countries, such as China and India, are projected to account for over 70% of the increase in electricity use in the decades ahead. This is reflected in Fig. 1.10 which shows that, because of their faster growth rate, developing countries, will overtake the industrialised (OECD) countries as users of electricity sometime between 2010 and 2020.

Today, in the industrialised countries, about 60% of all electricity is consumed in the residential and commercial buildings sector. The remainder is consumed in the industrial sector, except for about 1% used by mass transit systems.

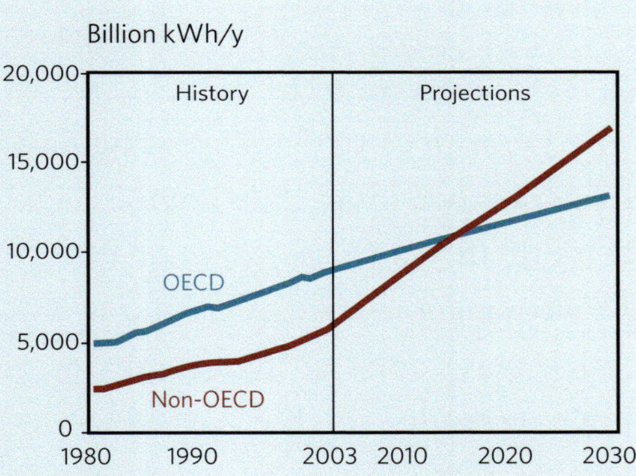

Fig. 1.10 Electricity consumption in OECD countries will be overtaken by the consumption in non-OECD countries in the near future.

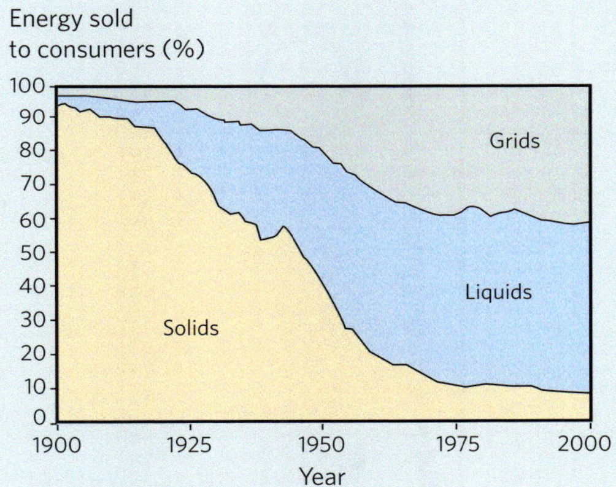

Fig. 1.11 The changing form of the energy delivered to consumers in the United States over 100 years. Solids consist of biomass and coal; liquids consist of petroleum products; grids include electricity, gas, and district heating.

All of these services could be provided by other means but electric motors provide a better solution to these tasks. Only the largest motors in specialised industrial applications use any other form of energy carrier. One quarter of electricity in the US is used by industrial motors[2] and it is thought[3] that another quarter may be used by other motors.

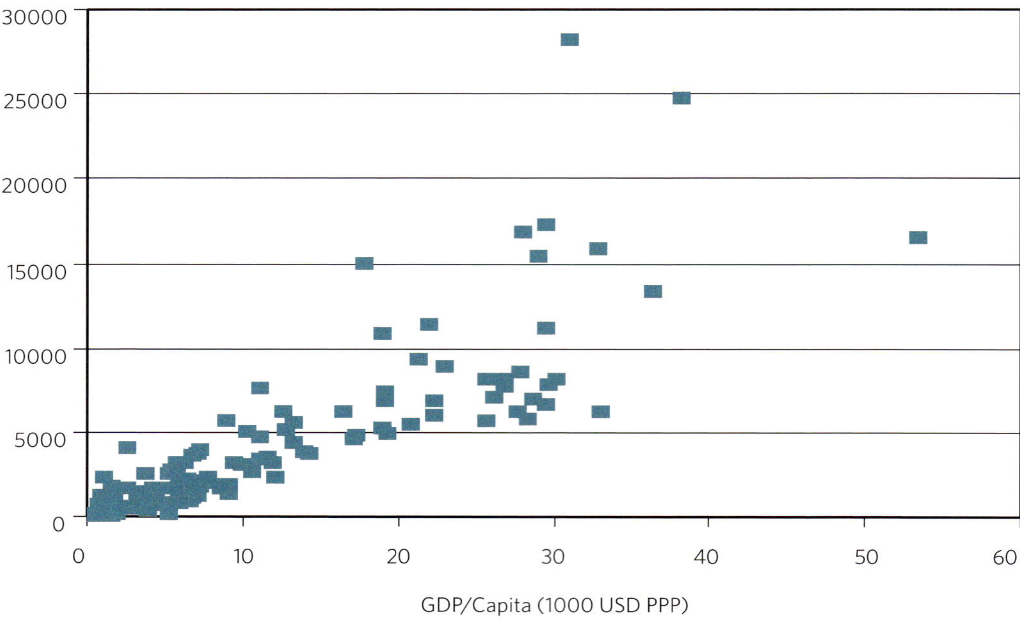

Fig. 1.12   Electricity use tends to rise with higher national income (GDP/Capita).

In addition to being used in motors, electricity has taken over the delivery of services in many areas of life (e.g. heating, lighting), as well as enabling a host of new services whose operation would not be possible without it (e.g. computers, televisions, stereos). The range of services provided by electrical technologies continues to expand. Electricity is a key means of delivering energy to the user, accounting for 18% of all energy delivered in the UK[4].

Electricity is attractive to the user not only because of its flexibility but also because it can be generated from a wide range of primary energy sources. Other energy carriers play a large part in delivering energy to the user, but tend to be less flexible. For example, although it is certainly possible to heat individual houses using wood, this would be better done via a communal heating service provided to a large number of buildings[5]. But this principle can only be carried so far – it seems unlikely, for example, that nuclear energy would be acceptable as a source of heating for buildings even in community-wide projects.

Production of energy carriers

Electricity is not available in the natural world, so it has to be generated from primary energy. This energy may come from a fossil fuel such as coal, gas or oil, or from a natural fuel such as wood or the wind. Or it could come from harnessing the energy made available by splitting uranium nuclei (nuclear fission).

Other energy carriers have a form much closer to the original fuels – petrol and diesel oil are widely used energy carriers which are extracted from crude oil. Increasingly, the chemical processing of crude oil is being used to make more of the desired energy carriers, as will be described in the next chapter.

The natural gas delivered to the user is virtually no different from what is extracted from the gas field – some cleaning up is done before the gas is piped to market and a "stench" agent is added to make it detectable in case of leaks, but relatively little is altered when preparing this energy carrier.

Another important energy carrier in some parts of the world is heat – in major cities such as Copenhagen, Stockholm and New York, heat is produced centrally as a by-product of electricity generation. This heat may be in the form of hot water or low pressure steam at a temperature of more than 100°C. At this temperature, it is useful for heating buildings but the efficiency of generating electricity falls slightly in consequence. Nevertheless, in this way, more of the energy in the fuel can be put to use than if electricity alone had been produced.

By analogy, another energy carrier is cooling – where buildings need to be cooled, central refrigeration plants may be used to supply "coolth" in the form of cold water. A central plant will be more efficient than the small, individual refrigerators (air conditioners) used in many buildings. As with heat, the coolth must be distributed through insulated pipework. One of the most efficient examples of a machine of this type is to be found in Stockholm – a heat pump, which can extract heat from the harbour water in order to heat buildings, but it can also be used to supply cold water to buildings for cooling.

Nuclear fission

It might be thought that releasing energy through nuclear fission contravenes the idea that energy is not produced, merely converted from one form into another. However, quantum physics has shown that matter and energy are, to a degree, interchangeable. So, in this broader sense, the principle still holds that energy is neither made nor destroyed, just changed from one form into another.

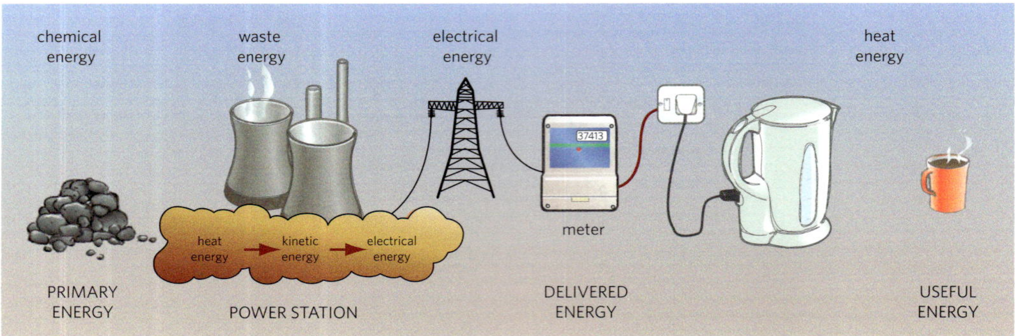

Fig. 1.13 Illustration of an energy chain from the primary energy source to the end use.

Supplies of primary energy

So where does all this energy come from? Worldwide, the most widely used source of primary energy is oil, whilst gas and coal are also important. Nuclear power is important, too, but in order to compare its role, it has to be treated as a special case in the statistics – by convention, its primary energy use is considered to be the same as its electricity production. Renewable energy sources such as the sun or the wind contribute some primary energy, mainly delivered as electricity.

In addition to these various commercial sources of primary energy, there is non-commercial energy, e.g. locally-gathered firewood, dried animal dung and methane from the digestion of waste. This is especially used in less developed parts of the world, but is not easily measured so it is often absent in global energy statistics.

The dominant type of fuel has changed with time. Until about 300 years ago in Europe, wood was the dominant fuel but competition with other uses for wood (i.e. ships and buildings), coupled with the failure to replace all of the felled trees, led to wood being replaced by coal; coal had other advantages as well. Later on, the introduction of oil was stimulated by reasons such as its practicality as a liquid fuel. Natural gas has been used more extensively during the past fifty years because of its cleanliness.

New sources of energy typically take about 100 years to capture more than half of their market. This statistic is surprisingly similar for several of the major changes which have taken place in the past – the replacement of wood by coal, the introduction of oil-based fuels, the development of natural gas as a fuel, and

Fig. 1.14 Fossil fuels provided 81% of primary energy in 2003 and are expected to account for 90% of the growth in demand between now and 2030. (reference: World Energy Outlook 2006. OECD/IEA, Paris).

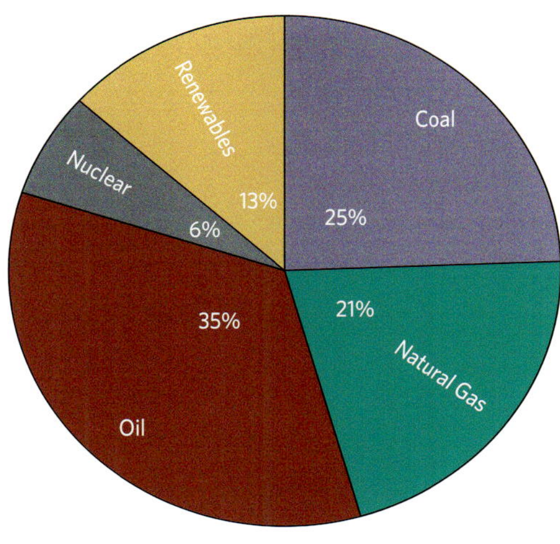

the introduction of nuclear power all happened at a similar rate (measured in terms of market share). This similarity in the rate of introduction may just be a coincidence but it could also represent the rate at which users are able to change their equipment or producers can fund investment in new production technology. If this is the case, future changes in energy systems may not happen much faster than in the past.

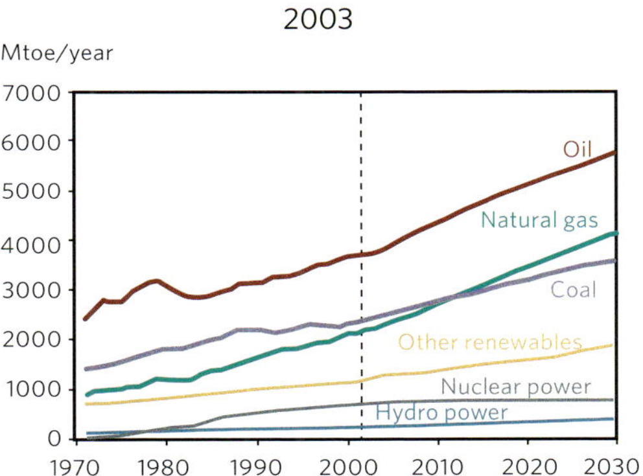

Fig. 1.15 There has been a remarkably similar rate of growth in market shares of different fuels; from this it can be inferred how gas and new energy technologies may grow in future (source: www.cesaremarchetti.org).

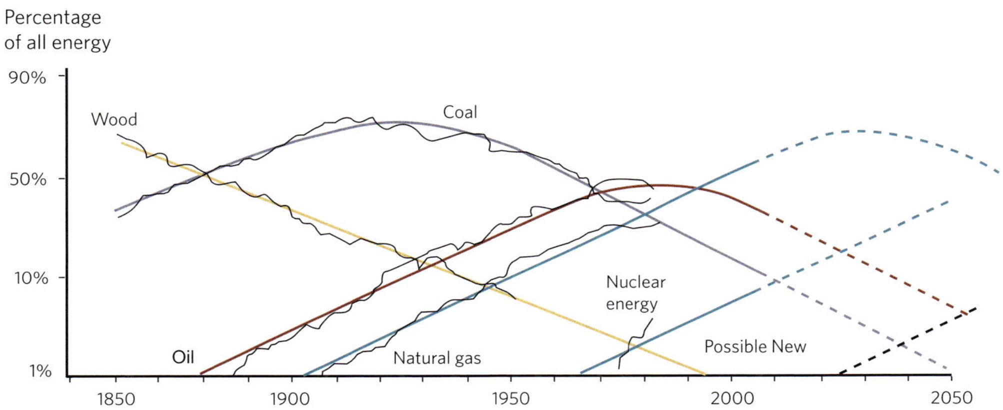

Where does primary energy come from?

Sources of primary energy are distributed unevenly around the world. The most widely available source is solar energy. Solar energy is available directly as well as indirectly via the wind and via the growth of plants which can be used as fuel, but solar energy varies from place to place and with time.

Large deposits of coal are to be found in many countries, providing secure local sources of energy; the wide availability of coal helps to ensure that supplies are relatively secure even in countries which have to buy them on the international market. Gas and oil are much more limited as regards the range of places which can supply them; a few countries have supplies which hugely exceed their own needs, which they can export to other parts of the world.

Today the industrialised nations are using a mixture of fuels – coal for power generation, particularly because of its low cost and because it can be handled in large quantities. Natural gas has replaced oil for domestic heating in many countries. In some others, electricity is used for heating, especially when it comes from hydropower, for example in parts of Scandinavia.

The price of primary energy, after allowing for inflation, has fallen with time, as new supplies became available and extraction processes and transportation became more efficient and less costly. Coupled with improvements in end-use technologies, this has reduced the cost of using energy which, as usual, has led to increased demand.

Fig. 1.16   The energy intensities of many industrial countries have fallen, indicating these economies have grown faster than their use of energy (this is the energy consumption, measured in tonnes of oil equivalent, per 1 million euro of GDP).

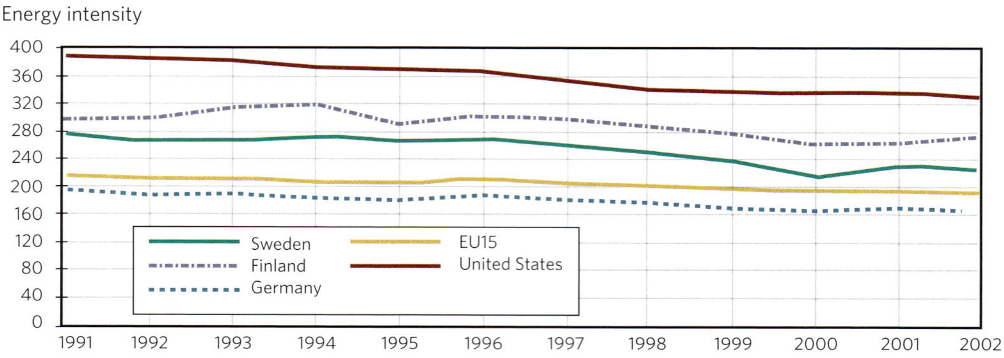

Forces at work that will change the picture

Fossil fuels, such as coal, oil and gas dominate the world's energy supply, not least because they are cheap and, in some cases, convenient means of providing energy today. We have learnt, through bitter experience, that using fossil fuels can affect our health and the environment. So we have employed technology to control these impacts, usually after we have seen the effects. This reactive approach means that fossil fuels are often associated with the bad things they do to the world around us, rather than with the value of the services they provide, which we have come to accept as the norm.

In recent decades, more proactive approaches have been adopted in order to deal with environmental problems. For example, in Europe, North America and elsewhere, laws were introduced to prevent the obvious pollution caused by burning coal. Many countries have now adopted regulations to control pollutants, such as mercury or greenhouse gases, because of the problems that they might cause in future. Using advanced technology to take precautions against future problems provides a recipe for exploiting the benefits of fossil fuels without penalising the environment; but does climate change signal the end of the fossil fuel era? This will be discussed in later chapters. The other challenge to the future use of fossil fuels is whether or not there are sufficient resources to supply the world for the foreseeable future, especially in view of the increasing demand for energy. This is considered next.

Endnotes

1   Primary energy is the energy content of the original fuel. (Data from Energy Technology Perspectives, OECD/IEA, 2006, p. 38).

2   "US Industrial electric motor systems market opportunities assessment", US DOE, December 2002.

3   "Digital signal processors usher in green motors." Kedar Godbole, Texas Instruments Inc., 2003.

4   "Energy Systems and Sustainability". G Boyle, B Everett, J Ramage. Oxford University Press, 2003.

5   For example, in Sweden, heating is delivered to community housing schemes from central wood-fired boilers.

KRUPP
BEA

Are we running out of fossil fuels?

It is obvious that fossil fuels are a finite resource. It is also clear that sooner or later the world will run out of them. Or will it? For many years, pundits have been prophesying doom, presenting pictures of the world running out of fossil fuels with ensuing calamity for everyone. It is relatively easy to raise such arguments since fossil fuels are clearly finite. However, closer inspection shows that the second half of this argument, namely that the world will run out of them, is not so obvious. To gain an insight into this seemingly contradictory statement, it is necessary to look in more detail at what fossil fuels are, how they are used and how this might change in future.

Fig. 2.1 Garzweiler brown-coal mine in Germany.

What are fossil fuels?

The phrase "fossil fuels" covers a range of substances produced by the decay of living material, which has been buried and then subjected to pressure and heat over very long periods of time. This process turns the decayed material into hydrocarbons (molecules consisting mainly of hydrogen and carbon) such as coal, oil and natural gas which can be combusted relatively easily.

One of the best known fossil fuels is coal, which is to be found in many parts of the world. Coal ranges from material which is partially converted plant matter (called brown coal or lignite) through harder, bituminous coals to anthracite which is almost pure carbon. Each of these has its own particular uses – lignite is available in large deposits but is costly to transport so, if it is to be used, this has to be done close to the mine. Anthracite, on the other hand, has valuable uses when making steel, so is worth moving over long distances to a steelworks. Bituminous coals are relatively cheap and can be moved long distances, by rail or sea, typically for use in power generation.

For a long time, there have been predictions about future shortages of coal – in 1865 William Stanley Jevons[1] pointed out that Britain's industrial strength

Reserves of coal

With 480 billion tonnes of anthracite and bituminous coal, plus 430 billion tonnes of sub-bituminous coal and lignite, the world is well endowed with coal reserves[3]. These are located in many countries.

To put the size of the reserves in perspective, the total use of coal was 5.8 billion tonnes in 2005; this rate has been increasing at about 5% per annum. Projections[4] suggest that China and India will account for about 70% of the increase in coal consumption by 2030. Both countries have substantial reserves of coal. Today, 55% of all coal in China goes to generating electricity. Most of the rest feeds the booming industrial sector because China only has limited domestic supplies of oil and natural gas. About 70% of all Indian coal is used for generating electricity.

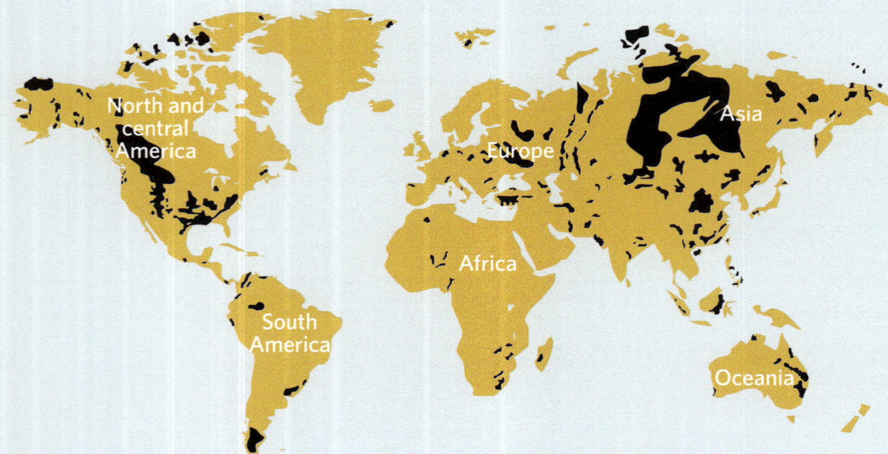

Fig. 2.2 Global distribution of coal reserves.

depended on its coal and so this would decline as the coal became exhausted; he predicted the price of coal would rise as the reserves ran out, which would encourage extraction from deeper seams. But Jevons failed to appreciate the fact that, as the price of energy rises, there is a strong incentive to use it more efficiently and to develop alternatives.

In fact, global supplies[2] of coal today are sufficient for hundreds of years of use at current rates. Because coal is available in many countries and can be extracted relatively easily, competition is sufficient to keep coal prices relatively steady, even during rapid swings in the price of alternatives, such as oil in the 1970s.

However, coal is also a dirty fuel – when burnt it emits solid particles and oxides of sulphur and of nitrogen, which cause local air pollution and acid rain (see next page). This has forced many countries to control how coal is used in order to improve air quality – initially, this was done for local benefit (for instance, to end the infamous London smog), then regionally and more recently globally, due to concerns about climate change, but that is a story for a later chapter.

Petroleum is another well-established fossil fuel; this term covers a multitude of different products ranging from crude oil, through heavy oil to shale oil and tars. What they all have in common is that they are a mixture of hydrocarbons, many of which are liquids.

The user does not buy crude oil itself but petrol, diesel oil or kerosene depending on his or her needs. These fuels are produced in a refinery which separates the different hydrocarbons and modifies them to make the required product. Each fuel has its particular uses – petrol for spark ignition engines or diesel oil for compression ignition engines, or aviation kerosene for the turbines in aeroplanes. Thus the refiner has to balance the combination of hydrocarbons he buys in crude oil with the demands of his customers for the various products. He does this by procuring oil on the world market and by using a range of conversion processes to convert the oil into products. At the same time, he can remove pollutants from the fuels (although the pollution problem is less severe with oil than with coal because the amounts of sulphur and nitrogen are lower).

The price of oil is subject to similar forces to those affecting the prices of other commodities – global economic change, the development of new supplies, the operation of cartels, the threat of war, speculation and substitution by alternatives although it does seem to be subject to more severe reactions than most. Figure 2.4 illustrates the ups and downs of the price of oil and other fuels.

Acid rain

Until quite recently, air pollution was seen as a local issue. An early answer to this problem was to build very tall chimneys. However, by the late 1950s, people in southern Scandinavia had begun to realise that they were being affected by pollution from far away – especially from Britain, and the heavily industrialised regions of Northern Europe. There was a similar experience in North America, and elsewhere in Europe, and around the Pacific rim. The common cause was recognised as being emissions of sulphur dioxide (SO_2) and nitrogen oxides (NOx) from the combustion of fossil fuels. This type of pollution has become known as acid rain.

Rainwater is slightly acidic due to naturally occurring oxides in the air; acid rain makes it even more so. The acidity[5] of rain can reach a pH value of 4; some rain has even been recorded at a pH value of 2, which is as acid as lemon juice!

The effects of acid rain are most obvious in streams, lakes and marshes as a result of water running off the land. As the acidity of a lake increases, the water becomes clearer and the numbers of fish and other aquatic animals decline. Eggs and young fish are the worst affected because the increasing acidity can cause deformities and prevent eggs from hatching properly. The acidity of the water can also cause toxic substances, e.g. aluminium, to be released from the soil, harming fish and other aquatic animals.

To assist policymakers in controlling acid rain, scientists have developed the concept of

Fig. 2.3 Using a helicopter to spread lime in a lake at Eksingedalen, Norway, in order to counteract the effect of acid rain.

the "critical load". This is an estimate of the amount of acid rain that a particular region can receive without significant damage to its ecosystem, taking into account the types of soil and rock and the ecosystem in the area. As a result, large power stations and other combustion plants in Europe and elsewhere have been subject to ever stricter emission controls, reducing SO_2 and NO_x emissions considerably.

As early as in 1874, the state geologist for Pennsylvania was raising concerns that there was only enough oil remaining in the USA to keep the nation's lamps burning for four years[6]. Ever since, there have been periodic scares about the future of oil supplies[7]. In 1919, the US Geological Survey (USGS) predicted that American oil would run out in 9 years. During the early 1940s, H.L. Ickes[8], the

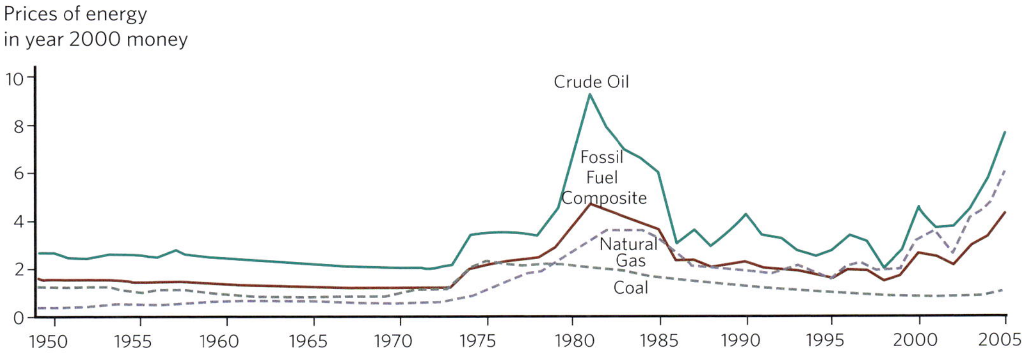

Fig. 2.4 Fossil fuel prices 1945–2005; the prices shown are after adjustment for inflation. During this period there were some major spikes in the price of oil.

US Petroleum Administrator for War, published an article entitled "We're Running Out of Oil." In 1977, President Carter said "we could use up all the proven reserves of oil in the entire world by the end of the next decade."

One of the reasons for these concerns is that oil supplies are concentrated in relatively few producing countries. In 1960, many of the oil producing countries came together to form the Organisation of Petroleum Exporting Countries (OPEC) in order to represent their own interests. As a reaction, the industrialised countries established the International Energy Agency (IEA) during the oil crisis of 1973–74. Nowadays, it is recognised that the stability of the oil market is a concern for both the (many) consuming countries and the (much fewer) producing countries.

After 1985, a combination of reduced demand and increased production from other sources saw prices fall back. Since then, most recently in 2005, a combination of increasing demand and constraints on oil exports has periodically pushed prices up again, bringing back fears that oil will run out. Nevertheless, oil production has never been higher.

Even so, there are concerns about the reserves of oil that we know about, and which we can extract economically. The US Geological Service (USGS) has estimated that about one third of all the oil that was technically recoverable has been produced to date. Other commentators suggest that, in fact, about half of

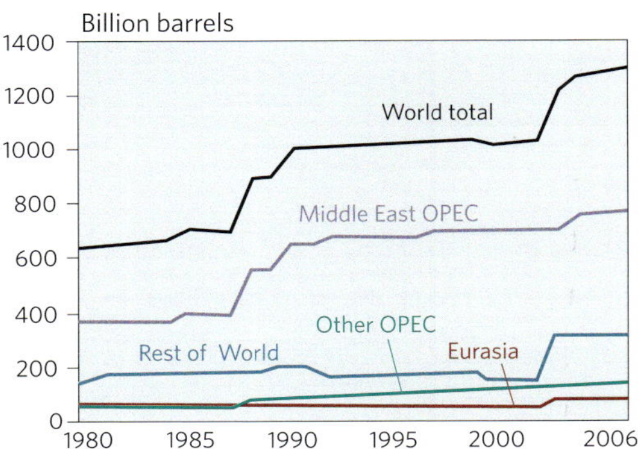

Fig. 2.5 The trend in world conventional oil reserves.

Resources and reserves of conventional oil

The total amount of hydrocarbons in the Earth has been estimated by various groups. The United States Geological Service (USGS) has made one of the most comprehensive assessments[9], concluding that global *resources* of conventional oil are between 7 and 8 trillion barrels, of which about 1 trillion barrels have so far been produced. Not all of the remainder can be recovered using current technology; some would be uneconomic to recover at current prices (the average amount of oil recovered from producing fields is about 35%[10]). This leaves the economically recoverable oil *reserves* – some of these are proven whilst the rest are probably recoverable but not yet proven.

The true level of the reserves will only finally be known once all of this oil has been produced. Proven oil reserves were about 1.2 trillion barrels at the end of 2005, up from 0.7 trillion barrels in 1980. Estimates of the probably recoverable amount range from 0.2 to 1 trillion barrels[11].

To put this into perspective, the world used 30 billion barrels of oil in 2005. Historically, the addition of new reserves has more than kept pace with the consumption of known reserves (although this clearly cannot go on for ever). This has given rise to considerable controversy regarding the future availability of conventional oil supplies. On the one hand, geophysicist Dr M. King Hubbert predicted, more or less correctly, in 1956 that onshore US oil production would peak in 1971, due to declining reserves.

Following his achievement, more recent commentators have suggested that world oil production peaked in 2004 or would peak in the near future. On the other hand, estimates by the USGS of the technically recoverable oil are somewhat higher than this. With improved technology and higher prices, as well as the use of unconventional oil, the amount of hydrocarbons in the world should be sufficient for many more years of oil supply.

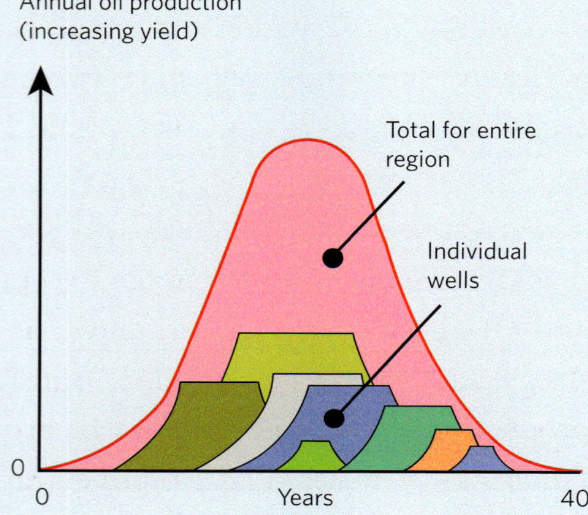

Fig. 2.6 Hubbert's peak – the oil production from each field in a region rises, reaches a plateau and then falls. Hubbert postulated a curve to describe overall production for the lower 48 states in the USA; it has been found this can also be used to describe oil production in other regions but there is disagreement about how well this predicts future global production.

it has been produced. The difference between these figures is not a disagreement about how much has been extracted but about the amount of oil in the ground, because it is likely that not all of it has been found yet. Also, as some oil is left behind at the end of production (perhaps half of the oil cannot be extracted using existing technology), there is clearly a limit on future production. At current rates, known reserves would last for about 30 years. But the same has been true for the past 30 years or more.

This picture reflects the situation for a particular type of crude oil, "conventional oil", which has been the basis of the oil industry since it began. This type of crude oil contains the largest proportions of petrol and diesel oil components. This makes it relatively free-flowing and so it is known as a "light crude". If its sulphur content is low, it is a "light sweet crude". This is the type of oil which is most in demand and is thus the target of most oil exploration. However, the oil prospector may not find any oil, or he may find gas or a heavier crude (i.e. a more viscous crude oil, which is more difficult to extract). Even worse, he may find a "heavy sour crude" which contains more sulphur. If the explorer finds heavy crude, he may leave it in the ground if he thinks he can find light sweet crude somewhere else.

Having found oil, geologists will work out its composition and estimate how much is present. If it is economic to produce, wells will be drilled into the field and the oil will be allowed to flow out of the reservoir, into pipelines or tankers. As the natural pressure declines, water may be injected into the field to maintain production levels or pumps may be brought in to extract more of the oil. Further fluids may be injected later on to extract even more of the oil.

There are also large amounts of oil in shales and tar sands; the oil is difficult to extract so, until recently, there was little commercial interest in these sources. Collectively referred to as "unconventional" crudes, they are now emerging as a major feature of the global energy picture. Because such crude oil is very viscous, it is necessary to heat it and/or use a solvent to make it flow to the surface. Heavy crude oil is extracted in the USA and in Venezuela. This type of crude has, in the past, been excluded from conventional estimates of oil reserves because it has not been commercially viable to produce. This picture may now be changing.

There are also large deposits of tar sands in Canada; these constitute the largest known oil resource in the world. Alberta, sometimes referred to as the Saudi of the North, is becoming better known today for its tar sands. The amount of tar (or bitumen) in the sand ranges from 1% to 20%. In the Athabasca area, the tar sands are close to the surface making it possible to extract the oil by mining, but about 80% of the tar sands in Alberta lie too deep for open-pit mining so the oil must be recovered by drilling followed by the injection of large amounts of steam

Formation and trapping of conventional oil and gas

Oil and natural gas were formed from the re-mains of plants and animals that lived in the ocean between 10 and 160 million years ago. When these organisms died and sank to the bottom, they were covered in mud and sand. Their rapid burial prevented the decay that would normally have occurred if they had been left exposed on the seabed. The lack of oxygen in some of the sedimentary layers caused the dead material to decay slowly into carbon-rich organic compounds. These compounds mixed with surrounding mud to form a shale. When further layers were added on top, pressure and heat acting on the shale turned the organic material into crude oil or natural gas (mainly methane).

Oil and natural gas are both lighter than the saline water that fills the pores and fractures in the rock. They will thus tend to migrate upwards (and perhaps sideways) as pores and fractures in the rock allow. Over millions of years, much of the oil and natural gas has escaped to the surface, where it has been broken down by bacteria and/or sunshine. The reservoirs that we find today are those where the oil or gas has been trapped on its way up.

Oil can accumulate in porous rocks, for example sandstone or limestone, providing there is an overlying cap and the structure of the rock traps the oil from moving sideways. Cap rocks are typically mud-stones, salt beds, or similarly impervious formations. Traps are typically formed by folds in the geological strata or by faults in the rock. Extracting oil from the ground thus involves drilling through the cap rock in order to access the underlying oil in the trap.

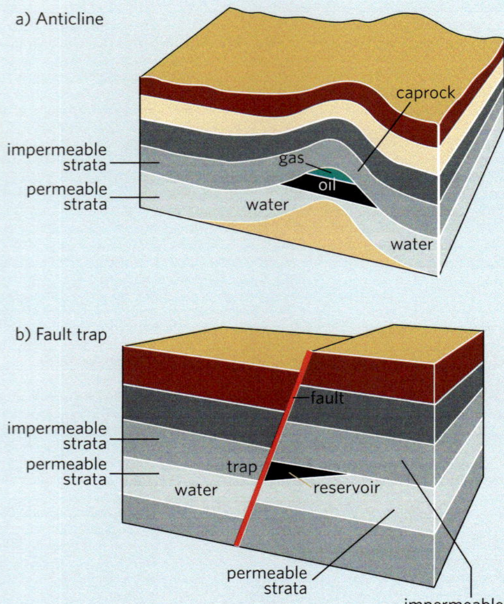

Fig. 2.7 Trapping of oil and gas beneath a cap-rock.

Fig. 2.8 A section of rock taken by drilling into a reservoir rock.

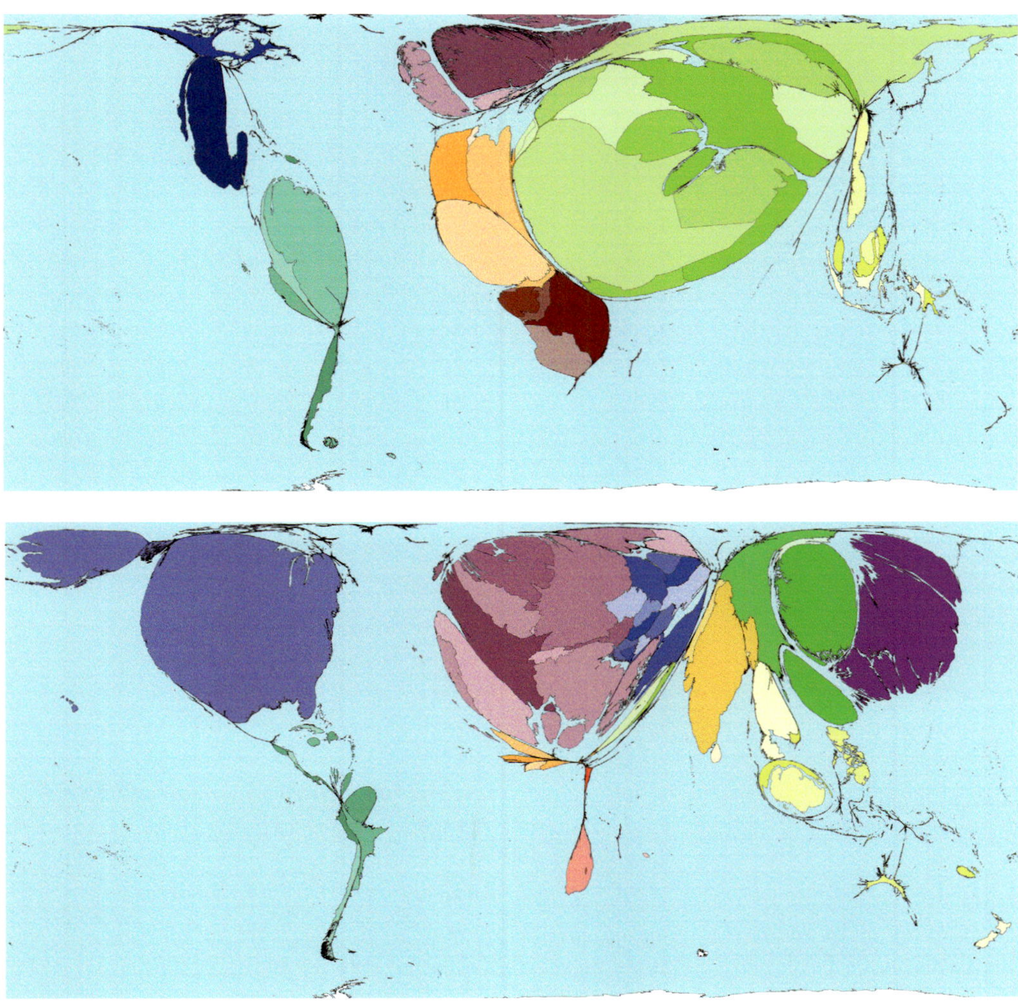

Fig. 2.9 Top: Map showing crude oil exports; areas of each country have been adjusted to represent that country's share of the global market. Bottom: Map showing crude oil imports by country. (www.worldmapper.org)

to make the oil flow to the surface. This approach may well replace mining as the principal means of production from tar sands in future.

The bitumen that is extracted in this way contains relatively more carbon and less hydrogen than conventional oil, so it must be upgraded before it can be sent to market. This is done close to the mine at large, expensive facilities where hydrogen is added and some carbon is removed. This makes a hydrocarbon product which is transportable and is more suitable for use in conventional refineries. Such upgrading facilities represent about two-thirds of the capital cost of heavy oil projects.

Tar sand, heavy crude and oil shales

Alberta's oil sands contain the largest known resource of oil in the world, estimated at between 1.7 and 2.5 trillion barrels of oil.

In Alberta, oil was first extracted by open-pit mining; this continues today using some of the world's largest trucks and shovels. But about 80% of the oil sands are too deep for open-pit mining. This oil can be extracted using *in situ* techniques – large amounts of steam injected through wells drilled into the sands; this makes the oil flow to the surface. Production from *in situ* methods already rivals that from open-pit mining and, in the future, may become the main means of production. Producing a barrel of oil from the Canadian tar sands can cost as much as USD 30.

Around 1.2 trillion barrels of heavy crude oil lie in a belt under the Orinoco River in Venezuela. President Chavez has declared "Venezuela has the largest oil reserves in the world" referring to more than 300 billion barrels of oil he believes is recoverable. The production of Orinoco heavy oil was not, until recently, deemed commercially profitable due to its adverse characteristics: high viscosity (like molasses), a high sulphur content (3.5%), and a high content of the metals vanadium and nickel. Improving the rate of recovery from the Orinoco reservoir has the potential to increase the reserves substantially. The recovery rate is currently as low as 7%, although the aim is to improve this to at least 22%, but this will require using more energy to make steam. The bitumen that is produced is unsuitable for treatment in a conventional oil refinery and has to be *upgraded* in very large and costly facilities before being shipped to refineries. Upgrading uses substantial amounts of energy, so producing a barrel of Venezuelan "synthetic crude" can cost USD 16.

Fig. 2.10 The Sincor plant near the city of Jose, Venezuela, upgrades heavy crude oil from the huge resource in the Orinoco belt.

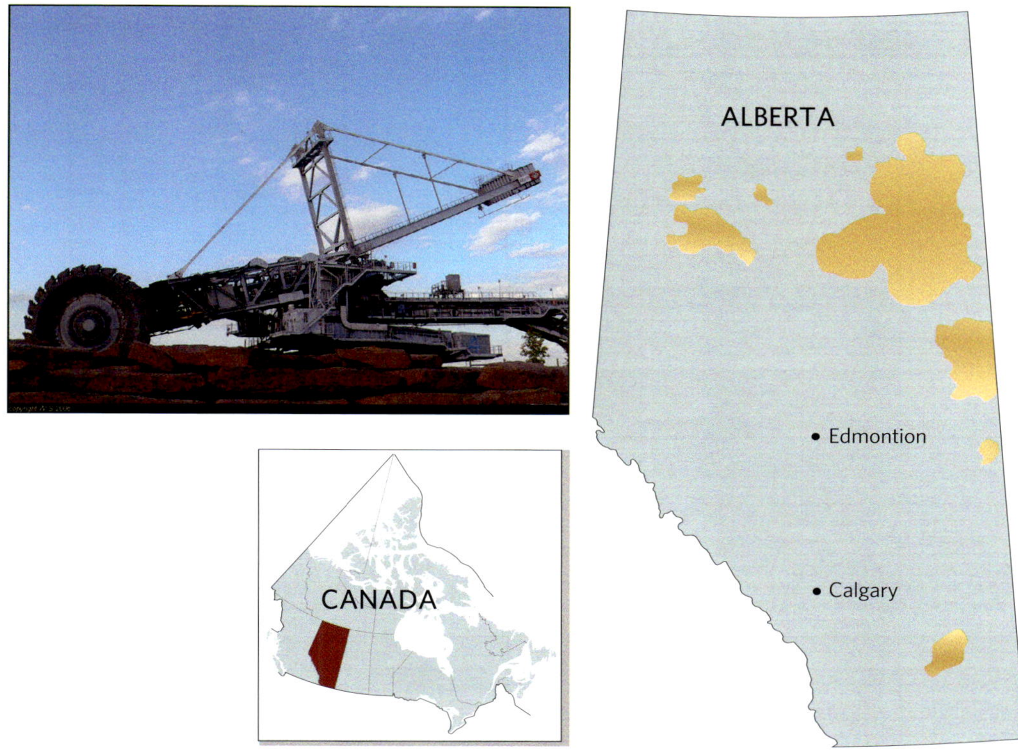

Fig. 2.11   Bucketwheel at work in the oil-sands of northern Alberta. The oil-sands are indicated in yellow.

There are numerous environmental concerns regarding the exploitation of the tar sands. The "footprint" of oil sands mining is very prominent, especially open-pit mining and its associated upgrading activities. Drilling and steam injection reduce this footprint slightly but add something of their own. In general, considerable attention is given to the care of the boreal forest and the animals around these sites, and to the management of water resources in the area.

The 2005 rise in oil price has increased commercial interest in unconventional crudes so substantial investments are now underway. The Orinoco and Alberta crude oils already provide a substantial and growing share of world oil supplies.

So, the answer to the question "how much oil is still in the ground?" is that this depends on which type of oil we want. Up to now, light sweet crude oils have been the basis of the oil industry, so it would be only reasonable to expect that new fields of this type would become harder to find. As the explorers turn their attention to the heavier crudes, techniques are being developed to extract them from the ground and refiners are investing in new technology to handle heavier

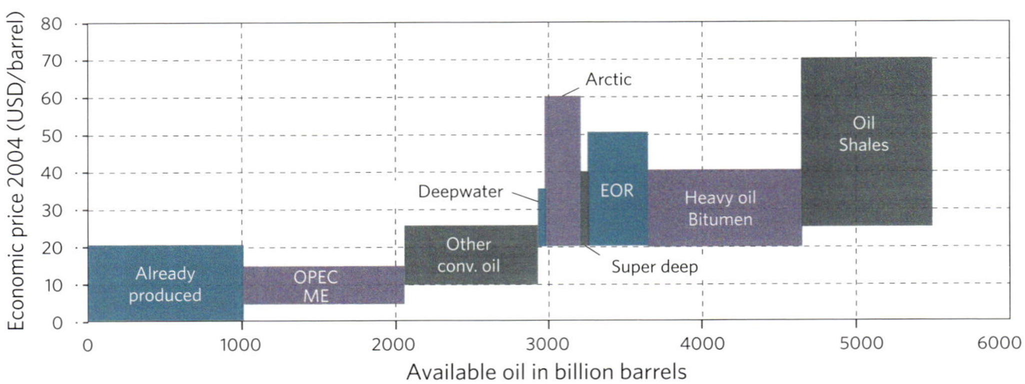

Fig. 2.12   Availability of oil resources as a function of cost, allowing for technological progress (redrawn from IEA, 2006).

and sourer crudes. With these capabilities, the oil industry can extract, transport and convert a wider range of crude oils in order to make the desired products. At the same time, the refiner can improve (upgrade) some of the less attractive components of crude oil, in order to make more valuable products from the oil that he purchases. However, because prospectors have not been deliberately looking for heavy crude oils, there is less knowledge about how much exists underground. It is thought that there is at least as much heavy oil as there was light oil before it was first exploited.

The third fossil fuel

The third type of fossil fuel is natural gas. This has become a major part of the world's energy supply during the past 30 years. Natural gas is found in many more places than oil and, typically, a larger proportion of it can be extracted. The greater range of choice in natural gas supplies should mean that there is more stability in gas prices than has been the case in oil prices recently. Whether this will be the case in practice remains to be seen. Unlike coal and oil, natural gas contains only faint traces of sulphur and no metals or ash-forming components, so it is very clean to use. It also emits less carbon dioxide (CO_2) than coal or oil during combustion.

Like oil, gas can be moved over long distances – the most economical method being through pipelines. Unlike oil, natural gas is delivered in a form that is ready to use – there is no need for a large refinery to prepare it for the user. Because of

Resources and reserves of gas

For a thousand years, the Chinese have been using natural gas to evaporate brine in order to make salt on an industrial scale. They found this gas leaking from natural reservoirs. Today, natural gas is extracted in many countries in much greater quantities, using methods similar to those used in oil production.

For a long time, gas was the unwanted sister of oil, because of the lack of a market for it and because it cost more to transport. The USA was the first country to use it on a large scale, extracting it from onshore fields. Europe started to deploy a natural gas network following the discovery of the Groningen gas field in the Netherlands at the end of the 1950s. In many places, natural gas is distributed through pipelines originally installed to carry "town gas" in the 19th century.

In the past 25 years, gas reserves have more than doubled[12] to 179 trillion m³ (equivalent to 162 billion tonnes of oil). Worldwide resources have been estimated by USGS at 450 trillion m³. Current production is 2.8 trillion m³ per year. Recovery from gas fields is typically higher than from oilfields, at between 70% and 80%[13].

More than half of the world's natural gas reserves are located in three countries – Russia, Iran and Qatar. Even now, there has been less exploration for gas than for oil, so it can be expected that total gas reserves will increase in the future. The production of gas is dominated by three countries – Russia (598 billion m³ annually), the USA (526 billion m³), and Canada (186 billion m³). As other countries with large reserves increase their production in the next decade or two, they can be expected to compete with these three producers.

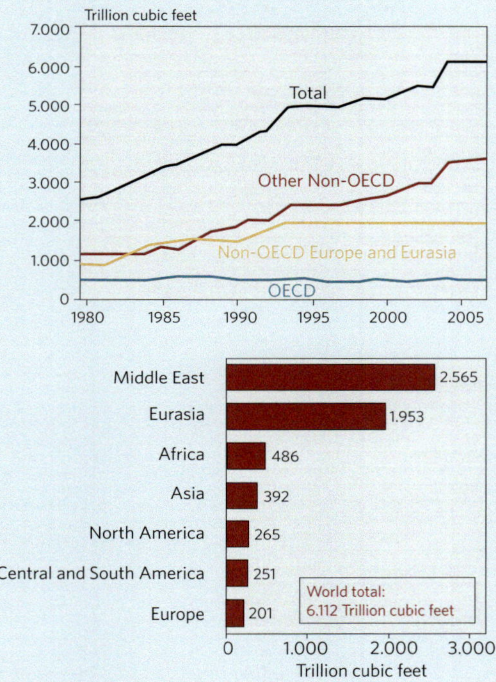

Fig. 2.13 Natural gas reserves are dominated by non-OECD countries as shown by trends 1980–2005 and by region (source: International Energy Outlook 2006, US EIA).

the high cost of transportation, producers are only inclined to make the necessary investment once a contract has been signed with a customer, e.g. a national gas company. Thus, the relationship between producer and customer is different from that in the oil market – in the gas industry, both the producer and the customer will have made substantial commitments in order to enable the project to take place, so both have a major interest in the continuation of supplies. It might be expected that this would reduce the risk of supply disruptions, compared with the oil market. However, the disruption in Russian supplies to the Ukraine during the winter of 2005/6 has called this into question.

Natural gas, because it is distributed by pipeline, is most conveniently used in fixed installations, such as home heating systems and power stations. Arguably, it is the easiest fossil fuel to use. For many years, there has also been some interest in using natural gas as a vehicle fuel, for reasons of cleanliness and cost, but particularly because it would avoid the importing of oil into some countries. There are many natural gas powered vehicles on the road today – about 5 million worldwide. The range of vehicles equipped to use natural gas includes motorbikes, taxis, buses and ships, as well as cars. However, natural gas is less convenient to use than gasoline, especially because of the larger amount of space needed to store it aboard the vehicle. For this reason, various methods of converting it into a different form have been tried. In Norway, it is used as liquefied natural gas (LNG)

C:H ratio and its relationship with solid, liquid and gas

Fossil fuels are made up of molecules of different sizes, with different proportions of carbon and hydrogen. These differences determine the physical form of the fuel. At one extreme, natural gas is largely made up of methane, a small molecule consisting of one carbon and four hydrogen atoms. Methane is a gas at room temperature.

At the other extreme, coal consists of relatively large numbers of carbon atoms in the molecule, with roughly 11 hydrogen for every 10 carbon atoms. Coal is a complex solid which also contains water and other impurities, including sulphur and mineral matter, so it is not open to such simple description as with gaseous or liquid fuels. Typical US coals contain between 70% and 80% carbon and 5% hydrogen.

In the middle, crude oil contains a variety of compounds, some of which are gases but most are liquids, e.g. petrol or kerosene. The gases are small molecules like methane and pentane with a high proportion of hydrogen. The liquids are larger molecules with typically between seven and eleven carbon atoms per molecule and roughly two atoms of hydrogen for each atom of carbon. At room temperature, some of these compounds (e.g. paraffin wax) are solid, a tendency which is emphasised by the increased number of carbon atoms in the molecule.

Any fuel has to be handled, moved and stored. Solids and liquids are easier to handle than gas but, for a given weight, the amount of energy available from a gas or liquid fuel is around twice as much as from coal; this factor influences how much work needs to be done to move the fuel. On the other hand, the amount of space occupied by a fuel is important with regard to storage, especially in a restricted space such as a vehicle. In this respect, liquid fuels require one thousand times less space than gaseous fuels at room temperature and atmospheric pressure. For this reason, in order to use gas as a fuel in vehicles, it is necessary to compress it hundreds of times, so that the energy available in a given space is similar to that available from liquid fuels. Such issues affect what is required of natural gas and, indeed, of any of the alternative fuels that we will discuss later.

Chapter 2 | Are we running out of fossil fuels?

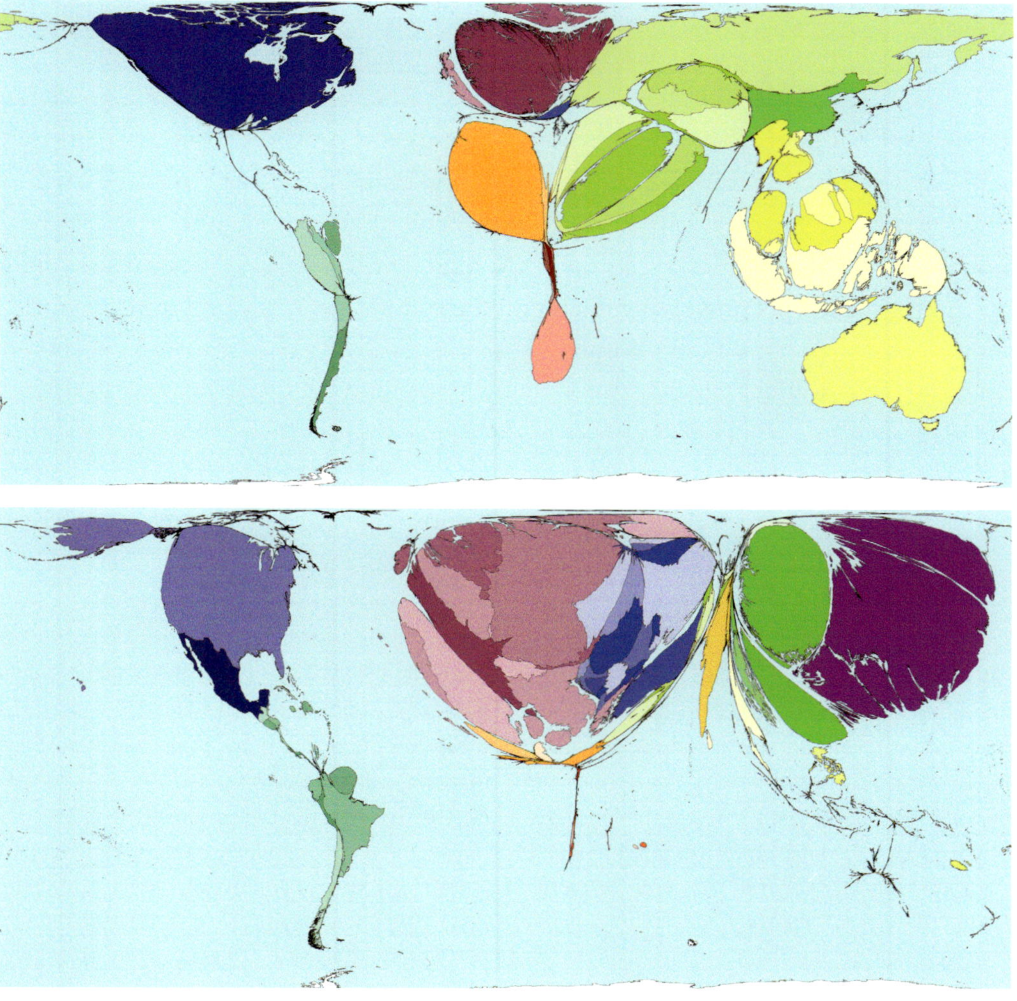

2.14 Map showing gas and coal exports; areas of each country have been adjusted for global shares. Map showing gas and coal imports by country (www.worldmapper.org).

in coastal shipping, but this is impracticable for other modes of transport. Many researchers have tried to convert it into more conventional liquid fuels for use in vehicles; large-scale production facilities of this type are now being built.

Make natural gas into something more convenient to use

The basic process for converting gas into liquids was developed in Germany in the 1920s in order to produce a range of chemicals from coal. Later, the same techni-

When gas becomes liquid

If natural gas is cooled to –162°C, it becomes a clear, colourless and non-toxic liquid which can be transported in specially-designed ships or even in tanker trucks. Liquefied natural gas, or LNG, enables the long distance transportation of natural gas in much the same way as for oil, overcoming some of the geographical limitations of moving gas by pipeline.

Twenty years ago, LNG was a niche product, representing only 4% of the trade in gas around the world. By 2020, this share is forecast to reach 17% as rapidly increasing demand drives the globalisation of the LNG business. In 1990, there were 13 liquefaction units, but now there are about 90. This development is most obvious in Qatar, the world-leader in the LNG business, which will soon supply one quarter of the world's demand for this fuel. Other countries exporting LNG include Algeria, Australia, Brunei, Egypt, Indonesia, Libya, Malaysia, Nigeria, Oman, Qatar, Trinidad, the UAE, and the US (Alaska). Within a short time, Russia, Norway and Equatorial Guinea will join their ranks.

In contrast to the transportation of oil in very large tankers, the transportation of LNG is characterised by heavy investment at both the producing end and the receiving end. In addition, the tankers themselves are expensive. This means that gas producers do not commit to developing their gas fields until the marketing of the gas has been decided upon.

Fourteen countries import a total of 140 million tons of LNG per year. Japan has historically been the largest importer; others will soon begin importing this fuel, which is expected to be one of the world's biggest growth sectors. However, as long as there are cheaper supplies of gas from pipelines, LNG will tend to be the "swing" supply, setting a ceiling on the price of gas.

Fig. 2.15 Natural gas liquefaction plant near Hammerfest in Norway.

que was applied in South Africa as a way of obtaining a domestic supply of liquid fuel from coal when external supplies of crude oil were likely to be disrupted. Improved versions of the same process are available today and are being applied to natural gas and coal. The conversion of natural gas can produce a liquid fuel which does not contain sulphur, so it is potentially attractive as a means of reducing sulphur emissions from conventional fuels by blending it with diesel oil. With ever-tightening environmental regulations, this may be an attractive proposition. Another attractive feature of the conversion of gas into liquid is that this could make it easier to transport from remote locations, thereby avoiding the need to build long gas pipelines.

Another method of long distance transportation is to cool the natural gas to such a low temperature (-162°C) that it liquefies. In this way, relatively large amounts can be transported over long distances using ships. A substantial amount of energy is needed to refrigerate natural gas. The energy demand, coupled with the cost of the ships and the terminals, means that liquefied natural gas (LNG) projects are expensive. They have been designed for supplying particular countries, especially Japan, but also Spain and some parts of the USA. As more countries recognise LNG as an additional option for supplying energy, more terminals are being built. At the same time, some producers are making LNG supplies available to the general market, not just to customers who have long-term contracts, which should broaden its use.

Because of these commercial constraints on the development of natural gas fields, the full potential of this fuel has only been recognised during the past decade. So there has been less exploration specifically for gas fields. As a consequence, our knowledge of gas resources is more limited than that of oil or coal. Substantially more natural gas is likely to be found in different parts of the world as further exploration takes place.

Are we running out of fossil fuels?

We have seen that a great deal of fossil fuel is available but that much of it is in a different form, and it is more costly to extract, than the fuel we use at present. But there is another aspect to this question, namely the rate at which we are using up the reserves. Let us now look into that.

An energy user is not particularly interested in which sort of fuel he or she uses as long as it provides sufficient energy in the desired fashion. So the rate at which fossil fuels are being used will be decided by the demand for energy and by the competition from other fuels which could be used in their place.

As we described in the previous chapter, the demand for energy continues to rise globally, although there is a shift in the balance between different uses. The principal demands for fossil fuels can be understood as falling into a number of main categories – electricity generation, buildings, industry, and transport.

One major use of fossil fuels is generating electricity. In most (but not all) of the developed countries, electricity generation is based on fossil fuels, particularly coal but also natural gas and, to a lesser extent, oil. Other energy-intensive industries use coal (e.g. cement, iron) or gas (e.g. petrochemicals, glass), although some use electricity (e.g. aluminium and the recycling of steel). Oil refining uses a small fraction of its raw material to run its plants.

Ever since the late 1980s, when natural gas was finally accepted as a major fuel in electricity generation, it has been displacing coal in this market. One reason for this is the use of the superior technology of gas turbines, as well as this fuel's clean-burning properties. With the recent increase in the price of oil (and with it that of natural gas), the rate of displacement of coal may decline in the immediate future. Even so, the amount of natural gas used in electricity generation is expected to increase further by 2030[14].

Domestic and commercial buildings are other major users of energy – this may include fossil fuels for heating, or electricity for lighting, air-conditioning and operating equipment. The fossil fuels used in many buildings, especially houses, are natural gas or heating oil (for reasons of convenience and cleanliness), or solid fuels.

Then there is transport – this is dominated by road vehicles, but air travel is growing and public transport systems are also significant in some places. Road transport is mainly fuelled by oil products, especially petrol and diesel oil. Similarly, air transport is exclusively fuelled by aviation fuel derived from crude oil. Public transport (e.g. buses, metros or trains) makes use of diesel oil and electricity, but natural gas has been introduced in public buses in some cities because of its low emissions.

This picture is true of the developed countries but the situation is somewhat different in the developing countries. Some have well-established electricity industries, with a rapidly growing demand for electricity, e.g. India, China and South Africa. The electricity industry in these countries depends on local coal for much of its fuel, although there is also substantial hydro-electric capacity and scope for further expansion. These countries only have limited resources of oil and natural gas, much of which has to be imported. Other developing countries which lack indigenous supplies of fossil fuels have to rely on imports for most of their energy needs.

In many developing countries, much of the energy needed for domestic purposes comes from non-commercial sources – this may be the combustion of locally grown plants or of methane generated by the decomposition of animal waste. Such contributions to the energy supply are not easily captured by statistics in the way that the energy supply is measured in the developed countries. Thus, the picture of the energy supply in the developing countries can be complicated by changes between the non-commercial and commercial sectors.

Alternatives to fossil fuels

In each of the four main areas of demand (i.e. electricity generation, buildings, industry and transport) alternatives to fossil fuels are being introduced. In electricity generation, nuclear power was established in many countries following the oil crises of the 1970s. France and Japan, in particular, built many nuclear power stations, displacing oil as a source of power generation. Other sources of electricity which have displaced fossil fuels include the so-called renewable energies, especially hydro-electricity, geo-thermal heat and more recently wind power. The energy source for most renewable energy is the sun or, in the case of geothermal heat, the centre of the Earth.

Fig. 2.16   Hydropower is the most important commercial source of renewable energy worldwide; the areas of each country are shown proportional to their shares of hydropower production. (www.worldmapper.org)

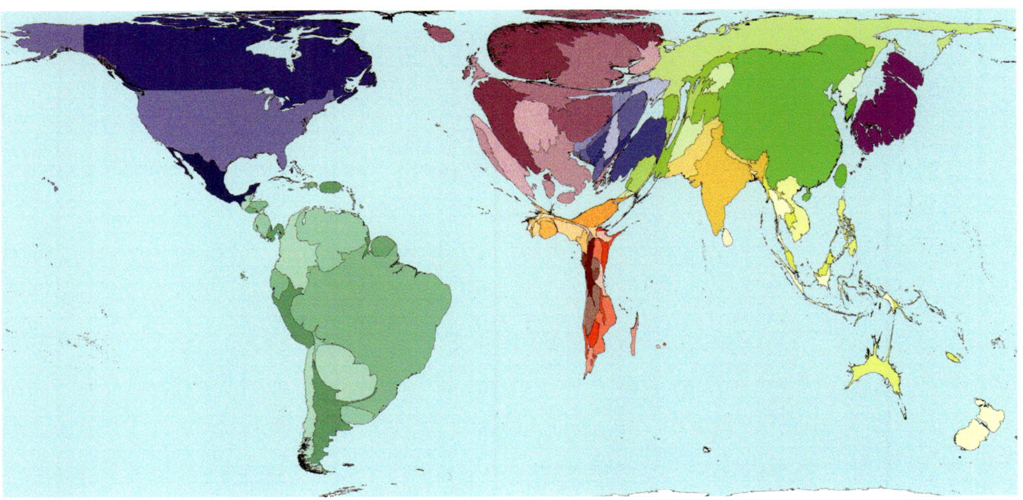

Fig. 2.17 Geothermal power plant – the Leathers geothermal power plant in the Salton Sea in California.

Hydro-electricity has been used in countries with suitable water supplies for many years – Norway's electricity supply relies almost entirely on hydro-electricity; New Zealand's South Island has so much capacity for hydro-electricity that it can export power to the North Island. However, in many developed countries, there is a limited potential for expanding hydro-electric schemes, so further growth in the demand for electricity will likely be met by the increased use of fossil fuels.

Geo-thermal energy utilizes heat coming from deep within the Earth to provide heat for buildings and to generate electricity. The most productive sources of geo-thermal energy are to be found where tectonic plates are colliding, so that rock relatively close to the surface is unusually hot (for example, Iceland, Indonesia or California).

Capturing energy from the wind is becoming more widespread as a means of generating electricity, which is then transmitted to areas of demand using high-voltage lines. The best sites for wind power tend to be remote from population centres. Large "wind farms" are being built in places like this, even offshore. Thus, the increasing use of wind energy is reducing the use of fossil fuels in electricity generation. This trend is expected to continue. However, there are constraints on the expansion of wind farms – for example, there is some resistance to the "industrialisation" of relatively unspoilt and wild parts of the countryside. Transmitting large volumes of electricity over long distances requires further encroachment into these wild areas using overhead lines. Once the most commercial sites have been exploited, it will become necessary to use less windy sites, so the commercial attraction may decline, although the costs of the technology should also fall with time. In addition, wind is an intermittent source which needs some back-up from other sources of electricity at times when there is less wind – in many places this back-up is most conveniently provided by the use of natural gas to generate electricity. Thus, the expansion of wind power will lead to a reduction in fossil fuel consumption but also to a (slight) shift away from one type of fossil fuel to another.

Fig. 2.18   Wind farm on the island of Hitra, off the coast of Norway.

Using wood as a fuel predates the use of fossil fuels; more recently, purpose-grown crops have been seen as a source of fuel (often called biomass). Another type of biomass is the waste material left after timber or other crops have been processed to make paper or food. In either form, biomass has a relatively low energy density which means it would be expensive to transport over long distances. Its high water content means less efficient combustion than for fossil fuels. Otherwise, it must be dried before use, which requires extra energy. Nevertheless, in many places where biomass is available or can be grown easily, it is attracting increasing attention as a source of energy. In Sweden, Finland and elsewhere, biomass is providing a fuel for electricity generation in place of coal.

Biomass is one of several renewable energy sources which make use of sunlight indirectly. Solar energy can also be captured for direct use – either as heat or electricity. Maximising the amount of solar heat captured in a building can be done by orienting the building in a suitable direction and designing the windows to take advantage of the sun's heat directly. Alternatively, the solar energy may be captured in a solar water heating panel for heating domestic tap water. Or a heat pump may be used during the winter to extract solar heat trapped in the soil during the previous summer.

Fig. 2.19   A photovoltaic array – the world's largest solar irrigation pumping system is powered by a 265 kW (peak) photovoltaic system at Borrego Springs, California.

Solar electricity generation involves using either the heat to raise steam to run a turbine or photovoltaic panels to convert light directly into electricity. The former may be used in a large power plant while photovoltaic panels can be used anywhere there is sufficient sunlight and on any scale. Indeed, the use of photovoltaic panels is most attractive for small installations if it can avoid the expense of connection to the electricity grid; for example emergency telephones beside motorways, radio transmitters in remote locations, or refrigerators in small villages in developing countries. Thus use of photovoltaics may displace fossil fuels, such as the diesel oil used in a generator, or provide a service which would otherwise not have been considered feasible, e.g. refrigeration.

The direct application of solar energy to power transport is unlikely to be competitive because of the intermittency of the energy supply (amongst other reasons). Indirect routes have more potential, e.g. in Brazil where sugar cane is grown to make ethanol to be used instead of petrol. Another approach is to extract oil from certain plants and seeds as a replacement for diesel oil; however, this process does not use all of the plant material – what happens to the rest will determine how wasteful the process is. So the demand for transportation fuel is beginning to be met by energy originating from non-fossil fuel sources, but the impact varies greatly from place to place, and the overall demand for fossil fuels continues to increase.

Many of the sources of renewable energy produce electricity, but electricity is (currently) unattractive to the road user in comparison with the convenience of liquid fuels. In principle, electricity from renewable energy sources could be used to produce hydrogen from water by electrolysis. This could be used to fuel an engine, and has attracted attention as the basis for the "hydrogen economy". A more intriguing possibility is using the hydrogen in a fuel cell rather than an engine. A fuel cell might be more efficient as a source of power for a vehicle, but it cannot use fossil fuels directly. Fuel cell technology is still very much under development. However, producing hydrogen by electrolysis is an inefficient process, so the whole system would be costly and such a transportation fuel would be expensive.

There are cheaper ways of making hydrogen. In oil refineries today, hydrogen is made in increasing quantities in order to upgrade the unwanted components of crude oil. The process is called reforming – it converts hydrocarbons, perhaps natural gas or one of the components of crude oil, into hydrogen and carbon dioxide (CO_2). The use of hydrogen in refineries is likely to increase as heavier crude oils become more widely used.

Other transportation fuels are made, for example from heavy oil, at upgrading facilities. Oil refining techniques have been developed for increasing the amount of the required products which can be made from a barrel of conventional oil. These techniques can be adapted for use with heavy oil. Broadly speaking, such processes consists of splitting the larger molecules (which make up the viscous residues from refining) into fragments and adding hydrogen to these pieces in order to improve the balance between carbon and hydrogen atoms. All of these techniques consume some energy and emit CO_2 which may be a problem, as will be discussed later. So, whether it is the deliberate manufacture of new fuels or the upgrading of more conventional ones, hydrogen is destined to play a major role in fuelling vehicles in the future.

Fig. 2.20   Hydrogen is produced at the Pernis refinery in the Netherlands.

Upgrading fuels in refineries

Conventional refineries separate out the main constituents of crude oil by distilling the oil and separating different "fractions", depending on their boiling points. The fractions with the lowest boiling points provide petrol, jet fuel and kerosene. Intermediate boiling point fractions provide diesel and gas oil used for heating; the highest boiling point fractions are used to fuel marine engines. A residue of materials cannot be distilled in this way and is treated separately.

The lower boiling fractions tend to be more valuable than the higher ones, so a number of techniques have been developed to convert the less attractive materials into more saleable fractions; as these processes involve breaking larger molecules into smaller ones, many are referred to as "cracking". In some cases, hydrogen is added to make more products with the right C:H balance. Thus, hydrogen is an increasingly important feedstock in refineries today; typically it is made on-site using oil or gas.

Another means of producing liquid products is to make them from natural gas. Where gas is found close to its market, it would be uneconomical to convert it into another fuel. For longer distances, because natural gas is more expensive to ship than oil, processes have been developed to convert natural gas into liquid products. Such conversions are based on a process dating from the 1920s invented by two German chemists, Franz Fischer and Hans Tropsch who converted coal into a synthesis gas, from which liquid fuels could be made. This technology helped fuel the Nazi armed forces but, after the war, with cheap crude oil available again, only coal-rich South Africa continued to construct such facilities. In recent times, Shell has used a similar process at a plant in Malaysia to convert natural gas into liquid fuels and other products; other companies also have plans to develop such conversion plants.

Because of the widespread availability of coal, its transformation into liquid products is enjoying increased interest. Since there are more impurities in coal than in natural gas, the process is bulkier and more expensive to build and run. South Africa has around 50 years' experience of this technology, which meets 28% of the country's oil requirements. Today, Sasol licences its process to countries and companies seeking to produce liquid fuels from coal.

Given its huge coal resources and its dependency on imported oil and natural gas, it is not surprising that the Chinese government is actively promoting the development of the coal-to-liquids (CTL) process. One such industrial plant, capable of producing 60,000 barrels per day, is due to come on stream in 2007. Others are planned. India is also interested, as is Indonesia.

A CTL process is very costly to build – a plant capable of producing 80,000 barrels of oil per day would cost about USD 6 billion. This means that the oil produced would cost between USD 30 and 35 per barrel or more, so investment can only be justified at times of high oil prices. A major problem with CTL conversion is that large amounts of CO_2 are emitted but, fortunately, there is a technical solution to this problem, as will be discussed in Chapter 5.

Oil made using a CTL process does not replace crude oil, but it is an interesting new component of the oil supply, one which is seen by coal-rich countries as contributing to the security of their energy supplies.

Whether vehicles are fuelled by petrol or diesel oil, gas, liquids made from coal, biomass, or hydrogen will largely depend on expectations regarding the price of oil. This is not just a matter of how expensive it is, but also whether it will remain costly for periods long enough to repay the investment in producing the chosen alternative fuel. Unfortunately, this demonstrates a basic problem which has hampered the development of alternative fuels for many years – once a new form of energy is sufficiently well established to capture a significant fraction of the market, the price of the conventional fuel falls (either because of an increasing supply or a reduction in demand), making the new option uncompetitive.

Whether or not this cycle will be broken in the near future remains to be seen, but there is an additional factor at work now – climate change. This will be discussed in the next chapter.

So are we running out of fossil fuels?

This complex picture contains one clear conclusion – the world is unlikely to run out of fossil fuels in the foreseeable future. Whether transportation fuels will be made in the future from unconventional crude oils or from natural gas, the availability of alternatives such as biofuels will extend the life of the fossil fuel supplies; at the same time, the increasing price of the alternatives and of the new supplies of oil will reduce demand, or at least slow its rate of increase.

Electricity generation will continue to rely on coal and natural gas, as well as on nuclear power and increasing amounts of renewable energy, but the vast resources of coal and gas that exist are sufficient to meet much of the demand for many years to come. Similarly, coal will continue to be available to the energy-intensive industries producing steel, cement and chemicals. The preferred fuel for heating buildings, especially houses, will continue to be natural gas in many places, for the simple reason that there are few practicable alternatives.

But a new factor has entered the picture during the past decade, namely climate change. This could mean the demand for fossil fuels being reduced even further, thereby increasing the life of the reserves. This will be discussed in the following chapters.

Suggestions for further reading

Energy Systems and Sustainability, by G Boyle, B Everett, J Ramage.
Oxford University Press, 2003. Oxford
Resources to Reserves. OECD/IEA, 2005. Paris.
Statistical Review of World Energy BP, London, 2006

Endnotes

1 "The coal question; an enquiry concerning the progress of the Nation, and the probable exhaustion of our coal-mines." 1865. William Stanley Jevons, Macmillan, London.
2 Much of the data used in this chapter is taken from the 2006 edition of the Statistical Review of World Energy published by BP.
3 Statistical Review of World Energy, BP, London, 2006
4 International Energy Outlook, US Energy Information Agency, 2006
5 On the pH scale, pure water has a value of 7 and unpolluted rain has a value between 5 and 6.
6 "Are We Running Out of Oil?" Policy Backgrounder No.159, January 29, 2003 by David Deming. National Centre for Policy Analysis and references therein
7 "The Age of Oil, The Mythology, History, and Future of the World's Most Controversial resource" by Leonardo Maugeri. Praeger, 2006.
8 Harold Icke's main job was as US Secretary of Interior; interestingly he believed that conservation was among the most important responsibilities of government and he greatly expanded the US National Parks.
9 USGC "World Petroleum Assessment", 2000.
10 "Resources to Reserves", 2005, OECD-IEA.
11 For contrasting views, see "The coming oil crisis" 1997, by C.J. Campbell (Multiscience Publishing) and the World Petroleum Assessment, 2000 by USGS.
12 Statistical Review of World Energy, BP, London, 2006.
13 "Resources to Reserves", 2005, OECD-IEA.
14 "Energy Technology Perspectives". 2006 OECD-IEA, Paris.

Ron Hagen 2006
CO₂
MAYDAY

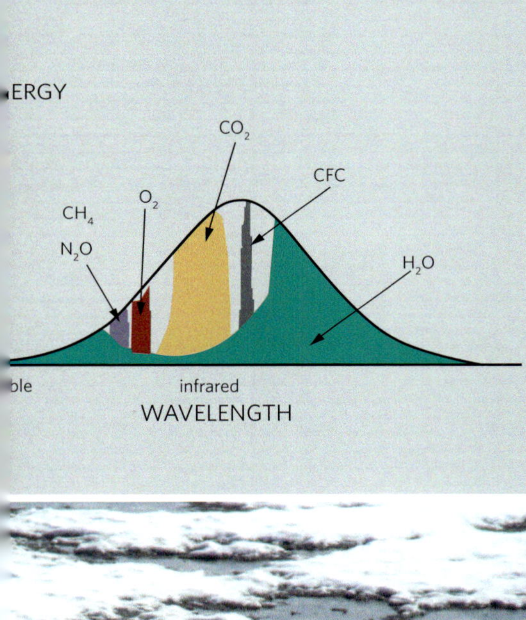

200 years of damaging the climate

Thanks to the natural Greenhouse Effect, our world is 33°C warmer than it would otherwise have been. Without this warming, almost all of today's species would find it difficult to survive.

Human activities are now known to be enhancing the Greenhouse Effect, leading to higher global temperatures and other changes in the climate. This could make living conditions difficult in some parts of the world in the future. In this chapter, we will examine how the climate is changing and why.

Fig. 3.1 Climate change has many forms.

How does the greenhouse effect work?

The Earth is warmed by radiation from the sun. Most of this radiation passes through the atmosphere and warms the Earth's surface. The Earth also radiates energy, but at a wavelength that we cannot see; this infra-red radiation cannot pass through the atmosphere as easily as sunlight and some of it becomes trapped, raising the temperature of the lower atmosphere and the Earth's surface.

The trapping of infra-red radiation is brought about by certain gases, especially water vapour and carbon dioxide[1]. Water vapour is responsible for about two thirds of the total greenhouse effect, followed by carbon dioxide which contributes another fifth, plus smaller contributions from methane and a range of other gases.

The amount of carbon dioxide (CO_2) in the atmosphere is steadily increasing and is thus enhancing the natural greenhouse effect. This has been happening for some time as a result of human activities. The main sources of this additional CO_2 are the combustion of fossil fuels and deforestation. The use of fossil fuels began to increase after the Industrial Revolution, 200 years ago. Since then, the amount of CO_2 in the atmosphere has increased by about 40%. This enhancement of the greenhouse effect is expected to lead to higher temperatures, which are expected to change the climate.

In contrast, allthough there is a large amount of water vapour in the atmosphere, the total quantity of water is virtually unaffected by human activities except to the extent that global warming enables the atmosphere to hold slightly more of it. So water vapour has little role in enhancing the greenhouse effect.

Fig. 3.2 Greenhouse effect: infra-red radiation from the Earth is trapped by the greenhouse effect, warming the Earth.

Fig. 3.3 The rising amount of CO_2 in the atmosphere measured at the Mauna Loa observatory in Hawaii.

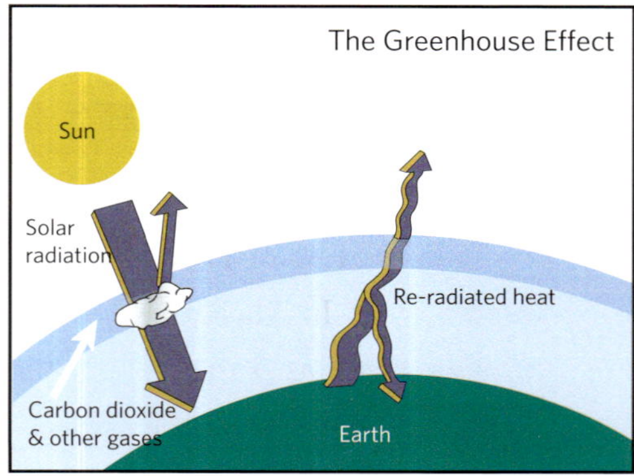

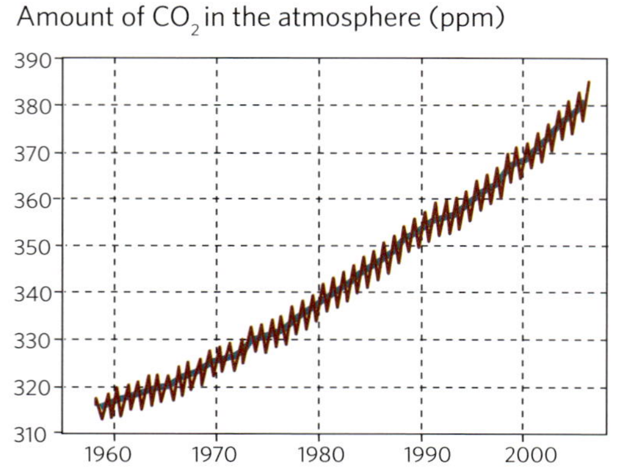

Chapter 3 | 200 years of damaging the climate

The weather is always different so how can we be sure the climate is changing?

Because we talk about weather and climate in similar terms, there can be some confusion about the difference between them. Mark Twain tried to explain the distinction thus: "climate is what we expect, weather is what we get", but today our expectations regarding climate have been disrupted by the new threat from the enhanced greenhouse effect.

The aim of this chapter is to provide a straightforward introduction to climate change and to explain briefly why it gives us cause for concern. As far as possible, scientific jargon will be avoided – more detailed descriptions of the phenomenon are available, for example in some of the books listed at the end of the chapter.

For a long time, many scientists were concerned about the possibility of human activities changing the climate but a major problem that they faced was establishing a clear link between changes in the amount of greenhouse gases, especially CO_2, and global warming. This is partly because the changes are so slow and also because there are always natural variations in the climate. Nevertheless, during the past few years, there have been an increasing number of observations of unusual events. Individually these might be regarded merely as statistical fluctuations but together they give credence to the belief that the climate is changing. As the amounts of greenhouse gases in the atmosphere have changed, and because such gases are known to have an effect on climate, the connection of the two sets of observations has steadily become stronger.

The Earth is now 0.6°C warmer than it was at the end of the 19th century[3]. This appears to be the warmest that the Earth has been for 10,000 years and yet it has happened in a very short period of time compared with natural fluctuations of this size. Some observers have been concerned that these measurements were distorted by the warming effect of cities but, in Japan, ground-level temperatures have been measured well away from cities for over a hundred years – in that time, the temperature has increased by 1.0°C. The planet's five warmest years in over a century have occurred during the past decade, with 2005 being the warmest of these. The European spring now comes earlier and autumn is delayed so the growing season is 11 days longer than it was 10 years ago. This has been matched by the length of ice-free periods on rivers and lakes. In Alaska and Western Canada, winter temperatures have increased by as much as 3 to 4°C during the past 50 years, but in Antarctica the East Ice Sheet is growing due to increased

Temperature values and CO$_2$ from the past

Temperatures are measured all over the world today, except for areas around the poles which are only covered in patches. Measurements are made at the surface and also from balloons at various heights and by satellites looking down through the atmosphere. However, these are relatively recent achievements – before about 1860, measurements were so limited that we do not know what the global temperature was from direct measurements. Indeed, even 150 years ago, thermometers were not as well standardised as they are today, so there is more uncertainty regarding how warm the Earth was then. Added to this is the problem that many temperature measurements were made close to urban areas; as these have expanded, the warmth of the cities has influenced the measured temperature, thus partly obscuring the trend in global temperature. Nevertheless, even after allowing for these effects, the trend in surface measurements over land and sea is generally

Fig. 3.4   Trend in global temperature since 1850. (source: http://www.cru.uea.ac.uk/cru/info/warming)

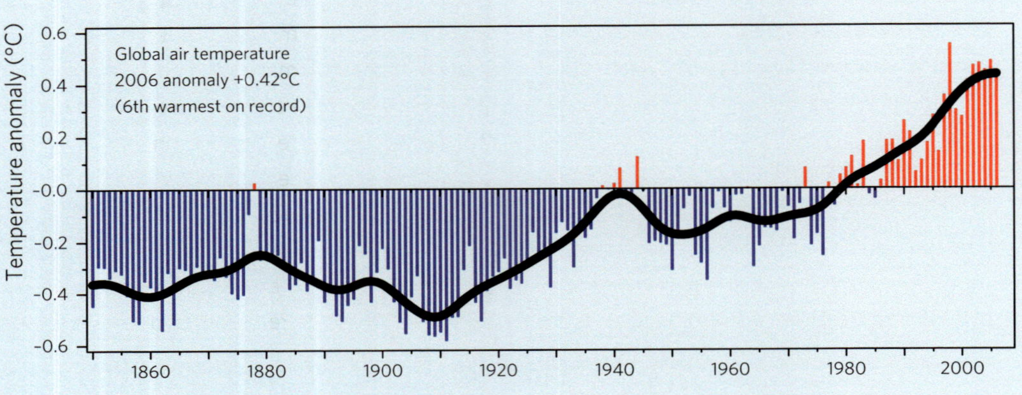

precipitation. Some of this must be natural variation but the scale and speed of these changes are sufficient to convince many scientists, and increasing numbers of governments, that the climate is changing in an unusual way.

Evidence of unusual change is not confined to temperature records. There are more dramatic examples. Glaciers in Northwest China, in the Andes and elsewhere have receded. The size of the Arctic ice sheet has shrunk. Land areas prone to drought have expanded, whilst other areas have experienced unusual

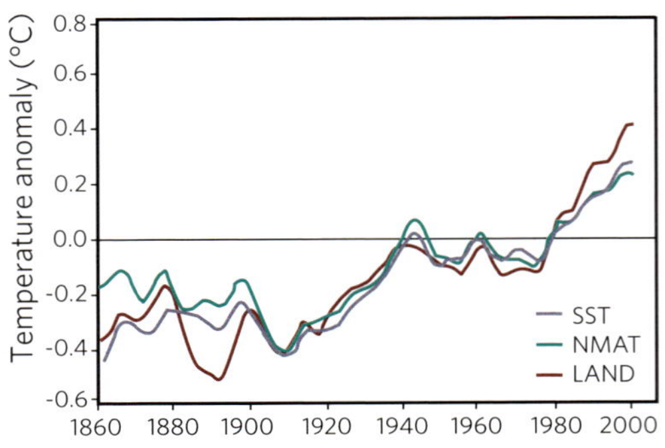

Fig. 3.5   Recent global temperature trends from three different sets of measurements – land surface, sea surface (SST) and air temperature over the sea at night (NMAT). (source: Hadley Centre)

consistent with a rise of approximately 0.6°C in the global temperature since 1860[2].

There are many ways of expressing the global temperature. In this book, we will mostly be concerned with the average temperature of the entire Earth over a whole year but other averages relate to minimum values, maximum values, daily values, etc. Changes in temperature are not uniform across the Earth's surface – temperatures at high latitudes have changed by 2°C or more since 1860, whilst the temperatures of some equatorial areas have not changed at all. Most reports of measurements seem to be consistent, but apparent differences between satellite measurements and surface temperature measurements have provoked much discussion, although it now seems that most of the differences can be explained.

Temperatures prior to 1860 can only be deduced from proxy measurements – these are natural phenomena which respond to temperature in a known way. For example, the annual growth of tree rings, the growth of coral, or the concentration of certain isotopes trapped in ice samples taken from deep inside the Greenland or Antarctic ice caps (the date is found by counting the number of layers of ice, as these are deposited annually).

None of these provide the extent of coverage that modern measurements provide, but they do give an indication of global temperatures although, the further back we look, the more uncertain the data. These records demonstrate natural variations in temperature, not only year on year, but over longer periods, making the discovery of trends more difficult – for example, there was a mini-ice age in Europe in the 1600s, when European temperatures were between 1 and 2°C below normal.

In the same way as for the isotopic measurement of temperature, the amount of CO_2 in the atmosphere has been found by measuring the amount of this gas trapped in ice. Samples of air trapped in the Greenland ice cap show no change in CO_2 content until about 300 years ago, after which the industrial revolution led to increases.

flooding. The sea-level has risen faster than expected based on historical trends. Corals are displaying the effects of bleaching due to higher temperatures. Seabirds failed to breed in the Shetland Islands in 2004, which has been attributed to disruption of their food supply because of the warming of the North Sea. These events may not be as obviously linked to human interference with the climate as the changes in temperature but they do reinforce the view that something unusual is happening to the Earth.

How can we find out what is causing these changes? One way of addressing this question is to look into the scientific theory behind the climate. The physics of the greenhouse effect were established more than 100 years ago and, since then, a great deal has been learnt about what affects the climate. The state of the atmosphere is influenced by the oceans, which also affect what is happening on land, which also has an effect on the atmosphere, and so on. The huge number of

such interactions can best be represented in a mathematical model. Such models contain a large number of equations which describe all of the physical, chemical and biological processes that determine the climate. The models are so complicated that it is necessary to use some of the world's largest computers to solve them. Even then, there are substantial uncertainties in the results.

Is climate change a cause for serious concern?

So, if human activity is affecting the climate, what needs to be done? There are two strands to the answer to this question – on the one hand, it is necessary to have some idea about how much the climate may change in the future, not just today. Secondly, it is necessary to understand what these changes imply for life on earth, especially the human race.

Luckily, once a mathematical model has been developed and verified, it can be run again and again for different combinations of circumstances to see what might happen. Thus, we can postulate the level of greenhouse gas emissions over the next 100 or 200 years and put these figures into the climate model, which in return would tell us how the climate may change.

Having established the possible climatic changes, this information can be used in other mathematical models to calculate how much heating and cooling buildings would need, how much water would be available for human and animal consumption and for farming, what effect rising temperatures might have on agriculture, or any other aspect of the world which might be of interest.

Climate science, modelling and sensitivity

The concept of the greenhouse effect was first proposed in the 19th century. Scientists became interested in it whilst seeking an explanation for the ice ages. The Swedish physicist Arrhenius recognised that the greenhouse effect also meant that emissions from human activities could produce global warming (he calculated that doubling the amount of CO_2 in the atmosphere could increase global temperatures by 5 to 6°C, which is in line with modern calculations). But his idea was not widely accepted at the time.

In the early 1960s, measurements showed that the amount of CO_2 in the atmosphere was rising fast. In order to understand the climate and how it might change due to greenhouse gas emissions, mathematical models were developed. Using such models only became feasible once large, fast computers were introduced in the 1970s to solve the equations.

These equations contain expressions of the temperature and pressure which describe the behaviour of the atmosphere and the oceans, and their interactions with the ice sheets and glaciers, the land surface and the biosphere (i.e. living things). The global pattern of circulation in the atmosphere is driven by the input of energy, so climate models start with a calculation of the balance of energy reaching and leaving the Earth. The movement of the atmosphere of a heated, rotating planet produces trade winds, as well as rising air in the tropics that descends at higher latitudes, cyclonic storms, etc. Clouds not only reflect incoming sunlight but also intercept radiation from below, the amount depending on the height of the clouds. Smoke, dust, and other aerosols not only influence the formation of clouds but also interact with radiation. Because many factors vary with height, the variables in the model are represented on a three-dimensional grid. The spacing between the grid points in the atmosphere is typically a few hundred kilometres horizontally and 500m vertically.

These models can describe what is likely to happen, although they cannot predict precisely what will happen, not least because there is still considerable uncertainty about the response of the climate to changes in the greenhouse effect. For example, doubling the amount of CO_2 (including the equivalent effect of other greenhouse gases) is calculated to change the global surface temperature by between 2 and 4.5°C. Such a wide range arises from uncertainties in the climate models and their internal feedbacks, particularly those concerned with clouds and related processes.

When using these models to make predictions, it must also be borne in mind that this would be in circumstances outside their calibration, so there is a substantial risk of errors due to unforeseen circumstances.

G.S. Callendar, one of the parents of climate studies, wrote in 1961: "This is a difficult subject: by long tradition the happy hunting ground for robust speculation, it suffers much because so few can separate fact from fancy."

These models are influenced by a large number of factors, many of which are uncertain, making precise prediction difficult. In view of this, scientists have constructed "scenarios" for the future which allow us to conduct "what-if" experiments. These are not forecasts – there is just not enough knowledge available for that – but they do provide some idea of the scale and impact of the problem.

Scenarios

In its Special Report on Emissions Scenarios[5], the IPCC grouped the many published scenarios into four broad families, which are briefly summarised here.

A key feature of any of the scenarios is global wealth, since increasing wealth tends to bring an increased use of energy and hence fossil fuels. The scenarios are distinguished from each other by a number of factors – the rate of economic development (which affects whether poor countries develop faster); the attitude towards environmental issues; the emphasis on global affairs or on regional/local affairs; the type of industry (energy-intensive or not) and the type of energy technology (conventional fossil fuel dependent, or high technology, or a mixture of the two). The four families of scenarios can be briefly summarised as follows:

A1: Rapid economic development, in which the current differences between rich and poor countries eventually disappear. High rates of investment and innovation, as well as highly mobile populations and the exchange of ideas and technology. Three variants of this type of scenario are considered, each with a different type of energy technology.

B1: A high level of environmental and social consciousness combined with a global approach to sustainable development.

B2: Increased concern about environmental and social sustainability, plus a shift towards local decision-making and self-reliance. Improvements in human welfare, equality, and environmental protection vary between regions.

A2: Continued economic differences between regions, with lower trade flows than in A1, relatively slower capital stock turnover, and slower technological change. In addition, regions become more self-reliant. Economic growth is constrained and there is less international cooperation and less mobility of capital and technology.

Whether or not some of these scenarios are feasible was not discussed specifically by the IPCC. The A1 scenarios are basically business-as-usual but with assumptions regarding changes in energy technology. It must be doubted whether rapid change to the high degree of environmental and social consciousness, as in the B1 or B2 scenarios, is realistic without some explicit policies to achieve this. What the scenarios do is allow us to test our expectations for the future against a range of ideas about what might happen.

A number of scenarios have been developed describing various ways in which the world's economies might evolve over the next 100 years. They are based on assumptions about the main factors influencing growth in emissions of greenhouse gases, e.g. population, economic growth, and energy technology, amongst other things.

The Intergovernmental Panel on Climate Change (IPCC) gathered nearly 100 scenarios in its work on understanding climate change[4]. All of these scenarios assume an increasing world population which will peak around the middle of the 21st century, not least as a result of all parts of the world becoming wealthier. None of the scenarios assume government policies being specifically introduced to reduce greenhouse gas emissions, so they provide a baseline against which possible responses can be tested.

From the emissions in each scenario, the amount of CO_2 which will be in the atmosphere at the end of the 21st century can be calculated – in one scenario there would be only 25% more CO_2 in the atmosphere than there is today. At the other extreme, the amount of CO_2 at the end of the century could be twice as much as the current level and still increasing fast.

As a result, in broad terms, the temperature of the Earth will increase, especially at higher latitudes, resulting in earlier springs and later autumns. The global average surface temperature in 2100 is expected to be about 3°C higher than its value in 1990, but the increase could be as little as 1.1°C or as much as 6.4°C depending on the scenario. There will also be more heat waves but fewer severe cold spells. The frequency of storms will increase and individual storms will become more intense. This will lead to more floods, which would be exacerbated in coastal areas by rising sea levels. There will also be a further reduction in the amount of ice in the Arctic Ocean. The oceans will become more acidic. One of the most pernicious changes is likely to be an increase in droughts in susceptible areas.

Such changes in natural systems would affect mankind in many ways. Changes in temperature would bring longer growing seasons at the higher latitudes, as well as a reduction in cold-related illnesses but an increase in cases of heat-stroke. There would be increases in weather-related damage to people and property, including flooding, particularly of low-lying islands where whole nations may be under threat. On the other hand, a reduction in sea ice could lead to the opening of the Arctic to commercial shipping. Agriculture is likely to be widely affected by changes in temperature and rainfall, with widespread failure of crops in regions affected by drought but the introduction of new crops elsewhere, leading to an expansion of agriculture in those regions. The changes in weather patterns would also encourage the movement of some species of animals, including disease-carrying insects, to higher latitudes, but others would become extinct if they were unable to move or adapt.

So, the likely consequence of climate change is that many people's lives would be affected – some may benefit from new opportunities while others will die. The old idea of the climate as something which is more or less fixed and predictable will disappear and people will have to get used to expecting and preparing for change. If, as expected, these changes become more substantial, the consequences for many people are likely to be very serious.

Projected effect of CO$_2$ emissions on temperature and sea level.

The various effects of climate change occur over different timescales, some of which are so long-term that accurate modelling is, to say the least, problematic. Nevertheless, an illustration[6] of the impact of the enhanced greenhouse effect can be sketched out, as shown in fig. 3.7. In this illustration, the CO$_2$ emissions first increase and then decrease again, reaching a low level within the next 100 years. As a result, the CO$_2$ concentration in the atmosphere stabilises after between 100 and 300 years, and then slowly falls. However, the thermal expansion of the oceans continues for hundreds of years as the heat permeates the deep oceans. Depending on the extent of the melting of ice, sea-levels may continue to rise for millennia.

Fig. 3.7 CO$_2$ concentration, temperature and sea-level will continue to rise long after the reductions in global emissions begin. (based on sketch in "Avoiding Dangerous Climate change" 2006)

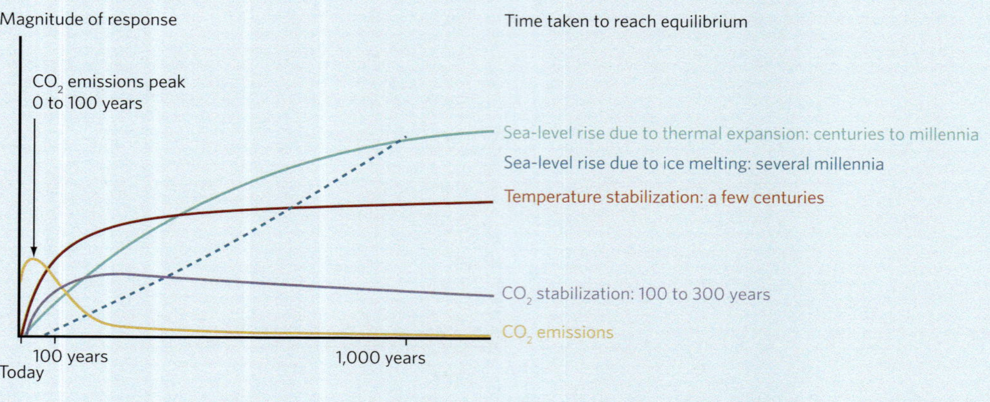

Prophetically, Mark Twain summarised the problem using another aphorism: "It is your human environment that makes climate."

More frightening still is the possibility of an unexpected outcome of climate change. Such an outcome may be a remote possibility but it cannot be completely discounted because the human race is conducting a worldwide experiment with the climate, provoking changes which may be greater and faster than any the world has seen during the last 10,000 years.

Two examples provide some idea of what is so frightening about this. For centuries Europe has been up to 8°C warmer than other regions on the same latitude (for example, Eastern Canada) because of the warming effect of the Gulf Stream. This current of warm water from the tropics is part of a worldwide circulation pattern which is driven by the difference between the salinity of the water in the northern seas and of that around the equator. If climate change leads to the

Chapter 3 | 200 years of damaging the climate

melting of ice in the north, thereby diluting the salt water with fresh water, this would reduce the force driving this circulation. So, European temperatures could fall towards the levels experienced elsewhere at this latitude. Even if the ice stopped melting, no one knows whether, or when, the circulation would revert to its original pattern.

A second example concerns the vast amount of methane which is trapped in ice-like crystals in the permafrost in the colder regions of the world. Methane is a very potent greenhouse gas and melting of the permafrost might release it. This could increase the rate of climate change, which in turn would lead to an even faster release of methane. Once the world got into such a situation, it would not be possible to make a simple recovery because it would be impossible to return the methane to the permafrost.

These are just two of the possible outcomes of climate change – there may only be a small chance of them occurring but, if they did, there could be major consequences for life on Earth. Changes in the global average temperature may give cause for concern but the unpredictable nature of some of the other possible outcomes is, perhaps, the most disturbing prospect of all.

How have governments responded to this?

Even in 1992, when much less was known about climate change, there was sufficient concern over the threat it posed to persuade governments worldwide to agree to an international treaty to protect the climate – the United Nations Framework Convention on Climate Change. This was put into practice in the Kyoto Protocol in 1997, which was eventually ratified in 2005. The objective of the Framework Convention demonstrates the degree of consensus achieved on goals, as well as indicating some of the obstacles to effective action on climate change. It aims to achieve:

> "stabilization of greenhouse gas concentrations in the atmosphere at a level that would prevent dangerous anthropogenic interference with the climate system."

Stabilization would occur when the rate of adding extra greenhouse gases to the atmosphere is balanced by the rate at which they are removed but it is not easy to say when and how this could be achieved.

Even more difficult to understand (and agree upon) is what constitutes a dangerous level of interference with the climate system. One measure which is often discussed is to assume that the amount of greenhouse gases in the atmosphere should be no more than double the amount in the atmosphere at the time of the Industrial Revolution. Is this the appropriate level to aim for? The simple answer is that no one knows.

The second part of the goal of the Convention states:

"Such a level (i.e. stabilization) should be achieved within a time frame sufficient to allow ecosystems to adapt naturally to climate change, to ensure that food production is not threatened and to enable economic development to proceed in a sustainable manner."

In other words, if change is happening, it must not be allowed to happen too fast. The signatories of the Convention saw merit in restraining the rate of change so as to allow plants and animals to adapt but, again, no one knows how fast would be too fast.

Do we need to take action?

Presenting a list of the likely effects of climate change, as we have just done, is all very well. It may serve to emphasise the dramatic effect that climate change will have on our lives. At one time, it could have enabled us to decide whether or not we were prepared to accept such change. But if, as seems likely, change is indeed now happening, we are beyond the point of being able to decide whether we want to accept it or not. Now the choice is about what we are prepared to do to control it and whether we can avoid any unacceptable changes. Broadly speaking, the actions available to us fall into two classes – either we can adapt to the changes or we can take action to mitigate their effects. But before we can do that, we need to understand how to strike a balance between the various aspects of the problem and the potential solutions.

How could we possibly decide whether, for instance, improvements in agriculture in northern countries due to the longer growing season would compensate in any way for the damage to Vanuatu or other low-lying nations in the South Pacific caused by rising sea-levels? Even King Solomon would have found such a judgement impossible. Global climate change presents many such issues so it is not surprising that politicians have called for help in deciding how to act. One approach which has been offered is to put an economic value on the benefits and damage using a "cost-benefit analysis".

This technique is very attractive because it appears to provide a single answer, expressed in monetary terms. This can be highly appealing to decision-makers

Cost-benefit analysis

Cost-benefit analysis is a well-established technique for testing whether or not a proposed project is of value to the community, for example a new sewage plant or an airport. All benefits and costs are expressed using a common unit of measurement – the most convenient one being money. Because money is worth more to us if it is available today than if the same amount were available to us at some time in the future, a discounted cash-flow calculation is employed to allow for this. The attractiveness of the project is determined by the difference between the discounted benefits and the discounted costs, with and without the project.

Some relevant factors are not normally expressed in monetary terms. In these cases, an equivalent monetary value must be derived if the cost-benefit calculation is to be complete. In conventional cost-benefit analysis, such a valuation is based on the choices which people actually make. For example, an improvement in the roads may allow people to save time on their journeys, so the monetary value of the time saved would be derived from observations of how people balance their time with the cost of, say, parking closer to their destination.

The benefits and damages of climate change can, in principle, be assessed in the same way. However, there are many differences compared with conventional cost-benefit analysis. For example, many aspects of climate change are not readily open to measurement, or cannot be easily quantified. Some of the possible effects of climate change are so far outside normal experience that a valuation based on the choices which people actually make would be a nonsense.

The most extreme aspect of conventional cost-benefit analysis is evaluating the benefit of saving human life; this causes much discussion, not least because there is widespread antipathy to the notion of placing a monetary value on human life. One way that conventional analysis gets round this concern is to consider examples where people voluntarily accept increased risk in return for higher pay. However, for climate change, the threat would be involuntary so such an approach would not provide a representative valuation of the threat to human life. Instead, the analysis is based on the statistical value of human life, even though this is based on the cost of saving life.

Another difference between conventional analysis and the climate change problem is the timescale – conventional projects typically have a lifetime of only a few decades and, importantly, they have substantial cash-flow during the early years, which will be a key determinant of the cost-effectiveness of the project. In the case of climate change, the major damage may not occur for 50 years or more and will get worse with time.

Indeed a basic problem when using cost-benefit analysis is the basic assumption of discounted cash-flow, namely that there is an acceptable alternative available for investment. In the case of the Earth, there is no alternative for the human race. If we make the Earth uninhabitable, there is nowhere else for us to live. So although, in principle, the techniques of cost-benefit analysis may be used to assess the effects of climate change, in practice there are severe problems associated with this approach. Even if a monetary value were to be derived for the net damage arising from climate change, it would be dangerous to compare this with the notional cost of action. The result could be very misleading.

but, in reality, this attraction is false since the numbers developed are, at best, inaccurate, and at worst represent only a part of the problem. A cost-benefit analysis places great emphasis on impacts which can be dealt with in the marketplace. It also attempts to deal with changes outside market systems, known as externalities, e.g. the effects of pollution on flora and fauna. But the values it places on some of the externalities are impossible to test, so we have no means of assessing how much confidence to put in the figures. For example, how could we decide whether the loss of unique assets such as the Arctic ice sheet, or the Monarch butterfly, or the coral atolls of the Pacific had been properly valued? Neither is it obvious how the distribution of impacts between different parts of the world (or between different generations) could be assessed in a satisfactory way. In addition the cost-benefit analysis framework cannot properly represent the effect of extreme climatic events, e.g. hurricanes of increasing strength, because so little is known about them that we cannot predict their occurrence with any confidence.

So it seems that decisions about taking action on climate change are too complicated to be subsumed into a simple analysis. It will have to be a societal decision, and a value judgement at that, regarding whether the damage we are doing to our environment is so severe that we need to take action.

At the very least, it would seem prudent to inform ourselves about the actions we could take, even to implement some limited measures, because the cost of action seems likely to be small in relation to the wealth that the world generates every year. A wealthy world should be able to take sensible precautions in view of the scale of the potential threat it faces. In essence, this is the subject of the rest of this book.

In preparation for a discussion about the actions we could take, it will first be necessary to equip ourselves with more information about where the greenhouse gases come from.

Emissions of greenhouse gases

Of the greenhouse gases arising from human activity, carbon dioxide (CO_2) is the one which has the greatest effect on the climate. There are large natural flows of CO_2 into and out of the atmosphere, yet the relatively small extra amounts originating from the combustion of fossil fuels and deforestation have caused the level in the atmosphere to increase by 40% during the past 200 years.

The second most important greenhouse gas is methane, which comes from a wide variety of sources. One of the most publicised sources of methane is the diges-

Carbon cycle

The amount of CO_2 which is added to the atmosphere each year by fossil fuel combustion and deforestation is dwarfed by the natural flows of carbon in and out of the atmosphere. Collectively, these natural processes are known as the carbon cycle:

- animals breathe in air, their bodies make use of some of the oxygen and they then exhale CO_2 and other gases;
- plants take up CO_2 from the atmosphere and release oxygen in small amounts during photosynthesis;
- half of the CO_2 assimilated over the year by plants through photosynthesis is released back into the atmosphere by respiration;
- decaying plant materials release CO_2;
- similar processes occur in the oceans.

The ability of the oceans to absorb CO_2 from the atmosphere is one of the main ways of removing the extra CO_2 that we are currently emitting. However, in consequence, we are dissolving large amounts of CO_2 into the oceans which is making them more acidic. Already, this has been observed to have slightly increased the acidity of the oceans (a change of about 0.1 pH units). This is the environment in which fish and other creatures live, so the impact on these species could be quite important for global fish stocks.

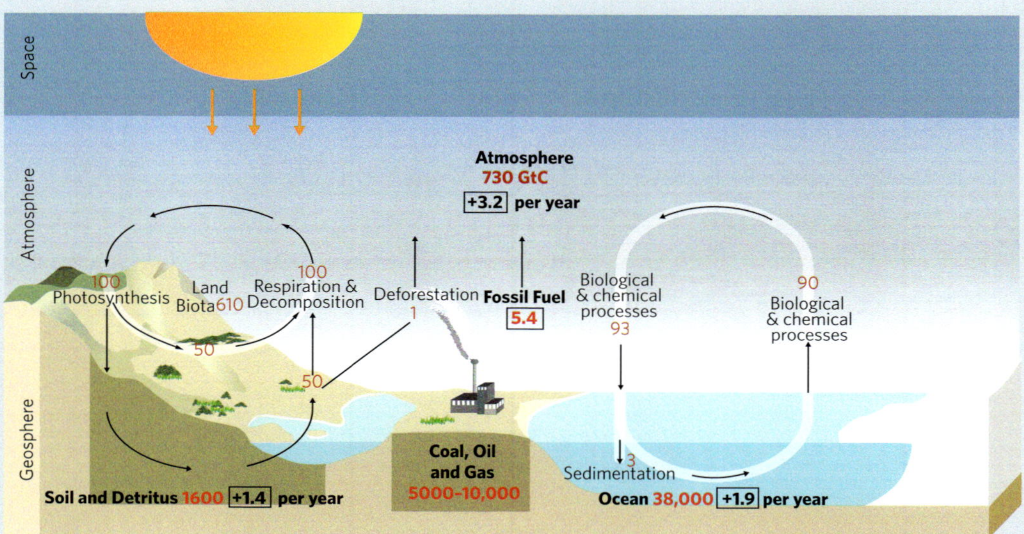

Fig. 3.8 Global carbon cycle: the natural flows of carbon into and out of the atmosphere. It should be noted that these flows are described in tonnes of C rather than tonnes of CO_2. The amounts of carbon in the atmosphere, ocean and soil are shown in red. (Redrawn from Australian government diagram)

tive systems of animals such as sheep and cows, but there are many others. There is now 150% more methane in the atmosphere than during pre-industrial times.

Other gases also contribute to enhancing the greenhouse effect, e.g. nitrous oxide and chlorofluorocarbons (CFCs), which are also known to be damaging the ozone

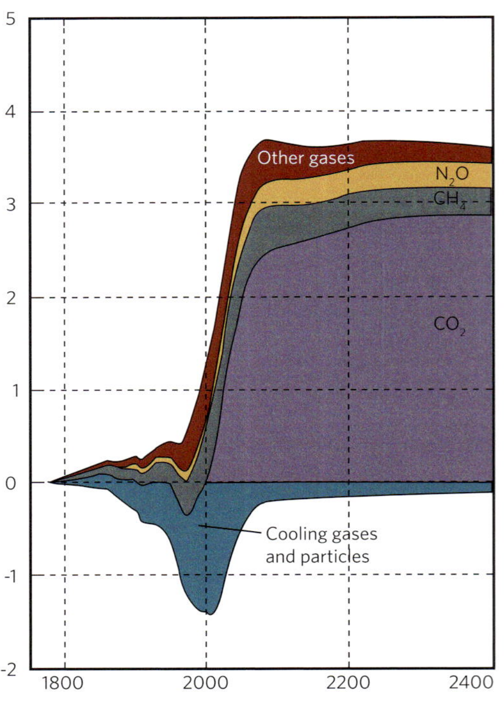

Fig. 3.9 The various greenhouse gases make different contributions to global warming. This illustrates one particular scenario for stabilising the amount of greenhouse gas in the atmosphere (Courtesy of Malte Meinshausen, ETH).

layer. The CFCs and other such gases are of particular interest because of their very long lifespan in the atmosphere.

In circumstances where more CO_2 is being emitted than is being removed by natural processes, the amount of it will increase in the atmosphere. This can be compared to a barrel being filled with water (see Figure 3.10) – if the rate at which water is added to the barrel exceeds the rate at which it flows out of the tap, then the level of water will rise. The level of water in the barrel is analogous to the amount of CO_2 in the Earth's atmosphere. Thus, adding CO_2 faster than it can be removed will cause the amount in the atmosphere to increase. CO_2 may stay in the atmosphere for 70 to 100 years before it is removed by natural processes, called "sinks". Methane may only last about 7 to 10 years but some of the other gases can last for thousands of years. These long-lived gases may be only a small part of the overall change, but because they will be there for such a long time, they will effectively reduce the amount of other gases which can be tolerated. In our analogy of a barrel this is equivalent to adding some pebbles.

Fig. 3.10   The level of water in the barrel is an analogy for the amount of CO_2 in the atmosphere; stabilisation occurs when the rate of adding water to the barrel is matched by the amount flowing out.

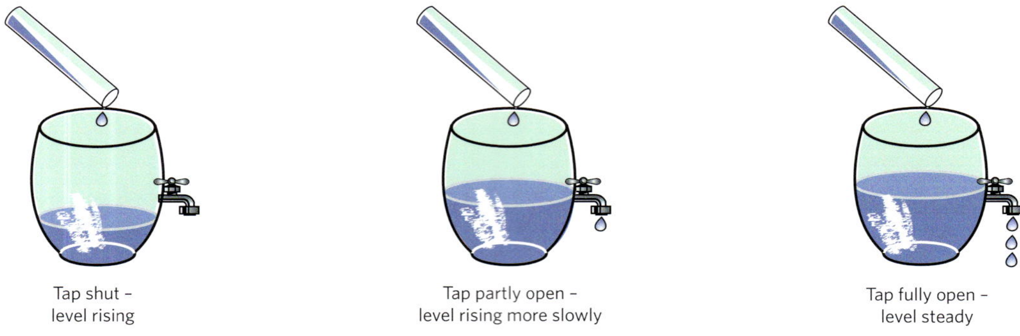

   Chapter 3 | 200 years of damaging the climate

Sources and sinks

The observed increase in atmospheric CO_2 is only about half of what is expected from the amount of fossil fuels burnt and the area of forests cleared. The reason for this difference appears to be that the increased concentration of CO_2 in the atmosphere has led to extra growth in plants and bacteria, which take up CO_2. These are called natural sinks for carbon. There is some physical evidence of the increased growth of forests, especially in North America, and the extra growth of phyto-plankton in the oceans.

Figure 3.11 indicates the main changes[7] in global flows of CO_2 during the 1980s and 1990s. These values have been derived from measurements of the atmospheric levels of CO_2 and O_2. There are significant uncertainties in all of these measurements, especially the CO_2 flux between land and atmosphere. The main difference between the 1980s and 1990s was the increase in the CO_2 emissions. Despite this, the amount of CO_2 in the atmosphere only increased during the 1990s by an amount similar to that in the 1980s. The role of the oceans in removing CO_2 from the atmosphere is thought to have declined slightly during the 1990s, which suggests that there has been a much greater net take-up of CO_2 by plants on land.

In order to work out the reasons why the land has been taking up more CO_2, it is necessary to distinguish between two processes: the natural sinks taking up CO_2 from the atmosphere, estimated at –7.0 Gt CO_2/year during the 1980s, and the emissions from land use changes (including deforestation) of 6.2 Gt CO_2/y during the 1980s. Separate estimates for these two processes during the 1990s were not published in the IPCC's Third Assessment Report. However, unless deforestation has been halted, the estimates suggest that the natural sinks have increased.

Fig. 3.11   Estimating the size of the natural sinks – the land and ocean sinks are smaller than the emissions of CO_2 from human activities but the uncertainties (shown in different colours) are large (positive figures indicate flow to the atmosphere; negative values indicate uptake from the atmosphere). (source: "Climate Change 2001: The Scientific Basis")

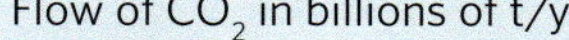

Flow of CO_2 in billions of t/y

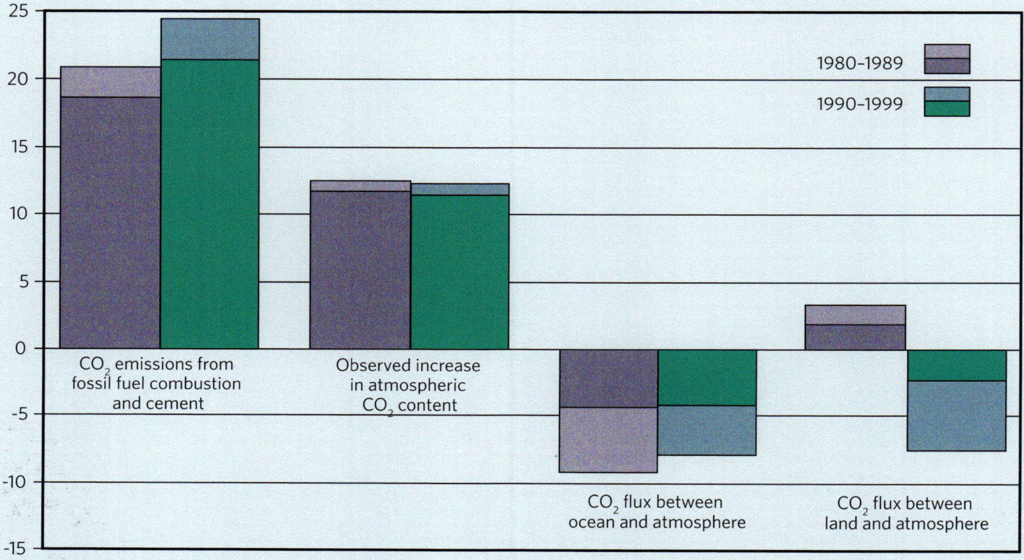

Who is responsible for emitting so much CO_2?

There are various ways of understanding who is responsible for CO_2 emissions. One way is to look at how much CO_2 comes from each of the main fossil fuels. The combustion of coal produces about 36% of the total – coal is mostly used in large industrial plants, especially for power generation. There are also significant amounts released from industrial processes, such as iron and steel manufacture and the production of cement.

Another important source is the combustion of natural gas. In terms of the energy released, the burning of natural gas only releases about half as much CO_2 as would come from the burning of coal to produce the same amount of energy. Nevertheless, natural gas is a major source of CO_2 and global emissions from the combustion of natural gas amount to over 20% of the total from all fossil fuels. Natural gas is used in large power stations but also to provide heating in buildings, as well as in some industrial processes such as chemical production and glassmaking.

However, the most important fossil fuel in terms of CO_2 emissions is oil, contributing more than 40% of the total. Oil is particularly important for powering cars and other vehicles, so the bulk of its use is in small engines. World demand for transport continues to increase, almost all of this being fuelled by petrol and diesel oil.

Fig. 3.12 The various fossil fuels emit different amounts of CO_2 in producing the same amount of energy (this diagram shows the amount of CO_2 in kg from production of 1 GJ of energy).

Fig. 3.13 CO_2-emissions in 2004 from the use of fossil fuels by the main sectors of the global economy (source: World Energy Outlook, 2006. IEA).

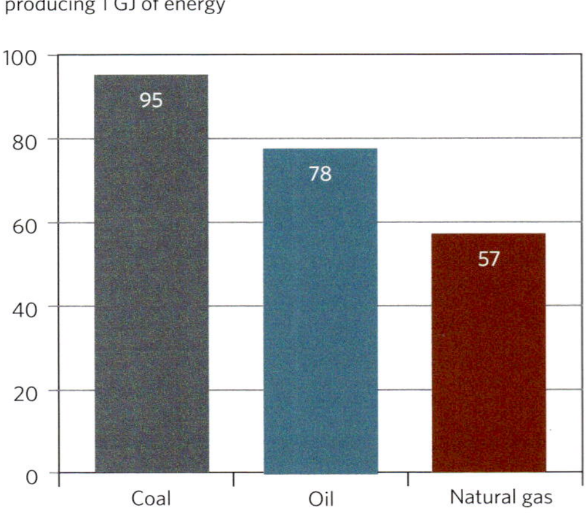

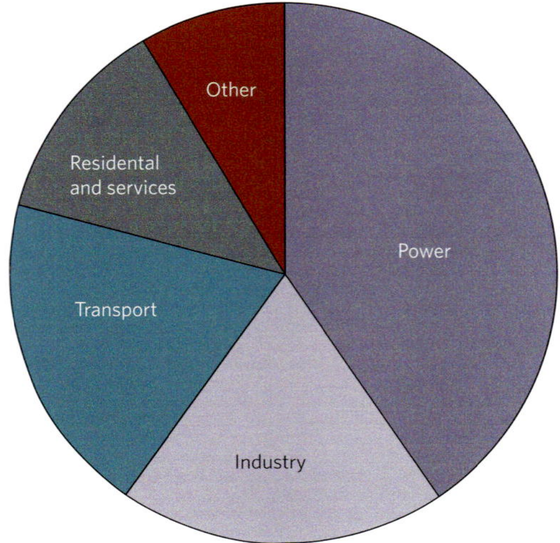

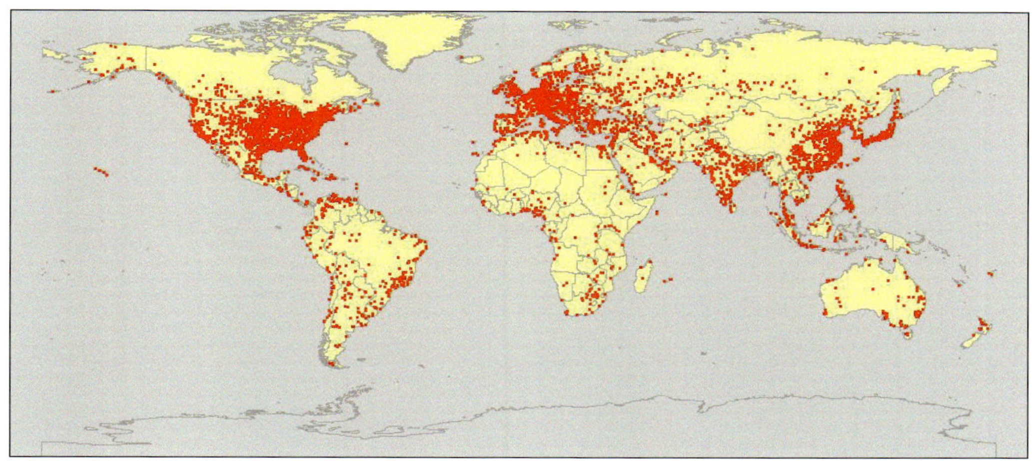

Fig. 3.14 There are many large, stationary sources of CO_2 around the world – each point indicates one source such as a power station, cement works, oil refinery, etc. (Courtesy: Ecofys).

The proportional contributions made by the different fuels have remained virtually constant over the past few years, as the increasing demand for energy has been matched by the increased supply of fossil fuels.

An alternative way of answering the question about responsibility is to consider which economic sectors are responsible for these emissions. The largest single source is power generation. Industry makes a substantial contribution, but transport and buildings are also major sources of emissions (fig. 3.13).

Yet another way of answering the question is to look at who causes these fuels to be used – each part of the global economy uses some energy/fuel directly and some in a more convenient form, especially electricity. Assigning emissions to the end-use sectors shows how the demands for energy services

Fig. 3.15 Different types of power stations produce different emissions of CO_2 – this shows the combined effect of choice of fuel and the technology used. (source: World Energy Outlook, 2006. EIA)

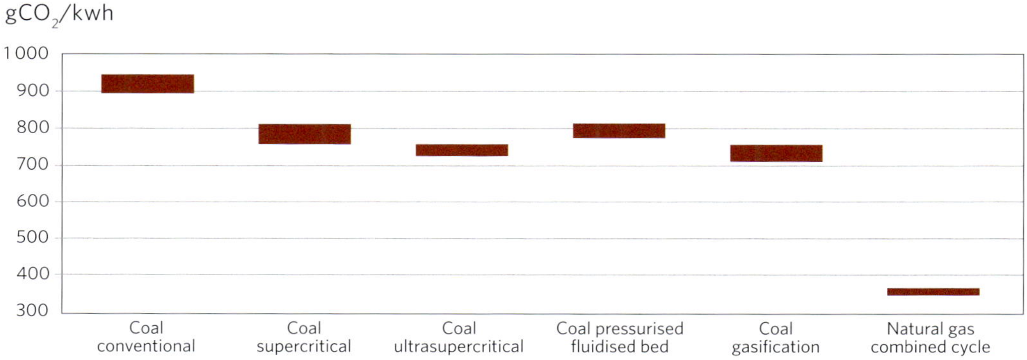

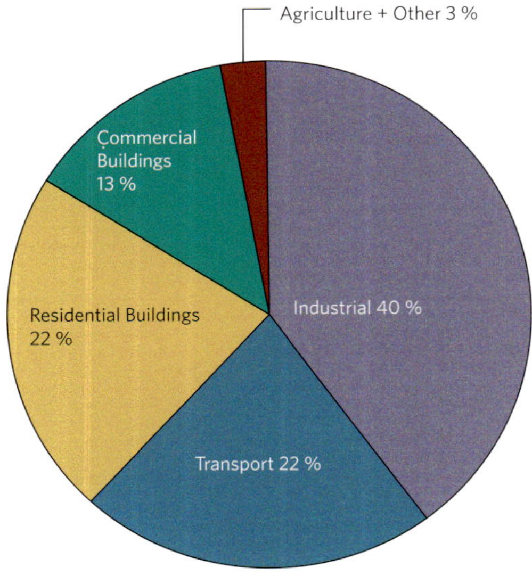

Fig. 3.16 CO_2 emissions can be attributed to each end-use sector by taking account of the emissions from primary energy supply, conversion and end use.

are creating the need for emissions. Figure 3.16 shows that the energy used in buildings causes at least one third of global emissions and probably more because the largest sector, industry, also includes some buildings-related emissions. A large part of the emissions due to energy being used in buildings is because of the amount of electricity consumed.

All of these answers provide some parts of the picture, but when it comes to action, the individual will be the key. The amount of CO_2 that each country emits per person varies widely because emissions are directly related to energy use, which is strongly influenced by national wealth. Thus the level of emissions per person largely reflects the wealth of the country. The greatest emissions per capita come from some oil-rich countries followed by many of the developed countries. Their emissions are five to ten times higher than those of some of the rapidly-growing developing countries, such as China and Mexico, which in turn have considerably higher emissions per capita than some of the other developing nations.

The larger and wealthier the country, the more it emits (fig. 3.18). Thus, the USA is responsible for more than 20% of global emissions but, as countries improve their standards of living, more emissions can be expected. Thus, China accounts for 14% of global fossil fuel emissions and the level is rising.

This picture is evolving all the time as countries increase their emissions in step with expanding their economies. At the same time, others may be reducing their emissions, for example in Eastern Europe during the 1990s, when uncompetitive heavy industries were shut down as these countries converted to market economies. Who will be emitting most in the future?

Recognising the ever-present danger of drowning any argument in statistics, some simple interpretations should be offered as to what some of these figures mean in terms of meeting the goals of the UN Framework Convention on Climate Change.

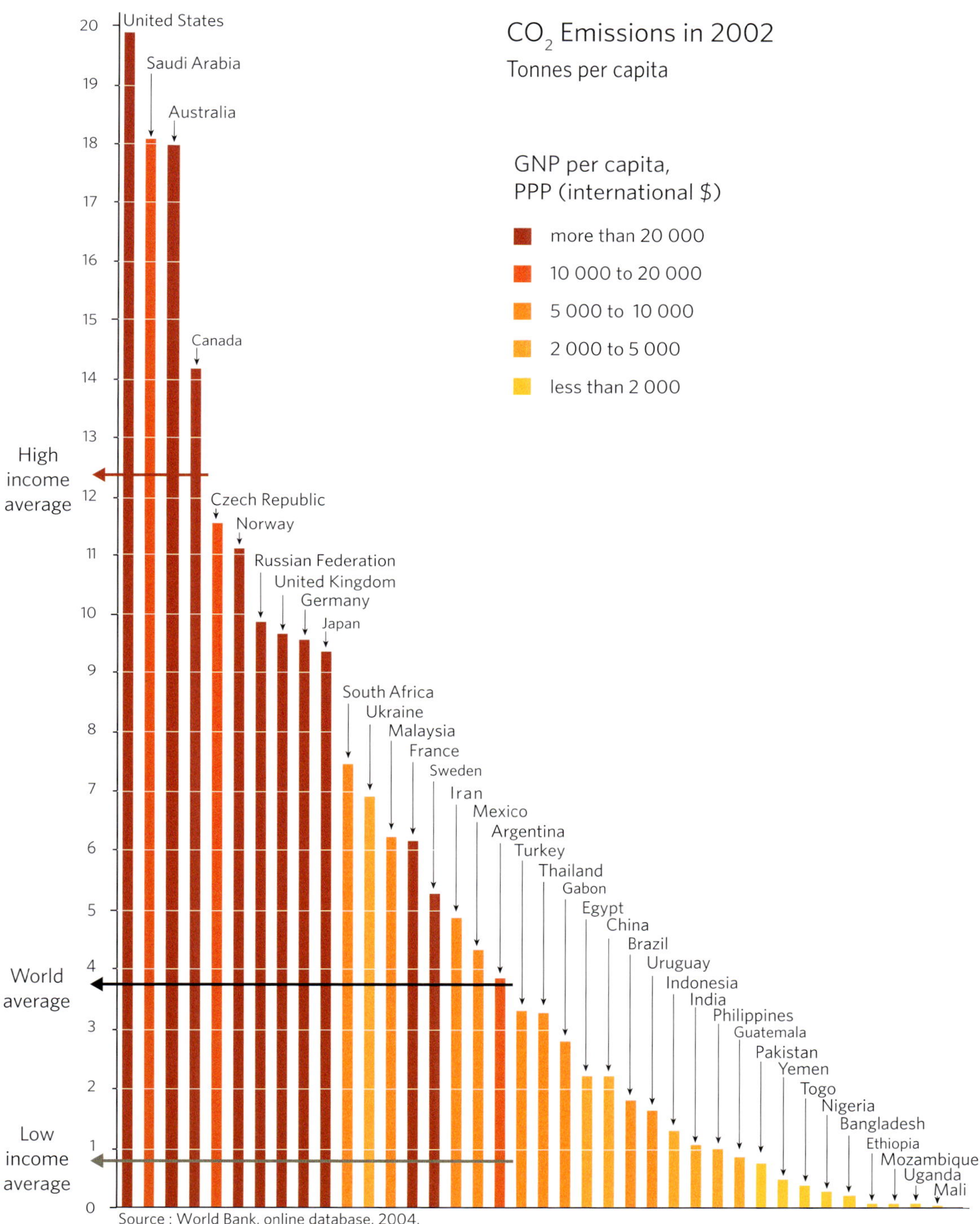

Fig. 3.17 CO₂ emissions per capita (in tonnes of CO₂) for various countries (source: GRID Arendal).

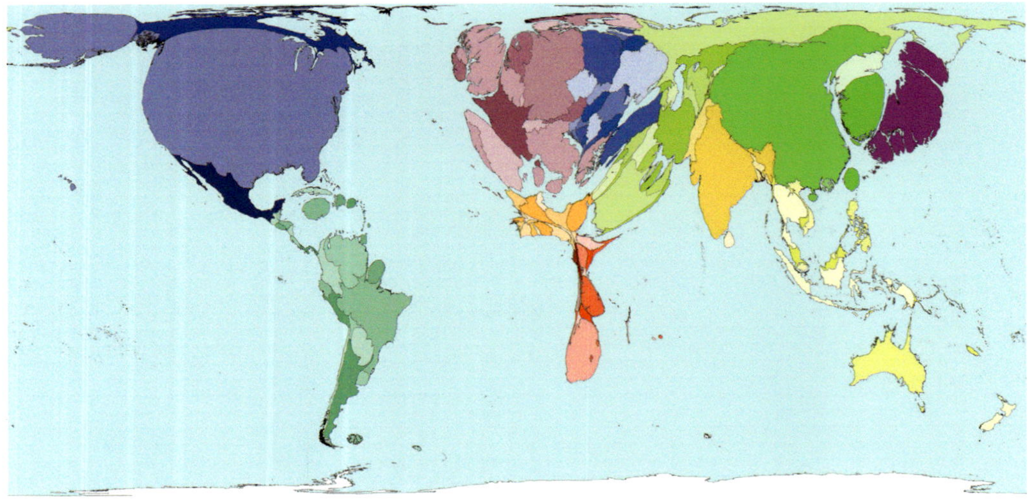

Fig. 3.18 CO$_2$ emissions by each country. In this map, the area of each country has been re-sized according to the amount of its emissions (www.worldmapper.org).

Broadly speaking, the world can only stabilise the amount of greenhouse gases in the atmosphere if emissions are reduced to a level where they are balanced by the removal by the natural sinks. With 6 billion people on the planet, and natural sinks absorbing about 8 billion tonnes of CO$_2$ annually (assuming deforestation continues at the rate seen in the 1980s), the world could achieve stabilisation if emissions worldwide were reduced to roughly 1.3 tonnes of CO$_2$ per person per

Trends in CO$_2$ emissions to 2050

Today, about 26 billion tonnes of CO$_2$ are emitted every year as result of people using fossil fuels worldwide. Estimates of how much emissions will increase in the future vary enormously, but one "business as usual" estimate made by the US Energy Information Administration (EIA) suggests that about 44 billion tonnes per year will be emitted in 2030[8]. About half of this increase is expected to come from the combustion of coal, with the rest divided equally between the combustion of petroleum products and natural gas.

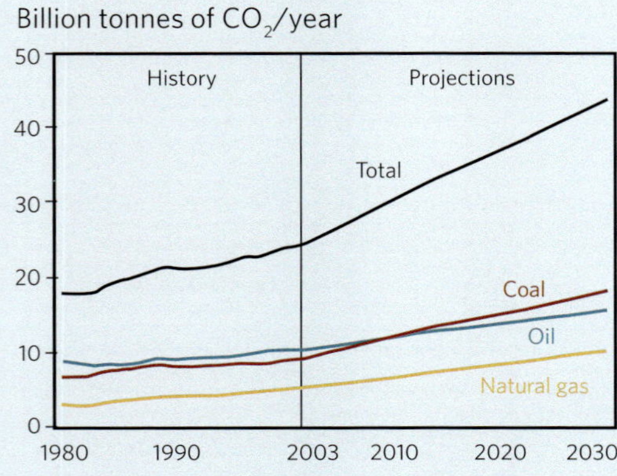

Fig. 3.19 World CO$_2$ emissions by type of fuel, 1980–2030 (US Energy Information Administration).

Chapter 3 | 200 years of damaging the climate

year with similar reduction in emission of other greenhouse gases. For example, in a European country, this would mean reducing current emissions by between 80% and 90%. For some developing countries, this might allow some increases in emissions but for others, already at this level of emissions, it would be necessary to constrain any further growth.

If such a level was accepted as a target, how soon would it have to be achieved? How would we go about it? Clearly no change of this magnitude can be made instantaneously. Figure 3.20 illustrates how the world might reduce its emissions of CO_2 in a managed way, reaching an annual level of around 1.3 tonnes per

Scenario of emission reductions

Figure 3.20 illustrates an emissions profile designed to achieve stabilisation in the atmosphere at 550 parts per million of CO_2 in 2100[9].

The effect on the global mean temperature, since pre-industrial levels, as a result of this strategy has been calculated for different values of the climate sensitivity assumption; the results are reproduced in Figure 3.21. The upper line in this figure indicates the temperature increase resulting from a climate sensitivity of 4.5; the middle line, 2.5; and the lower line,

1.5. The horizontal dotted line indicates a 2°C increase in the global mean temperature, the policy target adopted by the European Union.

Thus, in principle, the chosen pathway can limit the maximum increase in the global temperature to 2°C by 2100, with both medium and low climate sensitivities, but not with the high climate sensitivity. Even though the simulation ends at this point, both the increase in the amount of CO_2 in the atmosphere and the temperature will have stabilised by this time.

Fig. 3.20 Scenario of emission reduction in order to achieve stabilisation of the amount of CO_2 in the atmosphere by the end of the 21st century (this is the IMAGE S550e pathway)

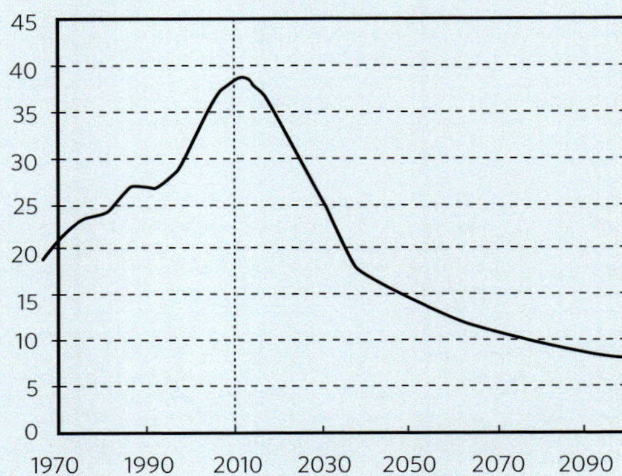

Fig. 3.21 Following the IMAGE S550e pathway may achieve temperature stabilisation by 2100 although there is significant uncertainty.[10]

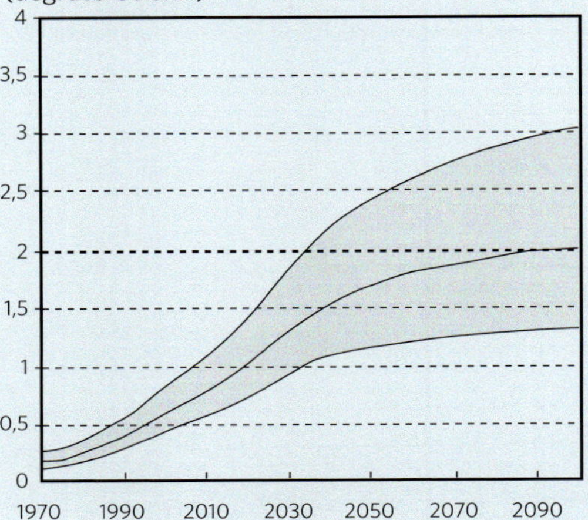

individual by the end of the century. Following this course would (just about) stabilise the amount of CO_2 in the atmosphere during this century. The result would be stabilisation at about twice the amount that there was before the Industrial Revolution. This might result in global temperatures rising by between 1.3°C and 3°C (the extent of the change is subject to all of the caveats expressed before). Whether or not that is an acceptable level is something which everyone will have to decide for themselves.

In order to follow this path, global emissions would have to be reduced every year by at least 3% until 2050, followed by smaller reductions after that. Such reductions would fall disproportionately on the major emitters, especially during the first few decades. These reductions may not seem large but, by historical standards, they are considerable. For example, consider the 15 countries of the European Union which accepted emission reduction targets under the Kyoto Protocol in 1997. Their joint goal was to reduce emissions to 8% less than 1990 levels by 2008–12. By the end of 2004 (7 years after the Protocol had been signed), their total greenhouse gas emissions[11] had only been reduced to 0.6% less than 1990 levels and were, in fact, no lower than in 1997.

So achieving global reductions of 3% per annum for 40 years is likely to be very challenging. This would involve each and every individual making changes, since the impact on the supply and use of energy would be substantial. Some emissions are directly under the control of the individual (e.g., heating buildings, individual transport) but there are other emissions which are not (e.g., power generation, public transport). These would have to be tackled differently. Some are easier to tackle while others are more difficult. Which ones should we start with?

Some sectors are inherently easier to address than others because they only have a few, large sources of CO_2 – for example power generation. These may be more susceptible to action than, for instance, millions of privately-owned vehicles. In the next chapter, we will describe some of the actions which could be taken to achieve major reductions in emissions.

Suggestions for further reading

Climate into the 21ˢᵗ century. 2003. W. Burroughs (ed.). WMO, Cambridge University Press.

Avoiding dangerous climate change. 2006. H. J. Schellnhuber, W. Cramer, N. Nakicenovic, T. Wigley, G. Yohe (eds.). Cambridge University Press.

Climate Change 2001: The Scientific Basis. Contribution of Working Group I to the Third Assessment Report of the Intergovernmental Panel on Climate Change [Houghton, J.T., Y. Ding, D.J. Griggs, M. Noguer, P.J. van der Linden, X. Dai, K. Maskell, and C.A. Johnson (eds.)]. Cambridge University Press, Cambridge, United Kingdom and New York, NY, USA, 881pp.

Fourth Assessment Report of The Intergovernmental Panel on Climate Change. http://www.ipcc.ch/

Endnotes

1   Much of the data in this chapter is taken from "Climate Change 2001: The Scientific Basis", the report of Working Group 1 of the Intergovernmental Panel on Climate Change, published by Cambridge University Press, 2001.

2   "Climate Change 2001: The Scientific Basis", the report of Working Group 1 of the Intergovernmental Panel on Climate Change, published by Cambridge University Press, 2001.

3   Ibid.

4   IPCC Special report on Scenarios. 2000. Published by Cambridge University Press.

5   IPCC Special report on Scenarios. 2000. Cambridge University Press.

6   Adapted from "Avoiding dangerous climate change." H. J. Schellnhuber, W. Cramer, N. Nakicenovic, T. Wigley, G. Yohe (eds.), Cambridge University Press, 2006.

7   "Climate Change 2001: The Scientific Basis", the report of Working Group 1 of the Intergovernmental Panel on Climate Change, published by Cambridge University Press, 2001.

8   "System for the Analysis of Global Markets." EIA, US DOE. 2006.

9   Adapted from "Multi-gas emission profiles for stabilising greenhouse gas concentrations – Emission implications of limiting global temperature increase to 2°C" by B. Eickhout, M.G.J. den Elzen and D.P. van Vuuren, RIVM report 728001026/2003.

10 Ibid.

11 This figure does not include the effects of land use changes and forestry.

Squaring the circle: accessing energy without damaging the climate

Some degree of climate change is inevitable. This will affect many parts of the world. The big question facing the human race is how far and how fast are we prepared to reduce emissions. In this chapter, we will examine whether the world may be able to obtain reliable supplies of energy whilst protecting the climate and without spending too much.

Fig. 4.1 Earth's lights by night (NASA).

What options does the world have to reduce emissions?

As we have seen, protecting the world against continuing climate change will require a considerable reduction in the emissions of greenhouse gases. Although the necessary timescale is not known with any certainty, it seems likely that most, if not all, of this reduction will need to be made this century.

Because of its substantial warming effect, CO_2 is the main cause of concern amongst the greenhouse gases produced by human activities, and is the focus of this book. In order to understand where changes could be made, it may be helpful to consider the main factors which determine how much CO_2 is emitted. These were captured in a simple identity by Professor Yoichi Kaya; this expresses the inter-relationships so clearly that we are willing to break our self-imposed rule (of not using equations) and present it here.

$$CO_2\ \text{Emissions} = \text{Population} \times \left(\frac{\text{GDP}}{\text{Population}}\right) \times \left(\frac{\text{Energy}}{\text{GDP}}\right) \times \left(\frac{\text{Emissions}}{\text{Energy}}\right)$$

What this says is that there are four main factors which jointly determine how much CO_2 the human race produces. These are:

- The population: everyone uses energy so the number of people on the planet is an important determinant of the total energy used and hence the level of emissions;
- Their wealth, expressed as average Gross Domestic Product (GDP) per capita: generally a higher GDP per capita implies a higher use of energy;
- The energy intensity of their activities, reflecting the fact that different individuals or countries use more or less energy than others; this is expressed as the amount of energy use per unit of GDP;
- The emissions produced by their energy technologies: each and every means of using or supplying energy can be associated with a certain amount of CO_2 emissions; this is expressed as the emissions per unit of energy supplied or used.

These four factors allow us to consider what changes we might make in order to reduce CO_2 emissions. It is worth reminding ourselves at this point that, for the developed countries, emissions may need to be reduced by as much as 80% or 90% in order to achieve stabilisation of the amount of CO_2 in the atmosphere.

Firstly, population: clearly, a wholesale reduction in the population would not be acceptable as a policy measure; indeed the global population is still increasing.

Secondly, wealth: generally, people aspire to improve their standards of living, for which wealth is one important ingredient. There is widespread acceptance of the idea that everyone has the right to expect higher standards of living in the future. In that context, it is hard to imagine that a deliberate policy of wealth reduction (as would be necessary to achieve an 80% to 90% reduction in emissions) would be an acceptable approach for controlling climate change.

Thirdly, energy intensity: in several countries, the energy intensity has been falling during the recent past but these reductions are quite small, often due to changes in the composition of national economies (e.g. switching from steel-making to software production). Nevertheless, this could be a contributor towards reducing CO_2 emissions.

Fourthly, technology: unlike the other three factors, there are many options for deep reductions in emissions – some technologies would enable reductions of 80% or more without affecting the service provided and with only a relatively modest increase in cost.

Consequently, we draw the preliminary conclusion that, in order to avoid drastic reductions in population or wealth, sharply reducing emissions will mainly depend on improving energy technology, although changes in the energy intensity could also help. Coupled with this, it would be desirable if these reductions could be achieved with the least cost to society.

It is also worth considering what this would imply if action were not taken to reduce emissions sufficiently. Without sufficient action, and sufficiently fast, the effects of climate change will be felt especially by people who are least capable of defending themselves, such as those in low-lying developing countries. This would mean a reduction in their standard of living or, in the extreme case, losing their lives. Thus, failure to take deliberate action to reduce emissions would still lead to a reduction in emissions but this would be by involuntary means – for example due to massive flooding or drought – ways that would be unacceptable to many civilised people. In comparison, the development and deployment of advanced technology to reduce emissions seems a much more acceptable approach to take.

Developing and deploying improved energy technology

A well-recognised action list for reducing the environmental impact of any activity is to:

- reduce (the demand)
- recycle
- substitute
- destroy
- dispose

The initial items in this list are preferable to the subsequent ones, if at all possible – i.e. reducing demand would be preferred whilst disposal should be avoided if possible.

Something similar can be applied to dealing with CO_2 emissions resulting from energy use. Let us examine in more detail just what could be done, for the main sectors of the global economy.

Option: Reduce demand

The first approach should be to reduce the demand for energy, which in turn would reduce CO_2 emissions. This can be achieved by changing the way that energy is used or by reducing our need to use energy, particularly cutting out unnecessary uses.

Changing how energy is used can reduce emissions, for example by using energy more efficiently. The efficiency with which we use energy is typically determined by a trade-off between the cost of inefficient use and the cost of improved technology. Thus a high-efficiency refrigerator may initially cost more than one with lower efficiency, but the extra cost can be recouped in perhaps two or three years. Investment in the high-efficiency appliance is thus likely to be cost-effective for most users. Such changes are likely to be long-lasting because, once the

Fig. 4.2 This front-loading clothes-washer uses half the energy and one-third the water of a top-loading washing machine. It also spins the clothes dryer than a conventional machine, saving energy in subsequent drying.

No-regrets measures

The fallacy that a substantial proportion of emissions could be avoided by measures which have no net cost appears to have arisen from the observation that certain efficiency improvements are cost-effective (based on assumptions about the rate of return on investment required by an investor, or by society).

For example, suppose we are purchasing a new refrigerator, and we are faced with a choice of two models – one being more energy efficient but more expensive than the other. If the extra cost of the higher efficiency model could be recouped within two years of operation, the rate of return on the investment after three years would exceed 20%, rising to 50% after 10 years, substantially more than can be obtained by leaving the money in the bank. This could even justify borrowing the money in order to buy the more efficient appliance. In this sense, we would save money overall by purchasing the more efficient unit. For most people, there would be "no regrets" about such a measure.

However, this is not a general rule regarding improvements in energy efficiency. Not everything will repay the extra money invested in it within a reasonable period of time. For example, insulating the external walls of an old, solid-walled house in Britain may need 20 or 30 years to repay the investment through savings in heating bills. In such cases, the rate of return might be only 4% after 30 years.

If the householder had to borrow the money from a bank, he or she would be spending more each year than prior to fitting the insulation, even allowing for the savings in heating costs. Worse still, some of the benefits of insulation might result in higher room temperatures (especially in rooms without thermostatic controls), so fuel bills would not be cut as much as expected. Government may consider that improved comfort should be valued as a benefit with the same worth as the heating that could have been avoided (another example of cost-benefit analysis at work). Indeed, in assessing such measures, government may decide that society requires a lower rate of return than the householder. From such a point of view, the improved insulation can have a positive rate of return for society, even though, in financial terms, it does not meet the investment criteria of the householder. Thus, it is described as a "no-regrets" measure.

However, in reality, this poor rate of return means that the householder typically looks to government for a subsidy before undertaking such a measure. The availability of a subsidy suggests that the investment would not have been made otherwise, which is hardly to be described as "no regrets". The basic problem seems to be that the rates of return required by people prior to investment in such measures are not typically used as the basis for these conclusions – rather, a "reasonable" assumption is made about what would be acceptable.

Fig. 4.3 Insulating the walls of a solid wall house may not be viewed as good use of money by its owners even if it makes sense from an energy saving point of view.

capital has been invested, the appliance will continue to provide service for several years up until it is replaced. Equally important, if an energy-efficient appliance is not selected at the time of replacement, the opportunity will not be available again until that appliance next needs replacing.

Unfortunately, many appliances are already highly efficient so further improvements will only achieve modest reductions in emissions; e.g. domestic gas boilers with an efficiency of 70% can be replaced by condensing boilers with an efficiency greater than 80%, thereby reducing emissions by between 15% and 20%. However, the law of diminishing returns applies here, with further improvements achieving ever smaller reductions in emissions.

A common fallacy is that a substantial proportion of emissions could be avoided by taking measures which have no net cost or which even make a profit for the owner. These are called "no regrets measures". Although some efficiency improvements are cost-effective for the user, many others cannot be justified on the basis of the savings made via reduced energy bills at the rate of return expected by many private individuals.

The other approach to cutting demand would be to reduce the need to use energy; this can be achieved, for example by switching off the lights when leaving a room, or by changing to a less energy-intensive way of working, for example by working from home. Unfortunately, reductions achieved in this way are not very robust – next time we leave the room, we might forget to switch the light off, or our employer might call us into the office next day rather than let us work at home. The financial cost of reducing energy use can often be low, but without consistent and repeated inducements to maintain these new habits, it will be very easy to slip back into our old ways and thus undo the changes achieved.

More long-lasting changes can be obtained through an investment that reduces the need to use energy. Investment in insulating the fabric of a building (i.e. the walls, windows, roof) would reduce the need for heating or cooling.

Fig. 4.4 Working from home saves energy but perhaps not as predictably as we might think.

Fig. 4.5 Low energy school at Butzbach in Germany. It was designed with large windows on southerly aspects, to harness the sun for lighting and heating purposes.

Fig. 4.6 Bryggen (the Wharf) is a series of Hanseatic commercial buildings in Bergen, Norway. Bryggen has been rehabilitated to house modern shops and offices. Rehabilitating old buildings for energy saving and other purposes will never be easy or cheap.

Although only poor statistics are available on the potential to make reductions in this way, it seems likely that emission reductions of 10% to 20% are feasible in the short-term, and perhaps as much as 50% with existing buildings in the long-term, but at much greater cost.

The easiest way to make changes to buildings is at the design stage. In many developed countries (where most of the emissions are currently taking place), new buildings are being constructed at a very low rate (for example, in the UK, new constructions add about 1% to the housing stock every year). Thus, existing buildings will continue to dominate emissions made by the property sector, but making large reductions in the energy use of existing buildings is difficult and expensive.

Particularly in commercial buildings, decisions about design and construction are made by different people than those who decide how the building will be used (typically, these are the owners of the building in the first instance and the tenants in the second). This lack of a connection during decision-making can result in a low-cost, but inefficient, heating or cooling system being installed. The inadequate provision of controls can be a particular source of waste. Once a building has been constructed, it will be much more costly to make major changes to insulation or systems than if different ones had been chosen at the design stage. This is often referred to as "lock-in", indicating that the consequences of such decisions will be with us for many years to come.

Reducing the amount of energy used in buildings, e.g. by appliances and equipment, is also important for reducing emissions from electricity generation. Global

Fig. 4.7 French TGV train at 300 kilometres an hour.

Fig. 4.8 Aeroplane over the London Eye.

Fig. 4.9 New York cabs lined up at Kennedy airport.

emissions from electricity generation are over 9 billion tonnes of CO_2 per year, out of the global total of 26 billion tonnes from all fossil fuels. Efficiency improvements at power stations could reduce emissions by a few percent for each unit of electricity produced and without any radical change in technology. More substantial reductions would require different approaches to generation. In addition, using some of the waste heat from power stations to heat buildings or industry would reduce overall emissions but, as will be discussed later, this depends on having suitable heat loads close by. Another way of achieving such a change is for end-users to generate their own electricity, in combination with heating their own buildings (this is discussed later).

Transport illustrates well the trade-offs involved in reducing energy use. The growth in air travel attracts much publicity but road transport is the main user of fossil fuels in this sector. Technical changes to road vehicles would involve

Vehicle energy use

Improvements in vehicle efficiency have been stimulated in Europe and elsewhere by changes in standards. For example, in the UK, the emissions per kilometre of new passenger vehicles have been reduced by about 12% over 10 years (fig. 4.10) – this is similar to the European trend, and should fall by another 17% in order to meet the standard set for 2010. New US vehicles, if built to the 2010 European emissions standard, would have emissions (per mile) of 48% less than at present. Whether or not this would be acceptable is open to question as vehicle weight and size play an important role in safety, comfort and noise, as well as in determining fuel consumption (and hence emissions).

Fig. 4.10 Trend in new car emissions in the UK (source: UK government).

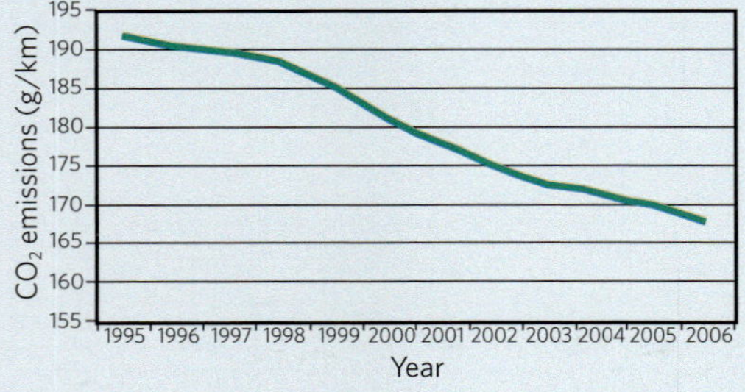

Chapter 4 | Squaring the circle: accessing energy without damaging the climate

switching to lighter and smaller vehicles or more efficient engines – these would reduce the amount of energy needed to achieve the same performance. At the same time, the trend towards larger vehicles, as well as the introduction of features designed to reduce other forms of pollution, e.g. SO_2, NO_x and noise, not to mention improvements in safety, tend to offset some of the reductions in CO_2 emissions achieved by improved vehicle technology.

Vehicles have relatively short service lives so turnover of the stock should provide opportunities to introduce radical changes in automotive design. Improved fuel economy would make a significant contribution to reducing emissions per km driven, although this also reduces the cost of driving which tends to increase usage, thereby offsetting to some extent the reduction in emissions[1]. A reduction in the demand for energy can also be achieved by switching from individual vehicles to public transport or, in the extreme case, by cutting out journeys altogether, but it is not easy to estimate the extent of the potential reduction in emissions.

Air travel is giving increasing cause for concern, not only because of the rate of growth in emissions but also because of where these are emitted, high up in the stratosphere. Unfortunately, the number of options for reducing demand is quite limited.

Heavy industry (e.g. iron and steel, chemicals, oil refining) should also be able to reduce its use of energy, but most of these industries already pay great attention to energy use because it is an important part of their budgets. Consequently, most of these industries have implemented cost-effective measures to reduce energy use. Nevertheless, the best current steel-making process uses 20% less energy than the world average when making a tonne of steel from the primary raw materials, so there is scope for improvement.

Cement-making emits about one tonne of CO_2 for each tonne of cement, with roughly half coming from the fuel used during the process and half from the raw materials. Changes in the way that cement is used could have a significant impact on emissions, if changes in the specifications for cement were acceptable. Process improvements could also reduce fuel-related CO_2 emissions, as will be discussed below.

Fig. 4.11 Steelworks at Scunthorpe, UK.

Fig. 4.12   The Citeureup cement plant located on the island of Java near to Jakarta.

Fig. 4.13   The Mongstad refinery on the west coast of Norway. This is one of over 600 refineries world-wide. Unlike most refineries, its storage capacity is underground in huge rock-caverns.

Oil refining releases CO_2 from the fuel used for processing the crude oil; the best modern refineries use about 25% less fuel than the average, which suggests there is considerable scope for reducing emissions from this industry, too.

The chemical industry is less susceptible to generalised remarks about the potential for improving energy efficiency and reducing CO_2 emissions but, because it largely uses the same type of equipment as oil refineries, it is likely that similar levels of emission reduction could be achieved there, too.

On a national basis, several countries have experienced reductions in national energy use as some of their more energy-intensive industries have closed down (e.g. steel making) and less energy-intensive industries have taken their place (e.g. computer software production). Such changes may enable individual countries to achieve their goals of reducing CO_2 emissions. However, if these goals are achieved by exporting, for instance, their aluminium or steel industry to another country, then the overall benefit to the planet could be negligible. Sometimes, the situation might become worse than before – e.g. if the electricity in the new location is produced using coal whereas in the previous location it had been made using natural gas. Examples like this should make us wary of broad claims regarding the potential for drastic emission reductions. In many cases, the problem may just be moved elsewhere.

Overall, the "reduce demand" option is likely to be able to reduce emissions by between 10% and 30%; many of these measures would incur little additional cost, but some, especially the inexpensive ones, lack intrinsic robustness.

Chapter 4 | Squaring the circle: accessing energy without damaging the climate

Option: Recycle

The concept of recycling is not as easily applied to energy as it is to some more substantial items such as bottles and packaging. As explained in Chapter 1, energy is neither created nor destroyed, but there is a degradation in its quality as it is used. Lower quality energy is available at lower temperatures than higher quality energy, and so is less useful if recycled.

In an industrial process, energy may be supplied at high temperatures because this is what is needed for that particular process. For example, an efficient gas turbine used in generating electricity burns the fuel at a temperature above 1,300°C. In the production of cement, the raw materials are roasted in a furnace at a temperature of 1,650°C. In such cases, the exhaust gas from the process is still very hot so it could be put to another use. For example, the exhaust from a gas turbine may be used to generate steam which could be used to drive another turbine and make more electricity. Consequently, although the gas turbine itself may be only 35% to 40% efficient at converting the energy in the fuel into electricity, the combination of a gas turbine with heat recovery and a steam-driven turbo-generator can be 60% efficient. As a consequence of recycling energy, emissions would be reduced by between 50% and 70%.

This type of recycling can be carried out in many places, especially in industry. Each industrial plant will provide specific opportunities which can be established through sophisticated analysis of the need for heat and the availability of waste heat. In general, this form of recycling is recognised as another way of improving the efficiency of energy use.

Fig. 4.14 The higher the temperature, the higher quality of the energy. This is a high temperature flame resulting from the combustion of a mixture of 77% hydrogen and 23% methane.

Fig. 4.15 Waste steam escaping from a process plant is an example of lower quality energy which is often released to air or water.

Fig. 4.16   A heat exchanger used in industry. This giant heat exchanger is used to recycle heat extracted during the cooling of natural gas to turn it into a liquid for transport by ship.

The pulp and paper industry has numerous opportunities to recycle its own by-products, which can then be used as fuel for generating electricity. This is done to a great extent at the most efficient plants today. In general, the larger and more complex the industrial site, the greater the demand for heat at different temperatures and the greater the opportunities will be for recycling.

Recycling scrap steel requires less energy than making steel from raw materials. The best recycling process uses 60% less primary energy (per tonne of steel) than the best process using primary ore[2]. Recycling is limited by the amount of scrap available but radical changes to the process for primary steel-making could also reduce the amount of energy used. Heat recovery during cement-making, whilst worthwhile, only addresses half of the CO_2 emissions, those which are derived from the fuel used during the process.

In buildings, waste heat is only available at low temperatures, which makes recycling difficult. If the building has mechanical ventilation, heat can be recovered from the outgoing stream to

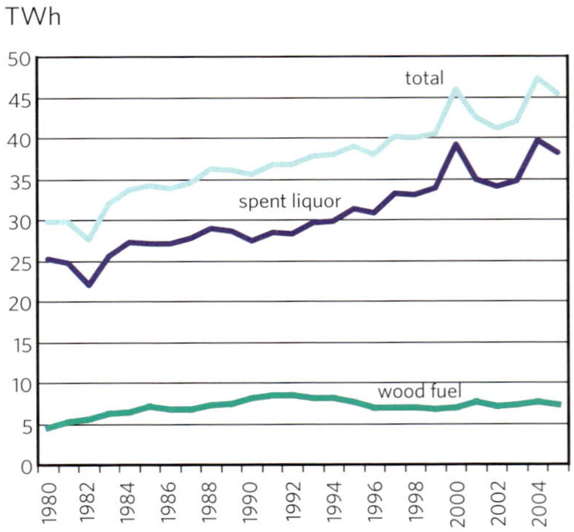

Figure 4.17   The Swedish pulp and paper industry is a leader in recycling, using its by-products (e.g. spent liquor) for energy, thereby avoiding the need to increase its consumption of wood.

preheat the incoming air. In well-insulated buildings, this can be a major part of the overall heating load.

It is difficult to generalise about the potential of the recycling option but demand could be reduced and emissions cut by between 10% and 60%, depending on circumstances; the cost would likely be significant but most of these measures would be cost-effective, especially at higher energy prices. Because they involve substantial investments in new equipment, the changes would be robust once implemented.

Option: Substitute

The combustion of fossil fuels supplies most of our energy needs today, as we saw in Chapter 1. A corollary of this is the emission of about 26 billion tonnes of CO_2 every year, with the potential for this to rise in the future. The substitution of different energy supplies that do not produce the same level of CO_2 emissions is being widely discussed as a way of combating climate change. The range of options is considerable but our discussion of the options can be kept to a reasonable length by recognising that similar measures can be applied in different sectors of the economy. However, there are some important differences between the various sectors, so it is worth considering the opportunities for substitution in each one.

Substitution in Buildings

A large part of the energy used in buildings is for conditioning the internal space – either heating or cooling; lighting and equipment also use substantial amounts of electricity. For most electric appliances, substitution at the point of use is infeasible but substitution options are possible during the production of electricity and will be discussed later.

Heating is provided by burning natural gas, oil or solid fuels, or by a district heating system, or by electric heating. The emission reductions produced by substituting natural gas for coal can be up to 50%. To achieve a greater reduction (or, in the case of natural gas, any reduction at all), it would be necessary to replace fossil fuels with wood or some other plant material. Although the combustion of plant-derived material (so-called biomass) releases CO_2, this is compensated for by the growth of replacement plants which draw down a similar amount of CO_2

Biomass – a neutral burden on the climate

Burning biomass as a substitute for fossil fuel does not avoid releasing CO_2 into the atmosphere. In order to minimise the impact on the climate, a similar amount of biomass must be grown which will capture an equivalent amount of CO_2 from the atmosphere over a period of time. This is the basic assumption underpinning the notion that biomass is a climate-neutral fuel. The validity of this assumption is often questioned. What is the truth?

Broadly, there are two conditions which must be satisfied – the amount of energy used for associated purposes (e.g. transporting the fuel) must be kept low, and the plants must be grown in a sustainable manner (i.e. without the excessive use of fertilisers, and by using land without depleting natural resources).

With the many and varied potential uses of biomass for energy purposes, there is nothing remotely like a single answer to the question of whether any particular source of biomass meets these requirements. If a farmer cuts down a tree for fuel while planting another, the assumption of climate neutrality may largely hold true when considered over the lifetime of the tree, especially if he does not use motorised equipment to cut down, transport, and chop up the tree.

Similar logic indicates that the growth of plants for fuelling power stations can produce an almost 100% reduction in CO_2 emissions over the entire cycle of growth and combustion.

On the other hand, when making bio-ethanol for fuelling vehicles, the answer may not be as straightforward – the number of crop cycles per year, the energy demand of the refinery, and the source of energy used for distillation will all affect the conclusion. So, in the best case, the emission reductions from using transportation biofuels may be 80% to 90%[3]; in other cases, the reduction in CO_2 emissions[4] may only be 40% to 50%, but there are confusingly wide differences between the claimed reductions, even for quite similar systems.

As to the environmental impact, this also depends on where the crop is grown and how it is processed, transported and used. As this process becomes more intensive, the pressures on the environment from the use of fertilizers and pesticides, the demand for water, especially for processing, and the competition with food production for use of land will all present issues which have to be considered when deciding on the merits of each case.

from the atmosphere. Thus, biomass could be a CO_2-neutral fuel when considered across the entire cycle of growth, harvesting and combustion.

In order to make the most efficient use of biomass, appliances will have to be designed specifically for this fuel. Biomass can be handled almost as easily as other solid fuels but supplies may not be available to everyone. The energy density of this fuel is relatively low, so a considerable storage volume would be needed. Automatic control of the fuel-burning appliance is not as easy as with natural gas, especially in small appliances; this could reduce the overall efficiency. Thus, biomass is only likely to be a substitution option for buildings close to a fuel supply

Fig. 4.18 Wood pellets are big in Sweden where the market, the world's largest, uses over one million tonnes per year.

which have adequate space for storage and where the appliance can be operated efficiently.

Many of these problems would be irrelevant for major users, such as industry, who are more likely to have space for storage on-site, be willing to invest in purpose-designed equipment and employ trained staff to manage the plant. Even so, there may be some shortfall in efficiency compared with fossil-fuel-fired equipment.

Waste materials may also be used as a heating fuel. If large amounts of waste were left to decompose under

District heating and combined heat and power

Sweden and the other Nordic countries have, for good reason, long been at the forefront of establishing networks for the central generation of heat and the distribution of the hot water produced around their major towns and cities. A good example (Fig. 4.19) is the district heating network in Southern Stockholm. This distributes heat from many different sources; some fired by fossil fuels, but most fuelled by renewable energy in one form or another. It is the largest district heating system in Sweden, with 710 kilometres of insulated pipework.

District heating provides a means of using biomass relatively effectively, but another major benefit arises where it can accept waste heat from large power stations, especially coal- or gas-fired ones. Although their main purpose is to generate electricity, by delivering much of their waste heat as hot water to nearby consumers in a district heating scheme, the overall energy efficiency of the stations rises from between 30% and 50% up to between 80% and 90%. These combined heat and power (CHP) stations come in many shapes and sizes. CHP stations are also used in large industrial complexes where the production and use of steam, hot water, and other process streams are integrated in intricate ways.

Fig. 4.19 District heating network in southern Stockholm. At 710 kilometres in length, this is Sweden's largest district heating system.

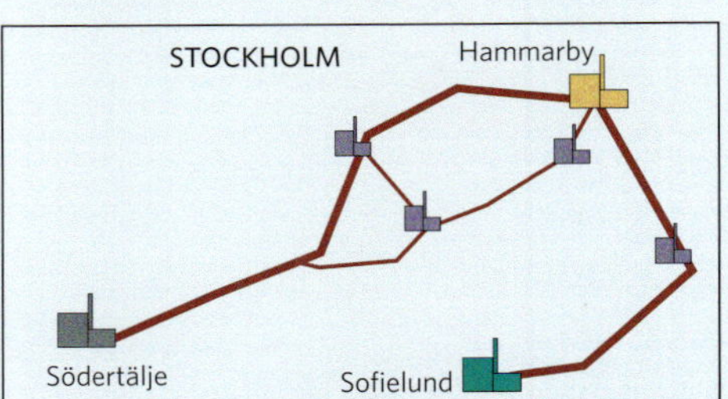

Small scale co-generation of heat and power

Increasingly widespread is the use of micro-CHP units, where small combustion engines (or other generators such as fuel cells) are used for the local generation of both heat and power. These units are located in an individual building or a complex and provide heat for that locality only. Figure 4.20 shows an internal combustion engine. Such engines may produce twice as much heat as electricity.

Small CHP units are less efficient when generating electricity than a large power station, but this is compensated by using waste heat in the building. However, the amount of heat that can be used puts a limit on how much electricity should be generated – producing more than this will just replace an efficient central power station with smaller, less efficient units, producing greater emissions.

Fig. 4.20 Micro-CHP unit based on an internal combustion engine.

anaerobic conditions, the production of methane could have a significant impact on the climate. This is what can happen when land-fill is used to deal with municipal waste. The use of waste as a fuel avoids this danger and provides a source of heat which can replace fossil fuels. Handling, equipment and control can present problems, so the most efficient installations are large incinerators, typically dealing with a variety of municipal waste. Usable heat can be recovered from these facilities, if the incinerator is connected to a district heating system.

District heating systems can make good use of the large volume of waste heat released by power stations and incinerators. A combined heat and power (CHP) facility, built to serve a large number of buildings, could be designed to use any fuel, including biomass. Smaller CHP units can be installed in a single building, where they would probably use natural gas.

Another substitute would be the use of geothermal energy, but this is not available everywhere – it tends to be most accessible close to major faults in the Earth's crust, especially where tectonic plates are colliding, e.g. Iceland, the west coast of the USA or Indonesia. In other places, although the temperature of the rock deep underground may be higher than at the surface, the temperature difference may be insufficient to justify sinking boreholes to exploit the heat.

At some sites, water is already present in the rock so that the heat can be extracted as hot water or steam; in other places, water has to be pumped down into the rocks to extract the heat. In either case, disposal of the water after use can present an environmental problem because of the dissolved salts and other materials brought up with it. In some geothermal fields, this water can also be a source of CO_2 which is released into the atmosphere in small quantities. After a period of time, which may be several decades, the rocks may have become cooled by the extraction of heat and then new wells will have to be sunk to tap into hotter rock.

Direct use of the sun for heating has been a part of building design for a long time – all structures benefit to some extent from such gains. The deliberate design of buildings to capture solar heat has been implemented in some locations, especially in the north, but this is not widespread. Such buildings also need to be designed to prevent overheating in mild weather and during the summer, which can involve the use of mechanical shades. In some cases, solar heat may be stored in the fabric of the building, or in purpose-made stores for later retrieval. Generally speaking, purpose-made inter-seasonal stores are very expensive.

A more attractive approach is to store heat at a low temperature (hence without the need for insulation); this can be done in the ground outside the building. The heat is later recovered by using a heat pump which can be an inexpensive source of heat. Alternatively, air-source heat pumps can extract heat from the outside air – again this is using solar heat indirectly (in this case using heat stored in the ambient air).

Fig. 4.21 House designed to make the most of solar energy in Maine; the south-facing roof incorporates solar thermal collectors and photovoltaic modules to form a single, uniform glazed surface. The house also incorporates passive solar heating and cooling, super insulation and advanced windows.

Fig. 4.22 Installing photovoltaic roof panels in San Ramon, California, USA.

Solar panels, mounted on the roof of the building, can provide heat in a much more controlled fashion. Such panels can be used to heat domestic tap water in the summertime but, at high latitudes, there is insufficient heat available at other times of the year to justify their use for space heating (i.e. in winter). Even when restricted to domestic water heating, this can be an expensive means of heating if the installation is done as a retrofit after the building has been constructed, unless groups of houses can be fitted at the same time.

The replacement of fossil fuels by biomass, waste, geothermal energy, or solar heating could achieve close to a 100% reduction in the emissions arising from heating buildings. Because of the investments involved, most of these reductions are robust but the capacity for emission reductions is constrained by the poor return on investment in most of these systems. The use of heat pumps reduces emissions to an extent determined by the emissions of the energy source used to drive the heat pump, which is usually electricity. Again, the capacity is constrained by the additional costs.

Substitution in Electricity Generation

A wide range of options is available for electricity generation. An important distinction must be made between those that are small-scale and those that are large-scale supply options. It is also important to recognise how costs are kept down by selecting different types of power station for different purposes; large efficient stations are built to run continuously and so are less expensive to operate, but expensive to build; less efficient stations, which are used occasionally, are cheap to build but are relatively expensive to operate.

Large power stations, generating hundreds or even thousands of megawatts[5] at one site are currently used to meet most of the demand for electricity. Large stations provide economies of scale which deliver electricity at the lowest cost. Emissions from fossil fuels (especially coal) used for electricity generation average about 919 kg of CO_2 for each MWh supplied to the grid[6]. Even if all fossil fuel power stations were converted to natural gas, at the standards of the best modern stations, it would only be possible to halve these emissions. For a variety of reasons, coal is expected to continue as a major fuel in power generation, so replacing coal with gas is only likely to bring about a limited change in global emissions.

One potential large-scale substitute for fossil fuels would be the use of nuclear power (as widely introduced in France and Japan during the 1980s). This requi-

Various types of power station are needed to balance the load on the grid

Large, capital-intensive power stations, such as nuclear or large coal- or gas-fired stations, have lower operating costs than smaller stations. The operators of the electricity system aim to use the large stations to the fullest extent possible in order to keep the cost of electricity down. However, if these stations are not fully utilised, the owners will lose out due to poor utilisation of their capital investment. So, no one wants to build more of these large stations than necessary. In order to strike a balance between the number of larger stations and the number of smaller, but more costly-to-operate, stations, it is necessary to understand how the load on the electricity system varies.

This can be expressed as a graph (Fig. 4.23), which shows how the demand for electricity varies during the year – this is not a time-based record, but a record of the frequency at which certain levels of demand occur.

Throughout the year, there is a base load on the system, which may amount to between 40 and 60% of the peak demand and which is present every hour of the day and night. This is supplied by running the large, capital-intensive stations almost continuously. Higher levels of demand occur for less than the whole year – this demand is met by some power stations running intermittently. To deal with such intermediate loads, it is appropriate to use stations with lower capital costs and higher operating costs – these may be less efficient than the large, base-load stations.

This picture is further complicated by the availability of some types of renewable energy sources on the grid, e.g. wind power, where the availability of the electricity is determined by outside forces. Luckily, the electricity supply from wind turbines may be correlated to some extent with demand (e.g. sometimes demand is highest when the wind is strongest). However, this is not always true (sometimes, very cold weather is associated with windless conditions). So, the effect of introducing wind power can be to change the balance of demand on the other stations on the grid.

Fig. 4.23 The frequency with which the demand on an electricity system occurs throughout the year.

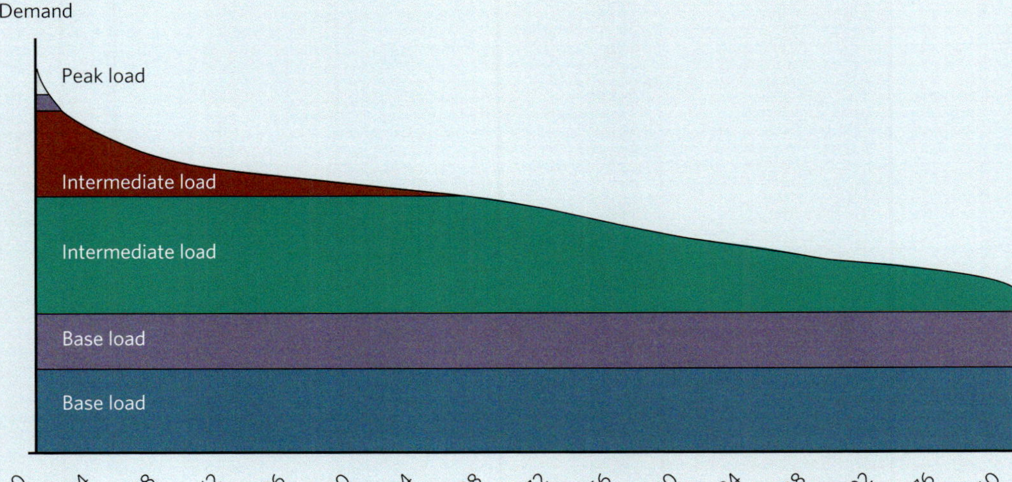

res dedicated facilities for the production of nuclear fuel, for using it to generate electricity and for the disposal of waste. There would be no CO_2 emissions from the nuclear power plant itself but, insofar as other parts of the fuel supply and the waste disposal system use electricity from non-nuclear sources, there may be a small amount of CO_2 emissions associated with the system as a whole.

Nuclear comeback

The prospects for electricity generation using nuclear power have improved considerably over the last few years. Not too long ago, the global nuclear electricity industry was seen to be in decline: several countries had decided to phase it out, staff recruitment had fallen, and the relevant university courses had been dropped.

Today, the nuclear industry is facing a brighter future than it has done for several decades. The US Energy Information Administration (EIA) projects an increase in global nuclear power from 361 000 MW to 438 000 MW by 2030[7]. New stations are being planned and built and existing plants are being renovated and up-rated. Amongst the industrialised countries, Finland, France, Japan, and the USA are expected to build new stations while the UK government announced in 2006 that it was prepared to accept new nuclear stations.

Figure 4.24 shows a 1,600 MW nuclear power station under construction on the south coast of Finland. This is the first new station to be constructed in Europe for more than a dec-ade. The reactor's uranium fuel will be mined in Canada, Australia and Africa and will then be enriched in Russia. Finally, it will be assembled and put into fuel rods in Sweden, Spain and Germany. The site also houses a laboratory deep in the granite rock to carry out tests on the final storage of highly radioactive waste.

This revival of nuclear power is the result of increasing energy prices in general, security of supply concerns, prospects that new designs will be less expensive and, not least, concern about climate change.

While the industrialised countries are moving rather slowly in this area, rapid growth in nuclear power capacity is expected in China, India and Russia over the next few decades. New construction in these countries may bring between 70,000 and 80,000 MW over the next 25 years.

However, this new dawn for nuclear power is not assured. The lack of capacity to train new staff could be a problem. Assuming that serious nuclear accidents are avoided, concerns remain regarding the actual competitiveness of such stations in a free energy market, and about the proliferation of fissile materials (which could be used to make nuclear weapons), especially when some countries are aspiring to establish themselves in critical parts of the fuel cycle.

Fig. 4.24 Olkiluoto3 – a new 1600 MW nuclear power station under construction in Finland.

Chapter 4 | Squaring the circle: accessing energy without damaging the climate

In principle, nuclear power stations could be built as extensively as fossil-fuel power stations, but there are political obstacles to their use in many countries. Nuclear power is most suitable for base-load generation, which means that it could replace 30% to 50% of electricity generation. The cost of the whole process, including fuel supply, use and waste disposal, is as high as, or even higher

Further ideas for using nuclear physics to make electricity

Conventional nuclear power stations use the fission of uranium nuclei to release heat. In the process, they produce other radioactive nuclei, not only from the fissile material in the fuel, but also by the conversion of inert uranium. The most advanced current designs can produce 70% to 80% as much fissile material as they use. Some of this fissile material may be extracted by reprocessing the waste to produce more fuel. However, there is some concern that the amount of uranium naturally available is limited. The fast breeder reactor was conceived as a way of overcoming these limitations (the term "fast" refers to the use of fast neutrons in the nuclear reactions). A fast breeder consumes fissile material and converts uranium and thorium into yet more fuel. This has been demonstrated in experimental reactors, where up to 20% more fuel has been produced than is fed into the reactor.

After its initial charge of plutonium, the fast breeder reactor only requires supplies of natural or even depleted uranium to produce electricity and more fuel. The used fuel is reprocessed externally to extract plutonium, but this could also be used to make nuclear weapons, which is one of the concerns about this system. Other concerns relate to the use of liquid sodium as a coolant, which has been a source of unreliability in the experimental designs.

Even further away from application is the concept of the fusion reactor. In this, some light

Fig. 4.25   The French Super-Phenix 1 prototype fast breeder reactor which closed in 1997 due to problems with its liquid sodium cooling system.

elements (typically, a form of hydrogen called deuterium which has a larger nucleus than hydrogen) are fused together at extremely high temperatures. This is the process which powers the sun, so making it work on earth would require containment of the fuel for long enough, and at a high enough temperature, for the deuterium nuclei to fuse together; this is done using very strong magnetic fields. When fused together, these nuclei release energy. To date, experimental reactors have not produced as much energy as was put into them to support the reaction. The next experimental reactor, called ITER (which will be built as an international collaboration), is intended to achieve greater energy output than input. In a commercial power station, this would be used to drive a turbine to make electricity, but it is unlikely that such a station will be available until at least the middle of this century.

Fig. 4.26 Hydro-power. a) The Churchill Falls station in Canada is the largest underground power station in the world. b) Devils Gate Dam in Australia.

than, the cost of fossil fuel generation in many countries. The size of uranium resources may also be a factor limiting growth in the use of nuclear power in the longer term. In the short term, in Western countries, growth in the use of nuclear power may be constrained by public attitudes and by a shortage of staff trained to design, build and operate these stations.

Hydropower is the most well-established large-scale alternative to using fossil fuels in electricity generation. Power stations of this type are used in many parts of the world. Often (as in Norway), the supply of water is determined by winter snowfall so, after dry winters, electricity has to be imported from other countries. The emissions of CO_2 from hydropower are nil but there has been some concern that vegetation in valleys flooded during the construction of hydropower dams decomposes and releases methane, which is also a greenhouse gas. There is little spare capacity in the developed countries for expanding large-scale hydropower, although more small-scale run-of-river stations could be built. There is a potential for the wider use of hydropower in some developing countries, which could be an alternative to new fossil-fuelled stations. Emission reductions would be up to 100%, compared with the fossil fuel stations, depending on the extent to which fossil fuel has to be used to make up for shortfalls in hydro-capacity at times of sporadic water supplies.

Another large-scale substitute is tidal power. The largest station of this type is on the Rance estuary in France – with a capacity of 240 MW. Tidal power is cyclical (roughly twice per day), but stations can be constructed with interim storage facilities to enable more continuous output. Major tidal power stations have been suggested for the Severn estuary in the UK and the Bay of Fundy in Canada. However, the availability of suitable sites, the capital cost of these projects and their environmental impact will restrict global application and hence the capacity for emission reductions. So tidal power has only a limited potential for global emission reductions, but it may be useful where it can be applied.

Fuels derived from biological materials (plants, trees, waste) can be burnt to make electricity, in much the same way as fossil fuels are used. Indeed, the co-combustion of biomass with fossil fuels is probably the least difficult way to make this substitution (for example, biomass may be introduced into the fuel supply of a coal-fired power station at levels of 5% or 10% of the total fuel). Purpose-designed biomass power stations can have capacity of more than 100MW. The scale of the plant is restricted, as much as anything, by the distance that the fuel has to be transported. If the fuel has to be grown so far away that transport costs dominate the economics of the fuel supply, then it may be more sensible to build more but smaller stations closer to where the fuel is grown.

Conventional agriculture is declining in many developed countries due to low revenues but, without subsidies, it seems unlikely that growing biomass would generate more income than growing food crops. Emission reductions from replacing fossil fuels would be virtually 100%, but biomass power could only replace a small fraction of the fossil fuel used in many developing countries because of poor economics and competition with the food supply over use of the land.

Biomass is one example of a fuel derived from solar energy. Harnessing wind power is another indirect use of solar energy. Solar power can also be used directly in suitable locations. Other natural sources may also be harnessed to generate electricity, e.g. ocean currents. Geothermal energy may be used for electricity generation in much the same way as for heating buildings.

Solar power would only be a substitute for fossil-fuel power during the hours of generation (i.e. during daytime)[8]. Large solar power stations, using arrays of photovoltaic cells connected together, are very expensive and are only likely to be competitive where the peak demand for electricity coincides with bright sunshine. Photovoltaic cells might also be mounted

Fig. 4.27 Biomass can be used in fairly large power stations. Burlington Electric's McNeil station gasifies wood to make a fuel gas for gas turbines which generate electricity.

Fig. 4.28 Modern wind turbines.

on the roofs of individual buildings. If this can be done as part of the construction of the building, the additional costs may be kept low enough to make this acceptable as a means of supplying electricity, providing there is a back-up from some other source (probably via the grid). Solar heat could also be used to supplement the operation of a fossil-fuel power station. The latter application is likely to have limited global capacity but, where applicable, it could be cost-effective. Other large-scale solar generation, for example using solar heat, is expensive and has limited prospects of cost reduction so the emission reduction potential is small.

In suitable windy locations, turbines on tall towers can harness the power of the wind to generate electricity. Typically, over a year, such units can supply an average of 25% to 30% of their rated capacity (i.e. a 3MW turbine supplies on average 0.9MW of electricity). The supply is necessarily sporadic but this can be compensated for to an extent by constructing many turbines at one site and by using turbines at different geographical locations connected to the same grid. Typically, the windiest areas of many countries are also the least inhabited so the turbines may not affect people very much although their impact on otherwise unspoilt landscapes is causing disquiet in some places. As the number of wind turbines increases, it becomes increasingly difficult to find suitable sites, especially in crowded countries such as Denmark and the UK. The solution in Denmark was to install turbines offshore and this practice has since been followed in the UK and elsewhere.

The intermittent nature of solar or wind power is not a problem for the first stations feeding into the grid because the electricity generated by the wind turbines merely serves to reduce the demand for fossil-fuel generated power. Thus, initially, the substitution of wind for fossil fuel reduces CO_2 emissions by 100%. However, as more wind power is introduced into the grid, and the number of fossil-fuelled stations operating falls correspondingly, there may be certain times when there is insufficient wind power to meet the demand. This situation can be managed by reducing demand, or by using electricity stored during a period of low demand, or by generating electricity using a rapid-response fossil-fuel power station, such as a gas turbine, installed specifically for the purpose. Experience of demand reduction is as yet insufficient to show whether or not this can be relied on; the large-scale storage of electricity is expensive; so the least-cost option seems to be to use a rapid-response fuel-fired power station. This means that, as the wind power capacity on a grid increases, the amount of emission reductions will fall below 100%, although not by more than about 10%.

Initially, the introduction of wind power in any country is likely to target the best sites. As the applications expand, less favourable sites will have to be used – these may be less windy or further away from centres of demand or connection to the grid. This means that the cost of using electricity from wind power will rise as the demand grows. At the same time, the cost of building and installing wind turbines will fall as more experience of their construction and deployment is gained, but this is insufficient to compensate for the increased cost of generation from the use of less favourable sites[9].

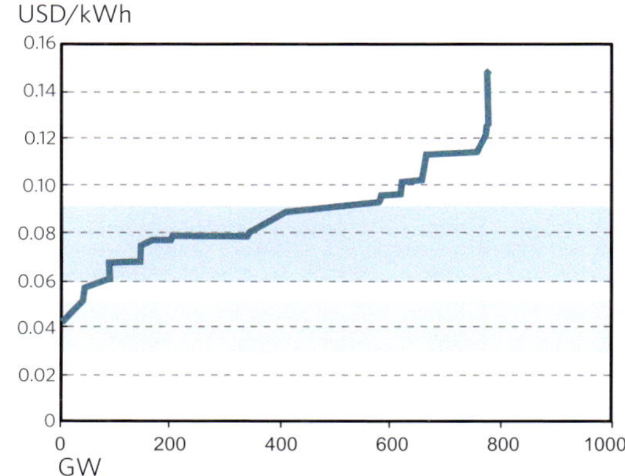

Fig. 4.29   Illustrative cost-curve for large-scale use of wind turbines to substitute for fossil fuel power generation in Europe. This illustrates a key issue for renewable energy supply that there is no single figure which is representative of the cost. (reference: IEA, 2006).

A somewhat similar technology may be used to harness ocean currents, whereby a turbine would be built under the sea. This has the potential to produce reliable power but connection to the grid would be a problem at least as large as that of offshore wind power. This technology is still under development. So too is technology for capturing wave-power for electricity generation – this must work in a very arduous environment and, so far, the most successful examples have been small stations built along the coastline. Both ocean current power and wave power would replace fossil fuel generated electricity with a 100% emission reduction for the amount substituted (subject to similar caveats in respect of sporadic supplies as for wind power). The capacity will be dictated by the geography of the country where they are used.

Many forms of renewable generation have a capacity of only a few megawatts for each unit. Thus, in order to generate sufficient electricity to replace fossil fuel power, thousands of them will have to be connected together. This also requires

Small is beautiful

The usefulness of different types of electricity supply technology varies with the scale of the unit. For example, natural gas used in a 400 MW gas turbine combined cycle power station can generate electricity at 60% efficiency. Small gas turbines are only 20% to 30% efficient, but an alternative approach, the fuel cell, may be able to achieve greater efficiency at capacities as small as 10kW.

Photovoltaic panels for solar electricity generation each have a peak capacity of 20 to 40W. In order to generate megawatts of electricity, many of them have to be coupled together, but the small intrinsic scale of this technology also allows it to be applied in unit sizes which match its use. For example, some important tasks in remote locations only require a small amount of electricity, e.g. domestic lighting in villages, refrigerators for storing vaccines, and radio repeaters. In such cases, the higher cost of electricity from a photovoltaic generator may be justified because it is less than the cost of running a small fossil-fuel-fired generator, as well as being more reliable.

However, solar power would only replace fossil-fuel generated electricity during the hours of generation (i.e. during daytime). Electricity can be stored, for example in batteries, but this is very expensive. This may be justifiable for small-scale remote applications, because the value of the product is high enough to warrant it, but not for large-scale use. Other energy sources, such as wind power, may be usable in a similar way.

Such small-scale sources of electricity may be more important because they are cost-effective for a particular, remote use than because of the emission reductions they achieve. Once the local demand for electricity rises sufficiently, connection to an electricity grid would be justified by the cost saving relative to using the small, dedicated source of electricity; the generator can then be moved to another location.

Chapter 4 | Squaring the circle: accessing energy without damaging the climate connection to a regional or national electricity grid in order to move the electricity to where it is required.

Substitution in Transport

Petrol, diesel oil, and kerosene are attractive fuels for individual vehicles because, as they are liquids, they can be handled relatively easily and stored in simple tanks without using much space. The technology for using them has been under development for over a hundred years and thus is now relatively inexpensive. This also means that a considerable infrastructure has been established worldwide to support them. The most acceptable substitutes for these fuels would be liquids that are compatible with the existing engines and supply infrastructure. Liquids derived from biological materials are similar in many ways to hydrocarbon fuels. For example, methanol, ethanol or butanol can be made from plant material and may be substituted for gasoline with only limited changes to vehicles; various plant-derived oils may be substituted for kerosene and diesel oil.

The extent to which these fuels would reduce CO_2 emissions depends on the method of use, the source of the plants from which they are made, and the ways in which they are processed. Ethanol can be blended with petrol to achieve minor emission reductions (5% to 10%), but major emission reductions would come from using these fuels in a more or less pure form[10]. With some alterations to engine management systems, plus the replacement of a few components, ethanol can be used in conventional engines blended with only a small amount of petrol (typically a blend of 85% ethanol with 15% petrol). Butanol is still in development but is potentially usable in the same way.

Both ethanol and butanol are produced by fermenting plant sugars. The liquid product is about 90% water, which must be removed before the fuel can be used; this is done by distillation. However, distillation consumes substantial amounts of energy. During the process, other parts of the plants (especially cellulose material) may be discarded as waste, which limits the extent to which emissions are reduced overall. In Brazil, the waste from sugarcane production is put to use during the distillation process, so the overall emission reduction can be high when compared with petrol. Improved processes, using new enzymes, may be able to produce ethanol from the cellulose, thereby reducing the amount of waste and improving the reduction of emissions.

Biofuels for transportation

The leading national producer of biofuels for transportation is Brazil, which produced 15.9 billion litres of bio-ethanol from sugarcane in 2005[11]. This was more than a third of the global production and required nearly 10% of Brazil's cultivated land. The energy efficiency (as well as net CO_2 emissions) of bio-ethanol manufacture in Brazil is as good as can be found anywhere; reductions in CO_2 emissions, compared with petrol, are quoted as being high as 80% to 90%[12]. The reasons for this include the prolific growth rate of the crop in tropical Brazil, and the use of a closed production cycle where the energy for the refinery and distillation process comes from burning the process residue, so little or no fossil fuel is needed.

For other sources and types of transportation biofuels, reductions in CO_2 emissions, compared with fossil fuels, are often quoted[13] as being in the range of 40% to 50%, but there are confusingly wide differences between the claimed reductions, even for quite similar systems.

In addition to the reduction in CO_2 emissions, it is also important to consider the environmental impact of the process. This will depend on where the crop is grown and how it is transported and used. The commercial growth of sugarcane is an intensive process which has impacts on the environment through the use of fertilizers and pesticides – in Brazil, the crushing mills require about $5m^3$ of water per tonne of sugarcane. Competition with food production for the use of agricultural land may cause higher food prices – while not a sizable problem today, this may become a controversial issue in the future with the expansion of biofuel production. These factors indicate that, even if Brazilian production from sugarcane has substantial CO_2 benefits, there is still a need to reduce its environmental impact.

Fig. 4.30 Sugarcane is used in great quantities to make bioethanol in Brazil.

Chapter 4 | Squaring the circle: accessing energy without damaging the climate

The separation of oils from plants, e.g. rapeseed or palm oil, provides a fuel which can be used by diesel engines, although it may need to be blended with conventional diesel oil to ensure it flows properly at low temperatures. The waste from the production process is even greater than with ethanol so emission reduction is less, at 40% to 60% compared with diesel oil[16]. In some cases, by-products can be manufactured for sale, which can improve the economics of the process. But, since the by-products are quite specialised, this added income is unlikely to be available if large-scale demand develops for this type of fuel.

The amount of biofuels which can be produced is determined by the availability of land so, in many countries, the growth of biofuels would be in competition with the growth of food crops. In Europe, a requirement for 5% of transportation fuels to be made from biofuels would require an area equivalent to all of the set-aside land, which is indicative of the limitations to supplying this type of fuel[17]. In the developing countries, more land may be available.

Gases could also be used as transportation fuels; for example, natural gas can be substituted for petrol fuels in suitably-adapted road or rail vehicles, but not in aircraft because its energy density is lower than that of aviation kerosene. Natural gas is attractive

Biofuels from cellulose

The CO_2 benefits of biofuels, e.g. ethanol, made from plant material depend, amongst other things, on which type of plant is used. Conventional processes ferment the starch in the plant to make ethanol, which is then concentrated by distillation. Sugarcane is one of the best sources of ethanol – 70 litres or more of ethanol can be produced from each tonne of sugar cane[14]. In cereal crops, much of the plant is lignin and cellulosic materials, which cannot be fermented, so only half as much ethanol can be made compared with sugarcane. New processes, including ones using novel enzymes, are under development to convert cellulose into sugar, which could then be fermented into ethanol. This has the potential to boost CO_2 emission reductions by up to 70%[15] when replacing petrol. Extension of this process to plants with even higher proportions of cellulose, e.g. wood, would encourage ethanol production in other parts of the world. At present, the production cost when making bio-ethanol from wood is almost double that when making it from sugarcane.

An alternative process would be to gasify the wood chippings at high temperature to make a mixture of hydrogen and carbon monoxide. This *synthesis gas* could then be converted into a number of fuels including diesel, oil, naphtha, methanol, Di-Methyl-Ether (DME) or hydrogen using a Fischer-Tropsch process. The CO_2 reduction benefits would be limited by the emissions from the process, but this could provide a route to developing an aviation fuel from biomass.

Fig. 4.31 A car fuelled by liquid hydrogen on the road in Germany. Other car manufacturers have chosen to store hydrogen as a high pressure gas rather than as a liquid.

because it reduces emissions of other pollutants as well as CO_2. It is already used in about 5 million vehicles worldwide. The reduction of emissions, compared with petrol, is about 20%, and cost savings to the motorist may be significant if there is a difference in tax, as is the case in several countries.

Hydrogen is potentially usable as a gaseous fuel. It is of interest for a number of reasons – it could be made from water by electrolysis, so it could be an energy carrier for any source of electricity, or it could be made from biomass or from fossil fuels (which is the current method). If the source of electricity were one of the renewable energy supplies, this would allow a 100% reduction in CO_2 emissions at the point of use (although the energy costs for compression are significant). Hydrogen could also be supplied as a liquid, requiring less space than gas, but the energy costs for liquefaction are considerable, undermining much of the advantage in terms of emissions.

As well as being usable in modified internal combustion engines, hydrogen is of particular interest because it is the fuel of choice for an alternative source of motive power, the fuel cell. Fuel cells generate electricity which could be fed to electric motors driving the wheels of a vehicle. The cost of fuel cells, motors and hydrogen storage tanks is still much higher than conventional engines and tanks, so the cost of emission reductions originating from this substitution would be substantial. Hydrogen requires dedicated handling and storage facilities, either as a gas or as a refrigerated liquid (which must be turned into gas before use), so a new fuel supply and distribution system would be needed. Thus, hydrogen has its good points, being free of carbon, but it also raises issues regarding where it would come from, how it would be handled, and how it would be stored and used. These problems are major obstacles to its use and have yet to be overcome.

Electricity is widely used as a an energy carrier in public transport, especially trains. For individual vehicles, the use of this carrier would be a radical departure from existing technology, not least because it would need a different means of storing the fuel – i.e. a battery. Conventional batteries have a relatively low energy density and high weight, making them uncompetitive for this task. Several manufacturers have improved this technology, but have not, at present, achieved sufficient capacity in a small space or been able to avoid large increases in vehicle weights. The reduction in emissions would essentially depend on the emissions of the electricity supply system but would be aided by the higher energy efficiency of the electric vehicle, when compared with a vehicle using an internal combustion engine. At present, this substitution would be an expensive alternative to conventional engines. But, if improved battery technology can be developed, the extra cost may be reduced.

A related development is the hybrid car, which uses an internal combustion engine in combination with a battery and an electric power-train[18]. Because the engine can be operated at its most efficient, or switched off, emissions are reduced. However, there are still substantial CO_2 emissions from it because the engine is in use a lot of the time, so the reduction in CO_2 emissions is small when compared with the emissions from advanced internal combustion engines.

Fig. 4.32 Electric delivery vans – the Citroën Berlingo used by the ELCIDIS goods distribution service in La Rochelle, France.

For air travel, suitable alternative fuels have not yet been developed. Some type of biofuel may offer a method of reducing emissions (if the low temperatures aircraft are exposed to can be tolerated), but emissions when processing the fuel will be significant, especially due to the demanding fuel specifications. Hydrogen has been considered a long-term option but its low energy density suggests that aeroplane design will have to change considerably to allow the storage and use of liquid hydrogen.

Substitution in Industry

Several of the major, energy-intensive industries are clearly open to changes that would reduce emissions substantially, but the most attractive approaches differ greatly from industry to industry.

For example, the aluminium industry emits a substantial amount of greenhouse gases (CO_2 and others) from the electrolysis process used to refine the raw material bauxite. This is partly from the electrodes, which are made of carbon, and partly from the generation of electricity (if fossil fuels are used). Besides the substitution of low emission sources in the generation of electricity (as discussed above), the emissions from the electrodes could be reduced almost completely by introducing inert anodes. This technology has been the subject of intensive research, but so far without a breakthrough.

An oil refinery is largely fuelled by its own by-products so fuel substitution might have little overall effect on emissions, depending on what happened to the displaced by-products. Some oil refineries already use combined heat and power, which cuts CO_2 emissions by half compared with simple power generation. The key to this application is the local need for heat (i.e. the refinery itself), something conventional power stations do not have. This, together with refinery fuel savings, could reduce worldwide refinery emissions by 20%[19].

In the steel industry, the use of natural gas instead of coke is being studied as part of the development of low emission processes[20]. If successful, the CO_2 emissions from making one tonne of steel might be halved (from about two tonnes of CO_2 per tonne of steel to one tonne per tonne). In the ferro-alloy industry, replacing coal with charcoal made from biomass might achieve a reduction in emissions of almost four tonnes of CO_2 per tonne of product.

Emissions associated with cement manufacture might be reduced if alternative product specifications were acceptable; this centres on a different product composition replacing the accepted Portland cements. Fuel used in cement kilns is often partly waste (sometimes biomass) so if that were replaced by another fuel it would just require a different means of disposing of this waste. Nevertheless, at least one Norwegian cement plant has found that it would be possible to increase the biomass proportion of its fuel to 60%.

Final remarks about substitution

Substitutes for fossil fuels, whether renewable or nuclear, offer the potential for as much as a 100% reduction in emissions across the entire cycle of production and use. However, the extra costs can make this an expensive way of achieving deep reductions in CO_2 emissions, and the capacity for producing many of these substitutes is constrained.

One of the realities of replacing fossil fuels is that the hydrocarbons will be left in the ground. So, unless their use is made illegal, it is possible that they will be extracted and used at some point in the future. Hence, replacing fossil fuels does not guarantee that they will not be exploited in the end, producing CO_2 at that time.

Option: Destroy

The destruction of CO_2 is barely conceivable but CO_2 is a very stable material so it would require large amounts of energy to break it into its constituent parts (carbon and oxygen). Any such use of large amounts of energy tends to involve the emission of large amounts of CO_2, so that the destruction of CO_2 is not relevant as an option for tackling climate change.

Option: Dispose

The final option, the disposal of CO_2, can be recognised as taking place in the natural process of plant growth, e.g. trees. This process draws down CO_2 from the atmosphere and incorporates it as carbon into wood. For trees that live for a long time, this will essentially be locked in for centuries. Thus, sequestering carbon as wood in trees is a potential method of reducing the amount of CO_2 in the atmosphere. However, trees have a finite lifespan – even if they are not cut down for commercial use, they may be destroyed by pests or fire. If these trees are destroyed, their carbon content will rapidly be released as CO_2, so this would be of no help to the climate.

On the other hand, once a commercial forest has been cut down, it would normally be replanted so that the removal of carbon from the atmosphere would continue. Cut timber keeps carbon out of the atmosphere for a certain period of time, depending on its eventual use. Thus, if the wood is made into paper, it is likely that the carbon will be returned to the atmosphere within months or years. If used for construction purposes, the carbon will be kept out of the atmosphere for decades or centuries. However, it is impossible to say how much carbon in total will be kept out of the atmosphere or for how long.

Another aspect of sequestering carbon in trees is that large areas of land will be needed – for example a forest area of about 100,000 hectares might be needed to sequester the equivalent amount of carbon emitted by a modern 400MW power station. Not only does this put a practical limit on how much carbon could be stored in trees, it also suggests there would be competition between this and other uses of land, especially agriculture. At present, such projects are underway in countries which have more land than they need for agricultural or other purposes. This is relatively inexpensive, so the cost of removing CO_2 from the atmosphere is low. However, as the number of carbon sequestration projects increases, the cost of land will rise and thus the cost of this method of drawing down carbon will increase considerably. This suggests that, whilst early projects are low-cost and look attractive, the long-term potential of this approach will be different, with a rather limited global capacity.

What does all this mean as regards stabilising the amount of CO_2 in the atmosphere?

Modest reductions of emissions from buildings (up to 20% to 30%) can be achieved by reducing energy use, especially cost-effective improvements to the efficiency of appliances; greater reductions could be achieved by reducing demand by means of building insulation, but this tends to be much more expensive.

Emissions from electricity generation can be reduced considerably, although there is only limited scope from improvements in efficiency in the short-term, at relatively high cost. Much deeper reductions in emissions (up to 100%) can be achieved by the substitution of renewable energy sources or nuclear power for fossil fuel generation. The cost of these methods of generation may be substantial; in particular, for the renewable sources once their best sites have been used.

Nuclear power, where acceptable, could be a substitute for base load generation although it is not as appropriate for meeting less frequent demand.

Small reductions in emissions from transport could be achieved through improved vehicle technology, e.g. improved combustion or the use of hybrid vehicles, but substantial reductions in emissions would require changes in fuel, for example replacement by biofuels or changing to a different energy carrier (e.g. hydrogen or electricity).

Emission reductions arising from the use of biofuels in transport could be as high as 60% or more, but the capacity will be constrained by the availability of land, especially in many highly-populated, developed countries. If there were limits to the amount of biofuels that could be produced, it might be the case that their use would eventually be restricted to areas where there is little alternative, e.g. as aircraft fuel.

Natural gas could reduce emissions from vehicles significantly, but there would still be considerable CO_2 emissions. The use of other energy carriers, such as hydrogen or electricity, shifts emissions away from the vehicle to the production stage, but much of the cost would be incurred when building the vehicles because of the complexity of the systems. Deep reductions in vehicle emissions are possible, but will be much more expensive than in large stationary sources.

Emission reductions in industry may be the most difficult to achieve in the short term because the energy-intensive industries have already raised their energy efficiency to high levels in countries where world market prices are paid for energy. In the longer term, new processes may be developed which could reduce emissions substantially. Replacement with biofuels may also be able to make a contribution in certain cases.

One final word of caution is needed regarding the extent to which emission reductions could be achieved in industry – depending on how this is introduced by government, the effect might be that some industries move to locations in other countries where the restrictions on emissions are less exacting. From a global point of view, emissions would not then be reduced to the same extent. The implementation of an emission reduction policy has to be coupled with other policies ensuring that industry does not relocate just to avoid these extra costs.

Most of the options discussed in this chapter will only work in certain situations – for example, biofuels are very successful in Brazil but less attractive in the colder parts of the world, or where less land is available for growing plants. Some parts of the world are better suited to solar power than others; some have good opportunities to use wind or tidal or ocean currents whilst other do not. Nuclear power would appear to be an option which has wide applicability, if acceptable. However, nuclear waste typically contains fissile material which could be extracted and used for other purposes, most worryingly for nuclear weapons. If weapons proliferation continues to be a concern, this may restrict the global expansion of nuclear power.

Is this the end of the fossil fuel era?

This chapter has demonstrated that there are many ways in which the world could reduce the CO_2 burden on the atmosphere by using new and improved technology. All of these imply that the role of fossil fuels will decline in the future. However, fossil fuels provide a very large part of the world's energy supply for the good reason that they are convenient to use and inexpensive. The attractiveness of fossil fuels will make it difficult for any of the alternatives to gain a large share of the market, at least initially. This makes it hard to imagine that a substantial reduction in global emissions could be quickly achieved without some drastic step being taken, e.g. outlawing the use of fossil fuels. But the economic impact of enforcing such a change would be dramatic and would likely cause considerable disruption to the world's economies, even if it could be agreed upon as an international policy (which seems most unlikely).

In these circumstances, the availability of an option to continue using fossil fuels, but with much reduced CO_2 emissions, would be potentially most important. Fortunately, there is such an alternative – this is to capture the CO_2 produced by the combustion of fossil fuels and keep it out of the atmosphere for a very long time, probably for ever. This may sound like science fiction but, in fact, it can be done using a novel combination of known and existing technologies, which are described in the next chapter. This would provide a means of allowing the world to choose how long it wished to continue using fossil fuels, whilst reducing its CO_2 emissions. It would provide the basis for an orderly and managed transition away from fossil fuels, at the lowest cost to society.

The climate problem is so large that the world will need to pursue all of the options because none of them alone can meet all of our demands for safety, security of supply, substantial emission reductions, low cost, and reliability.

Chapter 4 | Squaring the circle: accessing energy without damaging the climate

Suggestions for further reading

"Energy systems and sustainability" by G. Boyle, B. Everett, J. Romage. 2003. Oxford University Press. Oxford.

Energy Technology Perspectives. 2006. OECD-IEA. Paris.

Endnotes

1   This is an example of a wider problem resulting from reducing the cost of using the service – remember it is the service provided by using energy which interests the user. As the demand for some services, e.g. motoring, is constrained partly by cost, reducing the cost of the service will lead to increased consumption. So even cost-effective measures of emission reductions, perversely, may not reduce the use of energy as much as might be hoped.

2   "Future technologies for energy efficient iron and steel making." J de Beer, E Worrell, K Blok. Annual Review of Energy and Environment (1998) 2.3: 123–205.

3   "Biofuels for Transport", Lew Fulton, IEA, presentation 14 December 2004.

4   "Biofuels for Road Transport", Dr. Roger Cracknell, Shell Global Solutions, 19 September 2006.

5   A megawatt (MW) is a million watts, roughly the electricity needed to run 10,000 light bulbs.

6   Energy Technology Perspectives (2006). OECD/IEA. Paris.

7   US Energy Information Agency, International Energy Outlook 2006.

8   It would be feasible to store some of the electricity for use at night, but storing large amounts of electricity is very expensive and difficult to justify on a large scale.

9   IEA, 2006.

10 Almost-pure ethanol would not be used in this way in regions where temperatures might fall low enough for it to freeze.

11 "World Energy Outlook 2006". OECD-IEA, Paris.

12 As note 3 above.

13 Figures quoted for ethanol made from sugar beet crop in "Energy Technology Perspectives" 2006. OECD-IEA, Paris.

14 "Energy Technology Perspectives", 2006. OECD-IEA, Paris.

15 "Energy Technology Perspectives", 2006. OECD-IEA, Paris p 279.

16 "Energy Technology Perspectives", 2006. OECD/IEA, p 284.

17 In the UK, producing sufficient bioethanol to meet the European requirement of 5.75% of motor fuel would require the use of 25% of all arable land (source: Low carbon vehicle partnership: Board paper P 05-07).

18 The power-train is the engine, the gearbox, and the system for transmitting power to the wheels.

19 "Refining energy efficiency and environmental goods" by Z. Milosevic and W. Lowart. PTQ, Summer 2002.

20 ULCOS: Ultra Low CO_2 Steelmaking project, supported by EU R&D Programme.

Putting carbon back in the ground

How can we prevent the CO_2 produced by fossil fuels from reaching the atmosphere? Simply put, we first need to intercept it and then we need to store it somewhere. This storage has to be safe and secure for thousands of years. In order to make a worthwhile impact on the 26 billion tonnes of CO_2 which are emitted every year, it will be necessary to find some very large reservoirs in which to hold it. The only storage reservoirs capable of holding CO_2 on this scale are natural formations, especially underground ones, which we will discuss in this chapter.

Fig. 5.1 In Salah gas held with CO_2 capture for storage.

Natural reservoirs have been holding oil, gas, and CO_2 for millions of years

Holding CO_2 in geological formations is akin to what has been happening naturally for millions of years. Oil, natural gas, and even natural CO_2 have been held in geological formations for timescales which are unimaginably long, up to hundreds of millions of years. If this natural process can be replicated in CO_2 storage, then we would have the basis for keeping CO_2 out of the atmosphere for a very long time. Indeed, if these storage facilities are as secure as we expect, the CO_2 would be put away for ever, much like the hydrocarbons have been since they were first formed.

In principle, we could inject all of the gases from combustion into underground formations but the gases which emerge from the chimney of a power station not only contain CO_2 but also nitrogen and other gases. In fact, CO_2 only makes up about 13% of the gases originating from a coal-fired power station; from a gas-fired power station the gases contain as little as 3 or 4% CO_2. Thus, if we separate the CO_2 from these other gases, we can reduce the required storage volume by a factor of between 8 and 25.

Further to this, we can take advantage of a particular property of CO_2 that makes it behave like a liquid when put under sufficient pressure. In this state, cal-

Fig. 5.2 The flue gases from a coal-fired power plant consist of 14% CO_2, 72% nitrogen and 3% oxygen. Normal air is 78% nitrogen, 21% oxygen, nearly 1% argon and 0.038% CO_2.

Chapter 5 | Putting carbon back in the ground

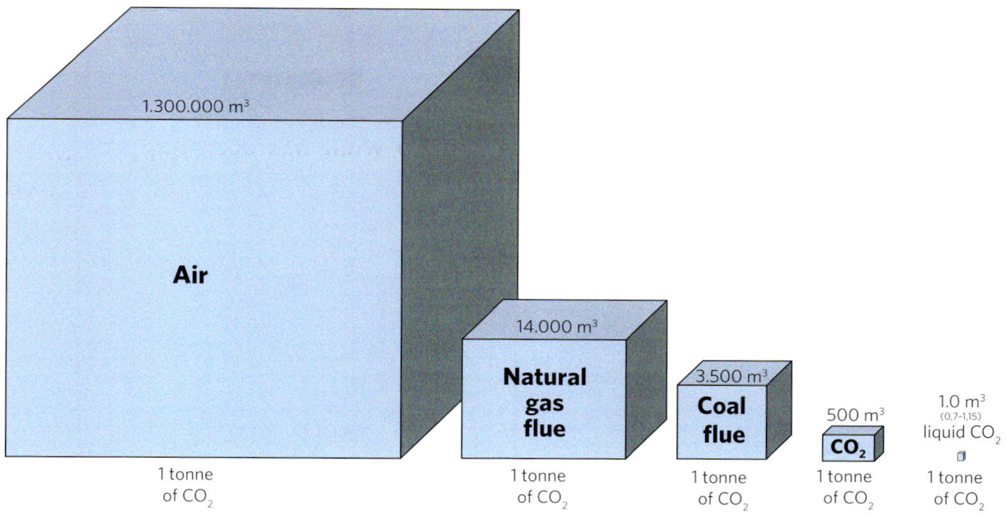

Fig. 5.3 Comparison of the volume occupied by one tonne of CO_2 – this illustrates why transporting CO_2 as liquid uses much less space than transporting the whole of the flue gas stream.

led the dense phase, its density is close to that of liquid water. This means that the required storage volume would be 300 to 400 times less than the volume occupied by a similar amount at atmospheric pressure. The necessary pressures are found at depths of 800m or more and these are easily accessed using the drilling techniques of the oil industry.

Both of these stratagems can also be applied to reducing the size of the pipelines used to transport the CO_2.

How to collect the CO_2 for storage

Separating the CO_2 from the other gases after combustion can be achieved using techniques developed 60 years ago for a very similar purpose, namely removing CO_2 during the production of town gas from coal. This method is also used by industry today for purifying hydrogen and ammonia. As a result, there is considerable industrial experience in methods of separating CO_2.

In much the same way that a large power station generates electricity more cheaply than a small one, a large plant for capturing CO_2 will cost much less per tonne of CO_2 than a small one. This phenomenon is known as "economies of scale". This has an important impact on how CO_2 would be separated, transported and stored. For example, it is about four times cheaper to move a tonne of

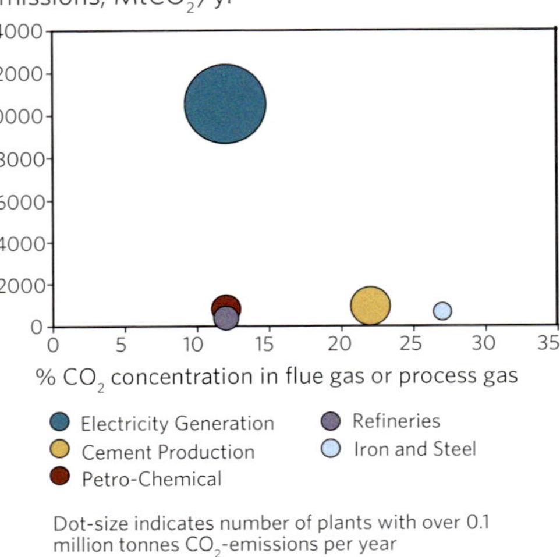

Fig. 5.4 Some CO$_2$ sources lend themselves to CO$_2$ capture better than others. The horizontal axis shows the CO$_2$ concentration in the flue gas stream, which is an indication of the relative ease or difficulty of capturing CO$_2$. The vertical axis gives the total emissions from each industrial sector. (Data from IPCC Special report on Carbon Dioxide Capture and Storage, 2005).

CO$_2$ by pipeline when moving 10 million tonnes per year, than when only moving one million tonnes per year. Similar reductions in cost also apply to the separation and storage processes. This has a profound effect on where the capture and storage of CO$_2$ is best deployed. The economies of scale differ greatly between a large power station, emitting more than two million tonnes annually, and a building heated by a gas boiler, emitting one or two tonnes per year. Broadly speaking, it makes sense to consider capturing the CO$_2$ originating from the large sources, but not from the small ones. Thus, the four main sectors responsible for CO$_2$ emissions can be characterized as follows:

- Large, central sources – electricity generation and much energy-intensive industry
- Small, distributed sources – buildings, vehicles

Roughly half of the CO$_2$ emissions come from large sources and half from small ones. This distinction is important when deciding how the capture and storage of CO$_2$ could be put into practice, as we will discuss later.

Where would we put the CO$_2$?

The idea of storing CO$_2$ underground is not as strange as it might seem because there are, in fact, geological formations which naturally hold CO$_2$ and have done so for thousands or millions of years. They do this in a similar way to how oil and gas have been trapped underground (see Chapter 2), but oil and gas fields are much more widespread than natural CO$_2$ fields. Because they have demonstrated their ability to hold fluids through geological timescales, they should also be suitable for holding CO$_2$ once the oil or gas has been extracted. The main proviso

Natural analogues of CO₂ storage

Three geological reservoirs in the USA each contain about 1.6 billion tonnes of almost pure CO_2. These are natural occurrences. They are just a few of many examples in the USA, Canada, Central America, Saudi Arabia, Australia, Southern Europe, and Eastern China and Russia. In addition, CO_2 is also to be found mixed with natural gas or dissolved in water. The largest known accumulation of CO_2 is the Natuna field in the South China Sea, which contains 9.1 billion tonnes of CO_2 together with 720 million tonnes of natural gas. Natural CO_2 in such formations has come from various sources, including from the decomposition of sediments and from volcanoes. In some cases, there is evidence that the CO_2 has been held in these reservoirs for thousands or millions of years.

Of course, none of these sites has been deliberately selected for storing CO_2 – the gas has accumulated in geological formations where some method of trapping exists to hold it in place. For this reason, it is not surprising that some of these reservoirs are leaking slightly, but others do not leak to any measurable extent.

In some volcanic areas, where there is continual replenishment of the CO_2, natural emissions of CO_2 occur in significant quantities. Some of these are referred to as spas, where carbonated waters are a consumer product. In others, bathing in carbonated springs is thought to help alleviate the symptoms of some illnesses. The most extreme case of the natural release of CO_2

occurs in Lake Nyos in Cameroon. The waters in such tropical lakes are stratified, so there is little natural mixing between the lower layers and the surface. Under these circumstances, CO_2 leaking into the lower levels of the lake accumulated until, in 1987, the whole lake overturned, with a massive release of CO_2. The gas filled the lower parts of the valley, killing 1,700 people in the process. This event reinforces the need for care when handling CO_2, but the circumstances of this unfortunate incident are so different from those surrounding the deliberate storage of CO_2 that there is no realistic danger from deliberate storage. In particular, no site would ever be selected which would hold CO_2 in this way. Nor are lakes in temperate areas stratified throughout the year, so they would not collect CO_2 in this way.

Natural CO_2 fields are good places to learn about the storage of CO_2. For example, where there are slight leaks, these provide the opportunity to develop techniques for monitoring storage. Also, the natural fields provide information on the long-term performance of the reservoir cap rock, which is the best test-bed for the types of geological seal that will be used in the deliberate storage of CO_2.

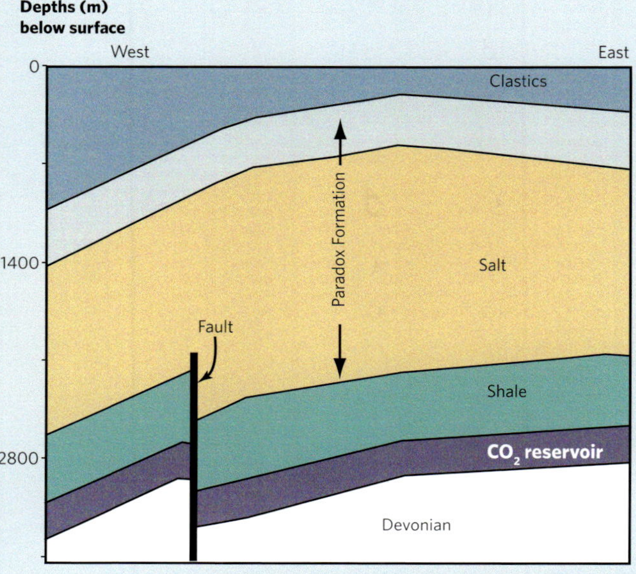

Fig. 5.5 Natural CO₂ reservoir – a simplified cross-section through the McElmo Dome reservoir and the overlying rock formations. (See fig. 5.8)

Man-made analogues of CO_2 storage

Various gases are already being stored underground. This has been done for many years. Such facilities provide the longest period of practical experience of a process closely related to the underground storage of CO_2. They can provide relevant information about the reliability, safety and regulation of underground storage.

Natural gas is stored underground in order to allow excess production during summer to help meet peak demand in winter, and to ensure that supplies are available in case of short-term disruptions (which may be a regulatory requirement on the gas supplier). This is done at 634 individual facilities in 25 countries. The total volume of stored gas is about 340 billion m³, which would be equivalent to the space required to hold 270 billion tonnes of CO_2 (if it was in the dense phase), so this is a relevant scale of experience.

Indeed, natural gas storage may be a competitor to CO_2 storage for use of some geological formations. The main formations used for natural gas are depleted gas or oilfields and, to a lesser extent, aquifers. The largest amount of natural gas storage is to be found in the USA and Russia. Most of the storage in the USA is at depths of less than 800m (i.e. shallower than required for CO_2 to be in the dense phase) but in Europe most of the depleted fields used for storage are at depths of more than 800m, although the aquifers used are at shallower depths. The maximum operating pressure allowed in such stores is carefully calculated from the characteristics of each formation. The injected gas is closely monitored through the use of observation wells in the target formation, and in adjacent geological formations.

Another close analogue is the injection of acid gases (i.e. CO_2 and H_2S) into geological formations in Western Canada and, to a lesser extent, the USA. These gases are extracted from natural gas before it is sent to market, mainly to remove the sulphur. Up to the end of 2003, 2.5 million tonnes of CO_2 had been injected in this way during 51 projects in Canada, mainly into deep saline aquifers but also into depleted oil and gas fields. Most of these facilities have performed satisfactorily, although some have now been decommissioned because they had used up their approved capacity; three of them have been suspended by the regulatory authority because the pressure was allowed to rise too much.

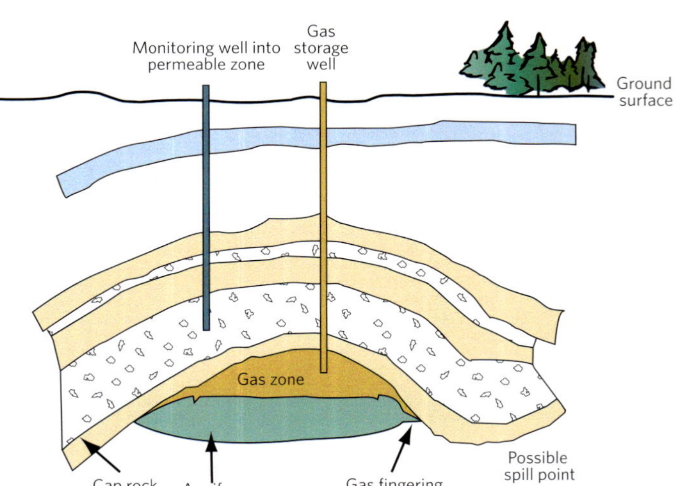

is that the seal on the reservoir (which trapped the oil or gas in the first place) must not have been disturbed by the extraction process. Providing that this is the case, the reservoir should be able to hold CO_2 for a long time.

This approach is already being used for the storage of natural gas, for ex-

Fig. 5.6 Natural gas storage in an aquifer beneath a cap-rock.

 **Chapter 5 | Putting carbon back in the ground

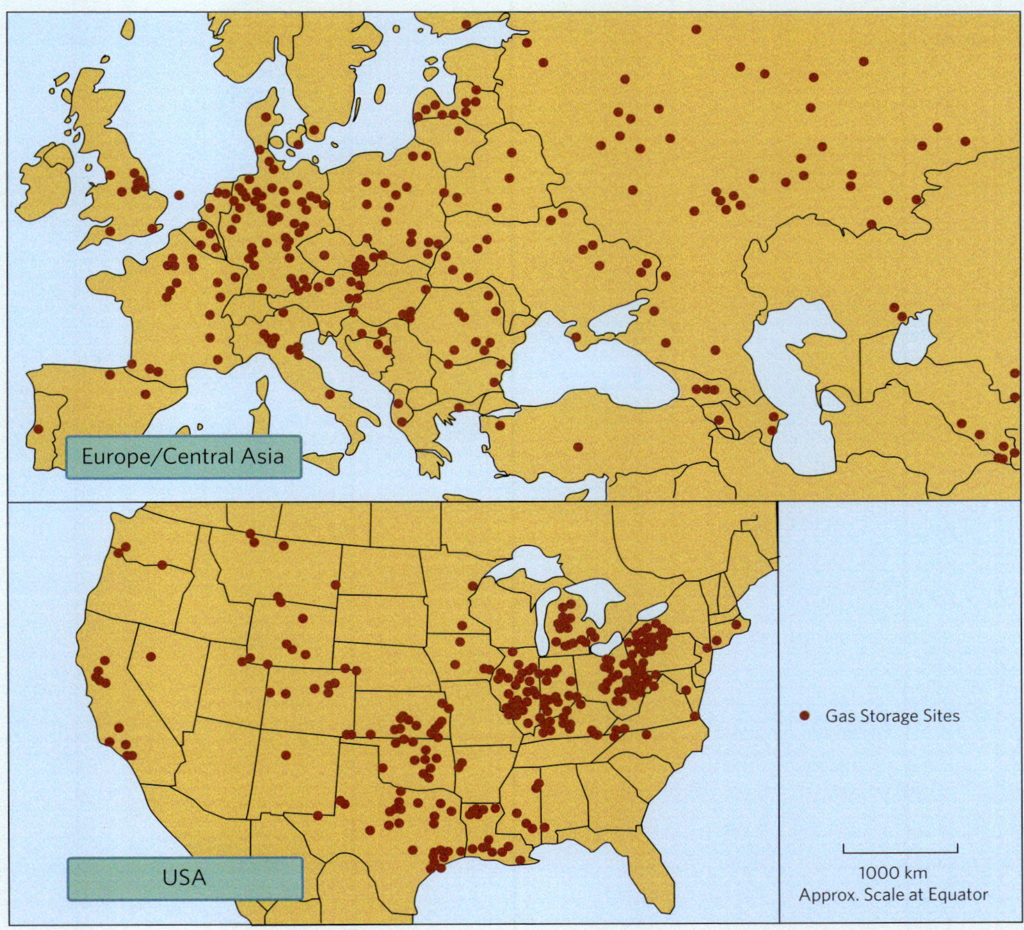

Fig. 5.7 Natural gas storage sites in Europe and USA.

ample to provide backup supplies of natural gas during winter. The major difference between storing natural gas and storing CO_2 is that the latter would be injected once and left there, whereas natural gas is typically stored for only a few months before it is extracted for use.

Perhaps the easiest way to visualise holding CO_2 underground is to consider doing this in a depleted gas field. Once natural gas has been extracted (pushed out of the pores in the rock by natural pressure) CO_2 can be injected, filling the pores and raising the pressure again. This must be stopped at a pressure short of the level at which damage might occur to the geological formation but this can be predicted and monitored, as is the case with natural gas storage.

Enhanced oil recovery using CO_2

Under appropriate circumstances, CO_2 dissolves into oil, making it easier to move the oil to the production well. The most frequent method of using it to enhance oil recovery is to alternate between the injection of CO_2 and the injection of water, which sweeps the oil to the production well. Some of the injected CO_2 will be extracted from the field with the oil – it is normal practice to separate this out and re-inject it.

In the USA, about 73 such projects inject more than 30 million tonnes of CO_2 per year. Ninety percent of this CO_2 comes from natural sources, with the remainder being captured during natural gas processing and fertiliser manufacture. The SACROC project in Texas was the first large-scale injection, starting in 1972. This used captured CO_2 until 1995, after which it has been using CO_2 from a natural source. In Canada, there are similar projects, including the Weyburn project which has been injecting captured CO_2 since 2000. Enhanced oil recovery using CO_2 has also been carried out in Turkey, Trinidad, Brazil, and in other countries.

US experience suggests that, on average, 0.3 tonnes of CO_2 are purchased for each additional barrel of oil produced (i.e. roughly 2 tonnes of CO_2 for each extra tonne of oil). On average, this is found to increase the amount of oil recovered by 12% (relative to the original amount of oil in place). In comparison, the worldwide average recovery of oil is about 35%[2] by conventional means, at best achieving 50% recovery.

The CO_2 remaining in the reservoir at the end of injection can be regarded as being stored, providing the field is not re-entered. The wells must be sealed, preventing the subsequent escape of CO_2. In addition, steps must be taken to prevent the steel tubing in any wells passing through the formation from being corroded by contact with CO_2, and to avoid degradation of the cement used to seal the wells. The storage of CO_2 in a depleted oilfield may benefit from any extra oil produced which can help to offset some of the cost of CO_2 supply.

It might seem conceivable that a similar approach could be used to enhance gas recovery, but an important difference here is that up to 95% of natural gas can be recovered by conventional production. In some circumstances, there may be some merit in injecting CO_2 into

Oilfields may also be used to store CO_2, but these are slightly different to gas fields because, following the initial reduction in pressure, water naturally enters some of the pore spaces and may also have been injected in order to increase the amount of oil recovered[1]. The injection of CO_2 into a partially-depleted oilfield has to push this water out again, which is possible in most fields because, typically, they are connected to a wider, underground aquifer. In addition, CO_2 has another useful property; under certain conditions, CO_2 dissolves in oil, making it easier to move the oil in the reservoir. This effect is exploited by the oil industry to increase oil recovery. By positioning the injection points so as to address the remaining oil, perhaps 10% more oil can be recovered from an oilfield. When production ceases, as much as possible of the CO_2 is extracted for use in another field. Something similar could be achieved if the purpose of injection was to store

Chapter 5 | Putting carbon back in the ground

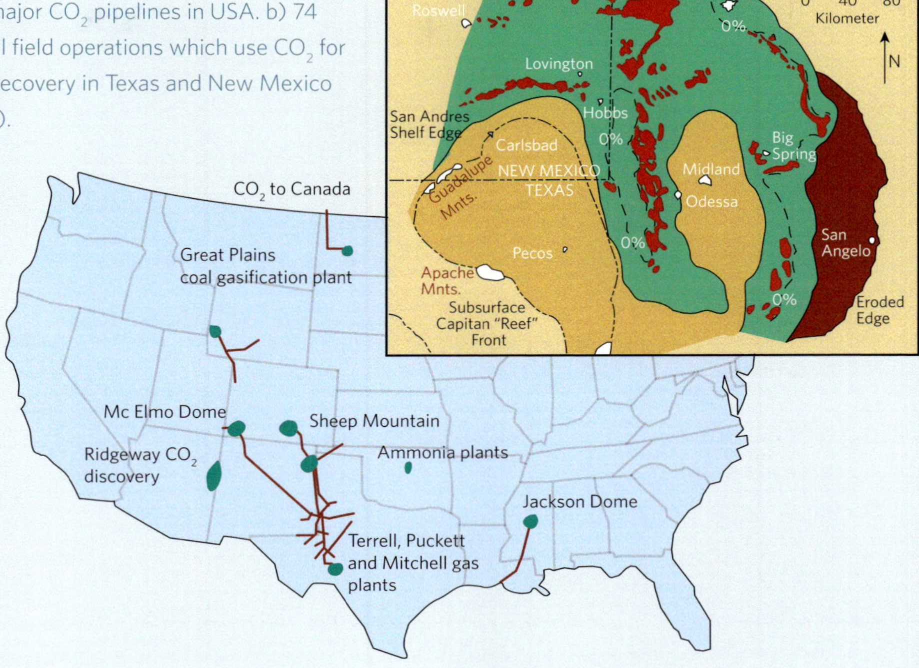

Fig. 5.8 a) Some natural and man-made CO$_2$ sources and major CO$_2$ pipelines in USA. b) 74 commercial oil field operations which use CO$_2$ for enhanced oil recovery in Texas and New Mexico (shown in red).

a gas field during the early years of its operation in order to maintain the pressure. This will help to keep up the rate of production, but will not increase the overall recovery of gas from the field. At some point, the CO$_2$ may mix with the natural gas – such contamination adds cost (for separation) which has to be traded off against the early benefit of maintaining production.

CO$_2$ in depleted fields, the main difference being that the CO$_2$ would be left in the field at the end of injection.

A third type of geological formation which could be useful for CO$_2$ storage holds only saltwater. These aquifers are deeper than those used to provide potable water. Because they contain saltwater, they have no commercial use. It seems likely that, worldwide, there is much greater capacity to hold CO$_2$ in deep saline aquifers than in oil or gas fields, but there has been little practical investigation as yet. Nevertheless, the world's first commercial-scale storage of CO$_2$ made use of a deep saline aquifer. This is the Utsira aquifer which stretches for hundreds of kilometres under the North Sea overlaid by a thick mudstone cap. Since 1996, roughly one million tonnes of CO$_2$ have been injected annually into the Utsira formation; this CO$_2$ comes from StatoilHydro's Sleipner West gas field. This pro-

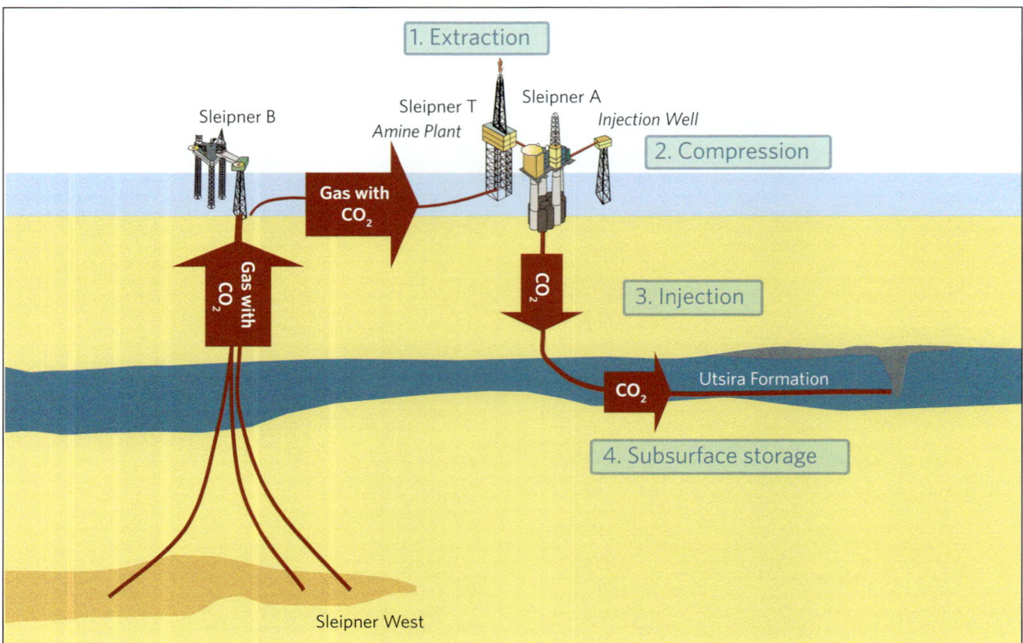

Fig. 5.9   In the Sleipner project, CO_2 separated from natural gas is injected at the rate of one million tonnes per year of CO_2 into the salt-water-filled Utsira formation under the North Sea (StatoilHydro).

ject was the first one to demonstrate that emissions of CO_2 could be avoided by capturing it and injecting it into a geological formation for storage.

Where are the geological formations we could use to store CO_2?

Oil and gas fields are not evenly distributed around the world, so only some countries would be able to use them for storing CO_2, once hydrocarbon production had come to an end. It is estimated that oilfields could hold between 100 and 400 billion tonnes of CO_2 and that gas fields could hold about 800 billion tonnes of CO_2[3].

It is likely that deep saline aquifers are more widely-distributed than oil and gas fields, but there is limited knowledge of their locations. The estimates of global capacity are more uncertain – it is expected that they could hold between 1,000 and 10,000 billion tonnes of CO_2[4].

But does this correspond to where the CO_2 might come from? A map of large sources of CO_2 shows there is a fair match in many developed countries between the sources of CO_2 and the possible storage locations, many lying within 300km of each other. Although the sources of CO_2 (e.g. power stations) are certain to

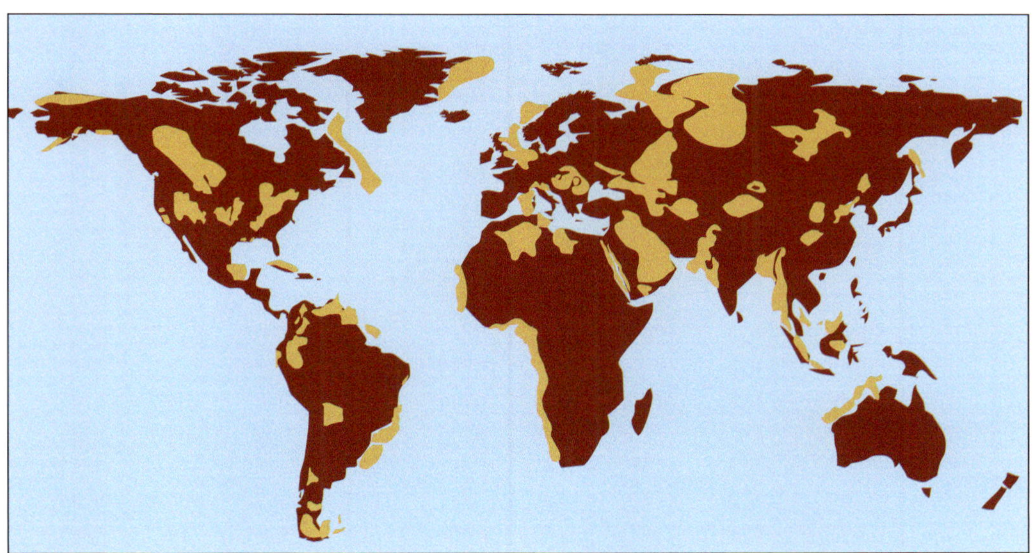

Fig. 5.10 Oil and gas regions of the world – because the sub-surface has been extensively surveyed, some of these could be the first places where CO_2 is stored in large amounts. (IPCC, 2005)

change in future, it is likely that, in developed countries, they will be built on sites already used for such purposes. However, in the developing countries, the situation is not so clear. For example in China, the amount of coal-fired generating capacity is increasing by about 12% a year, so it is likely that significant amounts of CO_2 might need to be captured at sites which currently do not produce CO_2. This means that, in rapidly expanding developing countries such as China and India, the map of the current sources of CO_2 only provides a rough indication of where CO_2 might be captured in the future.

Fig. 5.11 Places where CO_2 might be captured for storage are large, stationary sources of emissions. (Courtesy: Ecofys)

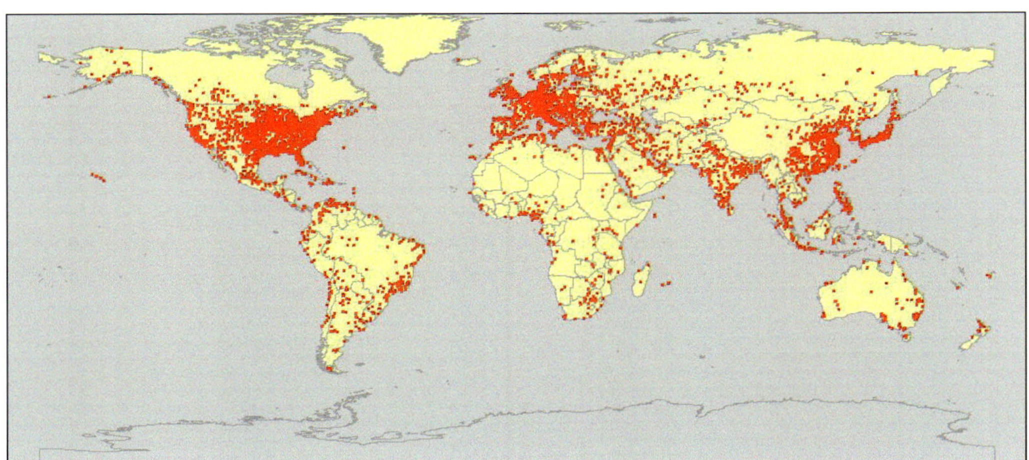

So, if we understand where CO_2 might be captured and where it might be stored, how would we get it from on place to another? Because of the large quantities involved, the most likely method of transport is by pipeline. There are already 2,600km of pipelines with the capacity to carry 50 million tonnes of CO_2/year in the USA; this provides a good indication of what might be done to transport CO_2 for storage. Such pipelines are built from carbon steel and operated at high pressure so that the CO_2 is in the dense phase. For power stations (or other sources) close to storage sites, it is likely that a pipeline would be built directly from one to the other, but for longer distances, CO_2 captured at several sources might be combined in a larger pipeline carrying tens of millions of tonnes per year. The final choice would depend on factors such as distance, cost, proximity to inhabited areas, etc.

Is this safe?

There may be concerns about the safety of handling large amounts of CO_2 in this way.

CO_2 is present in the atmosphere in very small amounts – the concentration of CO_2 is around 0.0038% at present (otherwise written as 380 parts per million). It is present in our breath when we exhale at a concentration of up to 4%. Neither situation presents any danger because we are still able to take in sufficient oxygen when we breathe. However, if we were to experience large volumes of CO_2 in a confined space, then there might be a danger that this would reduce the level of oxygen in the air to less than the 16% that we need. Or, by entering the bloodstream, the CO_2 could reduce the amount of oxygen we were able to take up when breathing. In view of these potential dangers, all handling and storage of CO_2 is carefully engineered and managed in order to avoid risk to life.

Separating out CO_2 in a power station will be achieved using processes designed and operated to modern chemical engineering standards. Any unintentional release of CO_2 would be inside the station; it would be detected and controlled immediately, so there would be no danger to the general public.

Outside the power station, the pipelines are a potential source of exposure to CO_2 so stringent design processes will be followed to ensure that the chances of leakage are very low. The choice of route for the line as well as the controls used are important factors in ensuring that no harm could come to people nearby. Current experience of leakage from CO_2 pipelines shows that they are similar to pipelines carrying natural gas, which are widely used in many countries. Both types have occasional accidents but the dangers of CO_2 are less than those of natural gas, because natural gas is flammable whilst CO_2 is not. The main disruption caused by such pipelines occurs whilst they are being laid.

Fig. 5.13 CO_2 injection at the Weyburn oil field. The wellhead for injecting CO_2 is protected by a weather-proof housing.

The injection of CO_2 into a geological formation will be just as safe as operating a pipeline. Once in the reservoir, there is a finite possibility that some CO_2 could escape but the chances of this happening will reduce with time due to a variety of natural processes which will help lock it in place. If the CO_2 were to escape, the most likely route would be via a well drilled into the reservoir (breaching the cap rock). Monitoring of the air above the reservoir would be carried out to detect whether any CO_2 was escaping in quantities which could be harmful. If such a leak were to be found, remedial action would be taken to limit the potential to cause harm – in the worst case, the CO_2 could be pumped out of the reservoir again.

How do we separate out the CO_2 to put it into storage?

Techniques for capturing CO_2 were first developed in the days when town gas was made from coal, and the CO_2 had to be removed before it was piped to customers. In those days, after the CO_2 had been separated out, it was just allowed to escape into the atmosphere. Now we can use the same technique to extract the CO_2 for storage, so that it does not reach the atmosphere.

One of the approaches that could be used in power stations is to remove the CO_2 after combustion – this is known as post-combustion capture. Another approach is to pre-treat the fuel so that the carbon-containing component is removed

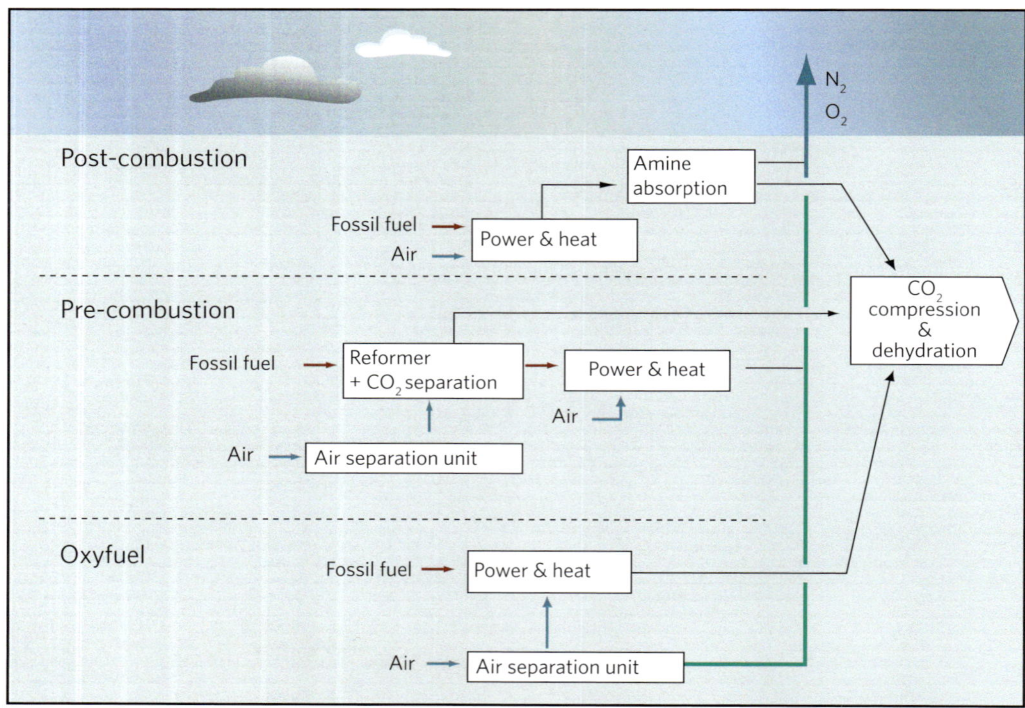

Fig. 5.14 Highly simplified diagram showing the 3 methods of CO_2 capture. The post-combustion technology is currently used for capturing CO_2 from flue gases for food-grade CO_2. The pre-combustion and oxy-fuel technologies are at less advanced stages of development but industrial scale demonstration projects have been launched.

before combustion – this is called pre-combustion capture. A third approach is to modify the combustion process to avoid mixing nitrogen with the CO_2 in the first place. In such a process, pure oxygen is used for combustion rather than air, thus avoiding the introduction of nitrogen into the combustion process. Then, all that is necessary is to separate out the CO_2 from a steam mixture, which is easily done. This is referred to as oxyfuel combustion. Using one of these three types of capture process can deliver a pure stream of CO_2 for storage.

A key factor which determines the ease (and hence cost) of separation is the concentration of CO_2 in the gas stream. Higher concentrations of CO_2 make it easier to separate out CO_2. Several industrial processes generate concentrations of CO_2 that are higher than the low levels found in power station exhaust gases (see fig. 5.4). Examples include blast furnaces, cement kilns and, in particular, ammonia and hydrogen production plants where the concentration of CO_2 can be as high as 100%.

All of this can be done with equipment which is already in industrial use, not least for supplying CO_2 to a range of users, including the food industry. The tech-

Fig. 5.15   An ammonia production plant, at Brunsbüttel in Germany. This plant uses hydrogen made from fossil fuels – an example of a possible low cost source of captured CO_2.

nologies and expertise are conventional chemical engineering. Suitably-trained designers and operators would be available from the pool of chemical engineers.

What can be done about small and mobile sources of CO_2?

Half of all fossil fuels are not used in large, industrial plants but in small burners (such as gas heaters), or in combustion engines in vehicles. Separating out, compressing, and transporting the CO_2 from small stationary appliances is conceivable but impracticable – this could not be implemented without radical change to the technology or without trained operators and supervision. It would be relatively expensive because of the economies of scale, as would transporting small amounts of CO_2, so it is not likely that it would be worth capturing CO_2 from small, fixed sources.

Food grade CO_2 and other industrial uses

CO_2 is used by a wide range of industries. In food production, it is used to carbonate beverages, to package foodstuffs, in chilling and freezing, and for temperature control during the distribution of chilled foods.

It is widely used in fire extinguishers, by the pharmaceutical industry, as well as others, to provide inert atmospheres, for supercritical fluid extraction, and for waste water treatment.

In some industrial processes, CO_2 is manufactured on site as an intermediate material in the production of certain chemicals. The main industrial use of CO_2 is in the manufacturing of urea, as a fertiliser. Large amounts of CO_2 are also used in the manufacturing of methanol, of inorganic carbonates, of polyurethanes, and, to a lesser extent, organic monomers and polycarbonates.

Most of these uses, especially food production, have very strict tolerances regarding the purity of the CO_2 – these requirements can be met by captured CO_2.

It should be noted that most of the CO_2 used for these purposes will be released into the atmosphere within days or months of use. None of these uses provides a means of combating climate change.

Fig. 5.16 Carbonated drink. The CO_2 in this drink may have been captured in an ammonia plant or from flue gases in a power station.

In addition, capturing CO_2 from vehicles would present the additional problem of recovering it from a mobile source. It is possible to conceive of technical solutions to this challenge but the cost would be very high. Whilst these arguments do not exclude the possibility of capturing CO_2 from small sources, it is unlikely that this would be cost-effective since another approach is more feasible; namely, supplying an energy carrier that produces no CO_2. One such "zero-carbon" energy carrier is hydrogen, another is electricity, while a third (for stationary uses) is heat.

All of these carriers can be made from fossil fuels using the capture and storage of CO_2 during their manufacture to avoid the emission of greenhouse gases. The process of generating electricity while capturing CO_2 has been described above; making heat while capturing and storing CO_2 would be done in a similar way. Cooling can also be supplied from a central plant using electricity, so this could also be made virtually emission-free.

Chapter 5 | Putting carbon back in the ground

Fig. 5.17 Hydrogen is made from natural gas as part of the production of methanol at the Tjeldbergodden plant in Norway.

Today, hydrogen is made from fossil fuels, especially natural gas, using a chemical process which initially produces a mixture of hydrogen and carbon monoxide. This can easily be adapted to produce hydrogen and CO_2, which can then be separated out for storage. Thus, small appliances and vehicles could be supplied with either electricity or hydrogen as a carbon-free energy carrier made from fossil fuels with the separating out of CO_2 (for storage) carried out at a central processing plant.

The provision of hydrogen as an energy carrier would require substantial changes in the way that energy is supplied and used. For stationary applications, hydrogen could be transmitted through pipelines, much as natural gas is distributed today. However the capacity of the current pipelines is insufficient to deliver energy at a similar rate to natural gas so there would need to be a considerable expansion of the pipeline system, unless the demand for energy could be reduced beforehand. There are also practical problems with using steel pipelines for hydrogen, which would have to be addressed.

Using hydrogen in vehicles would involve further departures from current practice. Hydrogen is a gas so it would have to be compressed so that it does

Fig. 5.18   Anders Hermansen filling a hydrogen-fuelled car with high pressure hydrogen gas at Stavanger, Norway as part of the HyNor project. This project is a public/private partnership to demonstrate real life use of hydrogen infrastructure along the route from Oslo to Stavanger.

not occupy much more space than petrol uses today. In order to achieve this, the pressure at which the hydrogen is delivered and stored would have to be 350 to 700 times atmospheric pressure which is very high.

Another option with hydrogen would be to cool it down (to −253°C) in order to liquefy it. Although this avoids the danger implicit in handling high pressure gases, the use of very cold liquids is also something which could be hazardous. The volume required for storage would be less but a substantial problem when using this approach is that about one third of the energy content of the hydrogen would be used to liquefy it, which seems a high price to pay for the convenience of having a liquid fuel. Nevertheless, several car manufacturers have vehicles on the road that use liquid hydrogen.

The hydrogen economy based on fossil fuels

In the decades since hydrogen was first demonstrated for use in powering space flight, the concept of the hydrogen economy has been embraced by some in the academic world, by environmental groups and, lately, also by industrial players. Why is there such interest in an energy carrier which does not occur in nature and which would require lots of R&D? The short answer is probably that hydrogen, as an energy source, can be envisaged as doing away with pollution. When burned or processed in a fuel cell, the end product is water – no CO_2, no SO_2, no particles and very little else to cause health problems or change the climate. Hydrogen is seen as a new energy carrier, comparable to electricity, which does not pollute at the point of use.

Up to now, the emphasis in research has been on fuel cell technology and on hydrogen storage, rather than on the hydrogen fuel itself and where it might come from. It was assumed

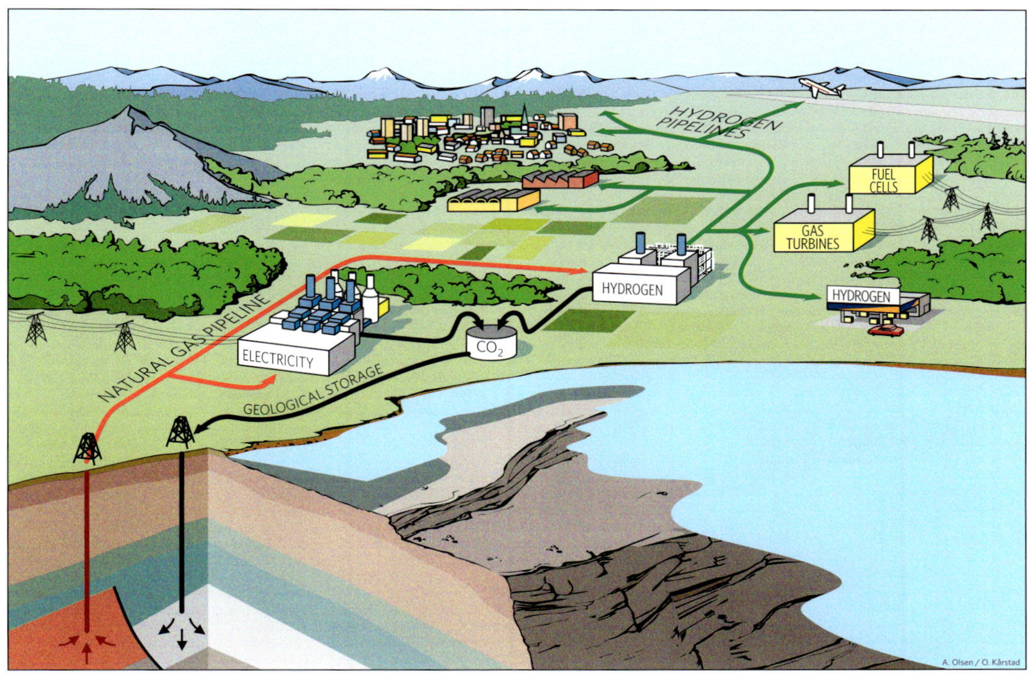

Figure 5.19   A "vision" of how fossil fuels might be de-carbonised in a climate-change-driven world, producing electricity and hydrogen as energy carriers with the resulting CO_2 stored underground (Source: Olav Kaarstad, 1993).

As mentioned before, hydrogen could be used with a fuel cell and electric motors to drive the wheels of a vehicle. This combination, whilst expensive, would be more efficient than an internal combustion engine with a conventional mechanical transmission.

that hydrogen would be produced using electricity from renewable energy sources to electrolyse water, from biomass, or from nuclear power.

Current world production of hydrogen is estimated at around 45 million tonnes per year. If used for energy purposes, this would be roughly equivalent to 1% of the global primary energy demand. The vast majority of this is produced by reforming fossil fuels, principally natural gas but also oil and coal. Roughly half of it is used in the manufacturing of ammonia-based fertilisers, with most of the rest being used in oil refineries.

The large industrial plants manufacturing hydrogen from fossil fuels mostly capture CO_2 as part of the process. This concentrated CO_2 is released into the atmosphere, although some is used in food or for making fertiliser. It is a short step from today's practice of making hydrogen to one where the captured CO_2 is stored. The added cost would be modest.

The alternative for vehicles would be to use electricity. Again electric motors would be used to drive the wheels but on-board storage would be achieved using batteries. Although quite different from the lead-acid starter batteries used in cars today, such batteries would occupy a large space and would be heavy, thereby affecting the performance of the vehicle.

Vehicles capable of using electricity or hydrogen carrier are currently under development. Only time will tell if one or the other will eventually succeed commercially.

How much would this all cost?

Compared with conventional power generation, the cost of capturing and storing CO_2 would add between 40% and 90% to the cost of base-load electricity generation[5]. This would not entail the price of the electricity delivered to the customer increasing by this much, because the rate the customer pays depends on how much electricity is used, as well as on transmission and distribution costs, etc.

This extra expense would achieve a reduction in emissions of 85% to 90%, compared with conventional power stations. Providing there is sufficient storage capacity for CO_2, the cost should be similar for most stations in a particular region of a country, the main variable being the cost of transporting the CO_2.

The addition of capture and storage to other industrial processes would increase costs by a similar amount, depending on circumstances. For example, hydrogen production costs would increase by between 6% and 50%, compared with conventional hydrogen production using fossil fuels, for almost complete avoidance of CO_2 emissions. The increase in cost for ammonia production would be even less because of the higher concentration of CO_2 in the exhaust gas (the precise cost would depend on how close the plant was to the storage facilities).

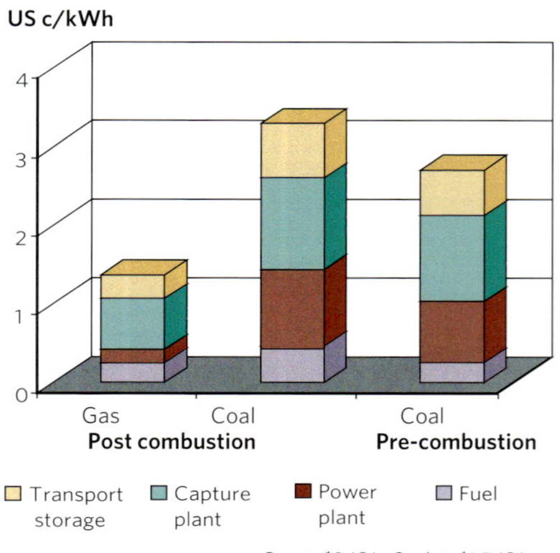

Fig. 5.20   Capturing CO_2 for storage increases the cost of generating electricity – additional costs will be incurred for purchasing and operating the extra equipment and for the extra fuel consumed.

   Chapter 5 | Putting carbon back in the ground

Other possible ways of using CO$_2$ capture

The concept of capturing and storing CO$_2$ only started to receive serious attention in the early 1990s. The first full-scale power stations may not be built until about 2012, so the full potential of this technique has probably not yet been understood. Nevertheless, a number of interesting variants are worth mentioning.

Application in power stations, as was described above, is most likely to be as base-load generation in the first instance. However, this will only address about half of the demand for electricity. One way of extending the application to part-load operation would be to use pre-combustion capture, whereby the fossil fuel is converted into an intermediate fuel gas consisting mostly of hydrogen. The hydrogen generated by a plant like this could be stored for later use[6], thus making it possible to run the fuel production and CO$_2$ separation parts of the plant continuously (thereby achieving the lowest production costs) whilst the hydrogen is stored for use in a generator whenever needed. Application in intermediate load generation would be more expensive but would allow this technique to handle, perhaps, 75% of the demand.

Another possibility would be to use the capture and storage of CO$_2$ in conjunction with a power station using biomass as a fuel (either on its own or in connection with fossil fuel). To the extent that growing biomass draws down CO$_2$ from the atmosphere, this application would transfer CO$_2$ from the atmosphere to underground storage. This offers a unique option for accelerating the speed at which the world could approach the goal of stabilisation. However, this option would be subject to the caveats expressed above regarding limits to the supply and transportation of biomass.

Alternative liquid fuels for vehicles may be manufactured from natural gas or coal using the Fischer-Tropsch process. This type of plant is sometimes referred to as a "CO$_2$-factory" testifying to the amount rejected to atmosphere. Capturing this CO$_2$ for storage would be more easily achieved than in power stations, so the additional cost would not be as great. Although the overall reduction in emissions (considering the whole system of fuel production and vehicle use) might only be 22%, compared with the best petrol vehicles, the low cost of this option may make this attractive during the next few decades as the world starts reducing greenhouse gas emissions. Fischer-Tropsch liquids are compatible with existing vehicles and distribution systems, making them much more acceptable to the user than zero-carbon energy carriers, but the fuels still contain some carbon so they cannot be the ultimate solution to the problem of CO$_2$ emissions from vehicles.

When will it happen?

The capture and storage of CO_2 is not just a theoretical concept – several projects are already in operation. These capture CO_2 separated out from natural gas and then inject it into geological formations. As yet, no power stations have been fitted with capture and storage facilities but plans have been announced for several such projects.

The world's first commercial-scale project for storing CO_2 in order to protect the climate was the Sleipner project, located 230 km off the coast of Norway. This started injecting about 1 million tonnes of CO_2 per year in 1996 and continues to do so. The CO_2 is separated from the natural gas produced by StatoilHydro's Sleipner West field. The CO_2 is injected into a deep saline aquifer, the Utsira formation, about 1,100m below sea-level. The Utsira formation is mainly sandstone and highly porous, so there is plenty of capacity. It is also highly permeable, so the CO_2 can move through it very easily. The CO_2 has been observed by seismic survey to have collected at the upper boundary of the formation and to have moved roughly northwards from the injection point.

Another project, off the coast of the Netherlands, injects CO_2 extracted from the natural gas produced by Gaz de France's K12-B field. From 2004, 60 ton-

Fig. 5.22   Monitoring of the CO_2 stored in the Utsira formation below the Sleipner platform shows it has collected under the cap-rock and has gradually spread out as more has been injected (Source: StatoilHydro).

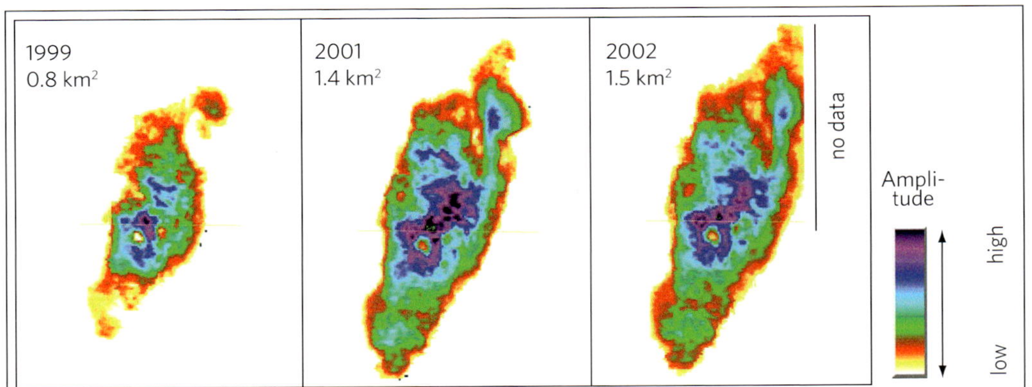

Fig. 5.23 This image shows how the CO_2 is distributed in the Utsira formation below the Sleipner platform 3 years after starting injection. The injection point is at the bottom and the CO_2 has reached the roof of the formation (Source: SACS Best Practice Manual).

nes per day were initially re-injected into part of the depleted field as a test. Subsequently, injection has begun into another part of the field.

At the In Salah natural gas complex in Algeria, the operators, started to re-inject about 1.3 million tonnes of CO_2 per year in 2004 through 3 horizontal wells. The CO_2 is being injected into a part of the reservoir well away from the gas production area, about 1,850m below the surface. A collaborative monitoring programme has been established to learn about the behaviour of the re-injected CO_2.

A different type of injection project is underway in Canada, where Encana is using captured CO_2 for enhanced oil recovery. Unusually for such a project, a detailed monitoring programme has been underway for several years in order to learn about the behaviour of the CO_2 underground. CO_2 is a by-product of the gasification of coal at Dakota Gasification's plant in Beulah, USA; it is transported by pipeline to Weyburn for injection. This began in 2000. Currently, approximately 5,500 tonnes per day of CO_2 are being injected, together with a further 1,300 tonnes of gas and CO_2 per day recycled from the oil produced.

Fig. 5.24 At the In Salah natural gas project in the Sahara desert in Algeria, CO_2 is separated and re-injected into the gas field. This project is operated by BP, StatoilHydro and Sonatrach.

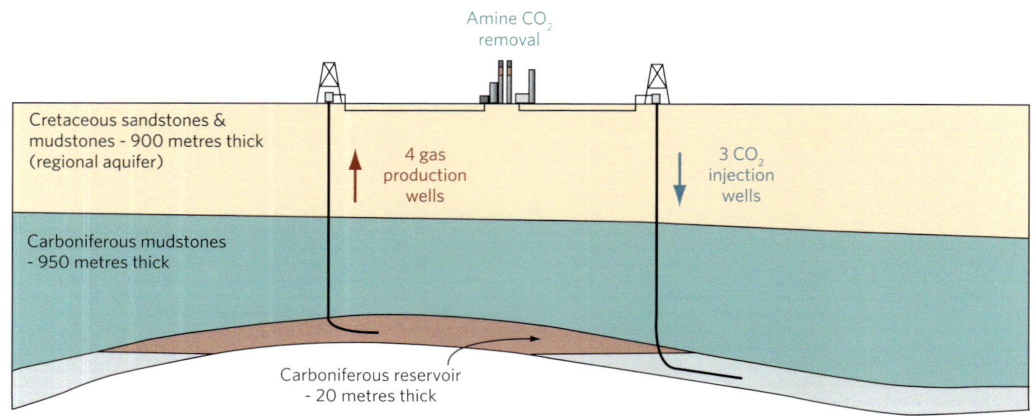

Chapter 5 | Putting carbon back in the ground

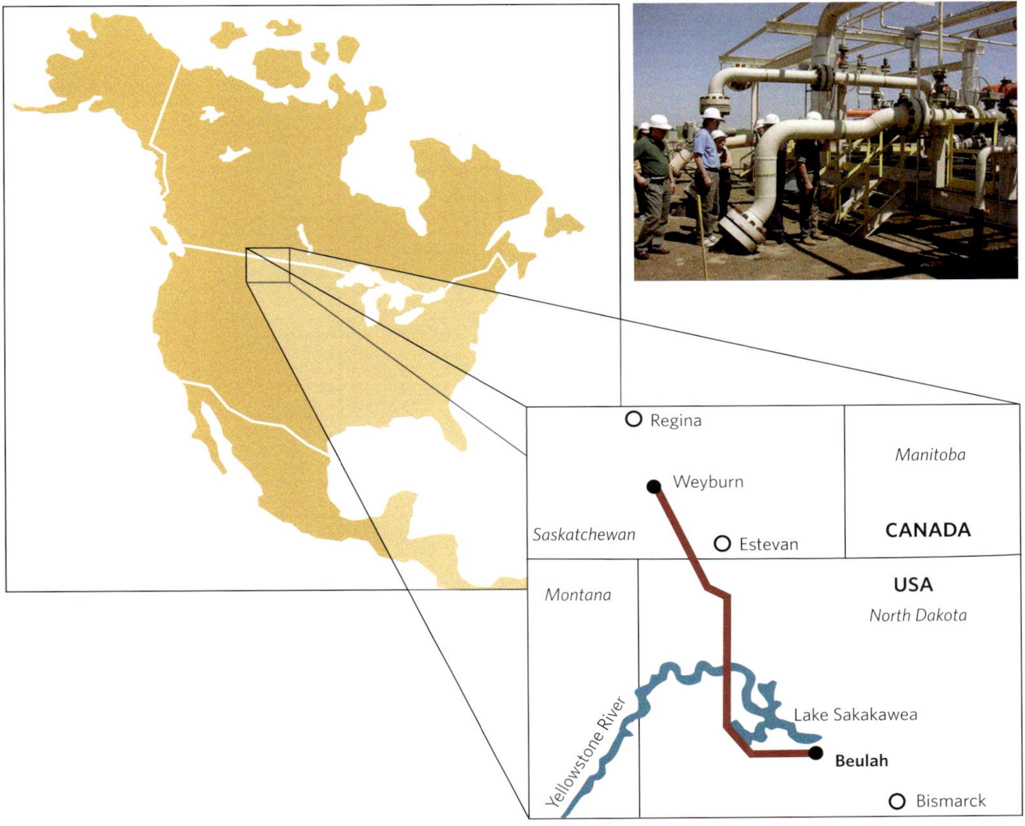

Fig. 5.25   The Weyburn CO_2 injection for enhanced oil recovery will result in CO_2-storage when completed. The CO_2 comes from the coal gasification plant at Beulah in North Dakota through a 320 kilometre long pipeline. The picture shows the CO_2-pipeline where it arrives at the Weyburn field.

Further commercial CO_2 injection projects are under construction but not yet in operation. Two of these will store CO_2 extracted from natural gas, but several will be power generation projects with CO_2 captured for storage.

Both of the natural gas projects will inject CO_2 into sub-sea geological formations – StatoilHydro's Snøhvit project in the Barents Sea, and Chevron's Gorgon project off the coast of Australia. The Snøvhit project is notable because it involves, amongst other novel features, a sub-sea wellhead for injecting CO_2, thereby avoiding the construction of a conventional platform. Initially, 0.8 million tonnes of CO_2 will be injected per year but expansion of the project with a second LNG production unit is anticipated. The Gorgon project, if realized, will inject CO_2 into a deep saline aquifer at a rate of 2.7 million tonnes per year. This was planned to start in 2009 but there is uncertainty at present regarding the timing due to a delay in receiving permission to build the associated LNG plant.

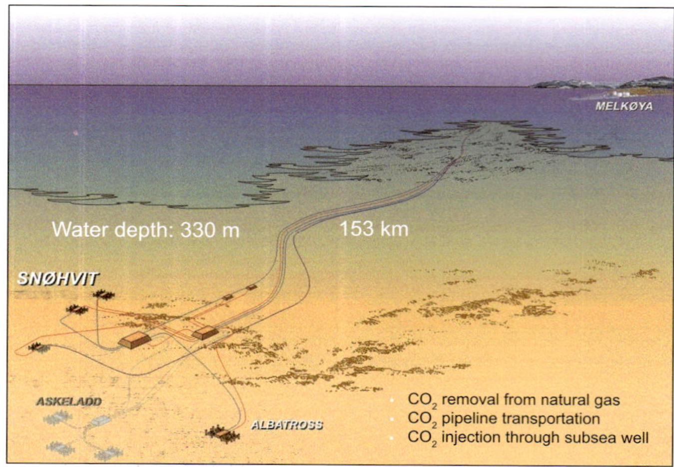

Fig. 5.26 Gas from the Snø-hvit field will be extracted using equipment on the bed of the Barents Sea off Northern Norway. This diagram shows the sub-sea equipment at the field and the 150 kilometre long sub-sea pipelines, one of which transports the gas to an LNG plant onshore and another which brings the captured CO_2 back for injection.

The first of the power generation projects will probably be the Kårstø gas-fired combined cycle power plant, now under construction in Southern Norway. This will have post-combustion CO_2 capture fitted after the plant has been built; the extra equipment needed will be financed by the Norwegian government who will also pay for the transportation of the CO_2 to a subsea storage site.

At StatoilHydro's Mongstad oil refinery, a gas-fired combined cycle plant is being built and will be in operation by 2010; this will subsequently be equipped with post-

Fig. 5.27 The Gorgon LNG project off Australia's North West coast is at the planning stage. The project will include injecting 2.7 million tonnes of CO_2 per year (recovered from the natural gas) into a geological formation (Illustration courtesy of the Gorgon Development project).

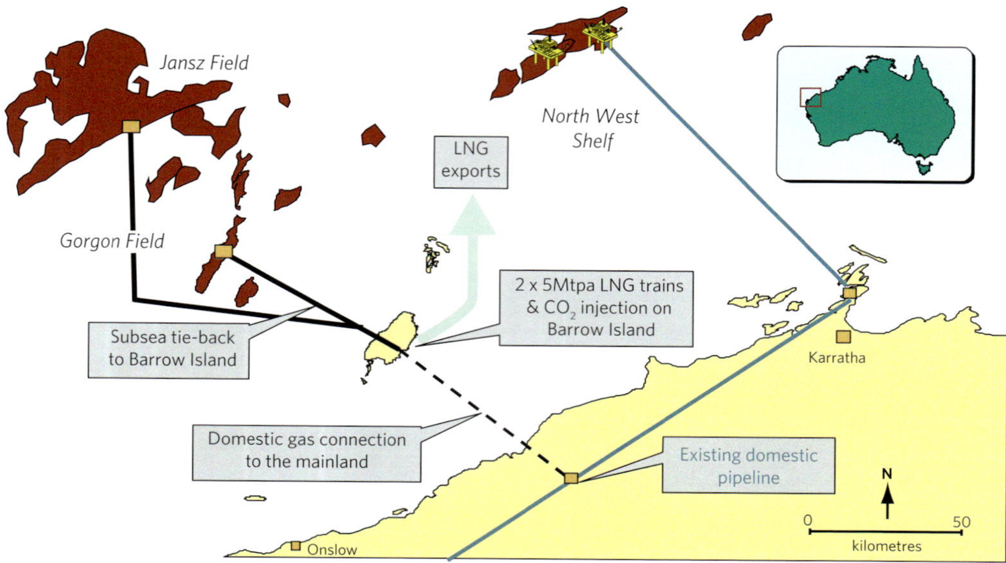

combustion capture which will be in operation by 2014. The Norwegian government will make a major contribution to both the capture and transportation of the CO_2 from this plant. An associated company will further develop the capture technology.

A third power generation project in Norway has been announced by Shell and StatoilHydro. This will be an 860MW$_e$ natural gas power station with post-combustion CO_2 capture. It will be located at Tjeldbergodden in a chemical factory producing methanol. The CO_2 will be piped to a subsea storage site. This will begin in 2011, providing that government support for the project is obtained. The electricity will be used by some offshore facilities (thereby avoiding emissions from them) and for compressing natural gas being exported from Norway. At the time of writing, the details of the financing of this project had not been finally agreed.

In the UK, BP and Scottish and Southern Energy in 2005 announced plans for a 350 MW combined cycle power station using hydrogen as fuel; this would have been produced by pre-combustion capture from natural gas. The CO_2 extracted

Fig. 5.28   At the Mongstad refinery, a new gas fired power station (illustrated in the picture) will supply 350 MW of heat to the refinery and 280 MW of electricity for two offshore platforms. The plant will have CO_2 capture and storage installed by 2014.

Fig. 5.29 A demonstration of oxyfuel combustion is being built beside the Schwarze Pumpe lignite-fired power station in Germany.

from this fuel would have been transported through an existing pipeline to the offshore Miller oil and gas field. A key factor in the choice of the Miller field for this project was that the gas it produces contains around 20% CO_2, so the platform and the pipeline to shore are already able to handle CO_2. Reversal of this pipeline would allow it to supply CO_2 for enhanced oil recovery. However, this project has recently been cancelled because of problems with funding. BP has also announced a project at its Carson City refinery in the USA which will capture CO_2 for enhanced oil recovery.

Another pre-combustion capture project, this one using coal rather than gas, is the FutureGen project in the USA. A consortium of companies will build a coal gasification plant to demonstrate the production of electricity and hydrogen. The US government will support this demonstration with much of the funding needed.

Chapter 5 | Putting carbon back in the ground

At the time of writing, the list of potential sites has been reduced to four – two in Texas and two in Illinois.

Another pre-combustion capture project is being planned at the Stanwell Energy Park, in central Queensland, Australia. The 100MW Zerogen project is intended to demonstrate base-load electricity generation by integrating coal gasification with CO_2 capture and storage. CO_2 will be transported 220 kilometres by pipeline and injected into a deep saline aquifer in the Denison Trough, where a test drilling programme is being undertaken by Shell. Public consultation and an environmental impact assessment are being conducted as part of the normal planning process for a power station like this. Construction is expected to start in 2008 with first operation in 2011.

A second Australian project may also involve the storage of CO_2 in the same area. This will demonstrate the retrofitting of oxyfuel combustion for CO_2 capture to one of the 30 MW units of the coal-fired Callide power station. The modified station should go into operation in 2009 with demonstration of CO_2 storage, perhaps, in 2010.

In Canada, SaskPower has announced plans for a 300 MW lignite-fired power station, to be built by 2012, which would supply CO_2 for enhanced oil recovery. This will also use oxyfuel combustion. Construction is due to start in 2007.

Future possibilities

In addition to the CO_2 capture projects announced to date, several other power generation projects will involve the capture and storage of CO_2 if suitable financial arrangements can be agreed with governments. Some of these projects will be built in stages, with the conventional stations being built first and the capture and storage being added later. The design of the new stations will provide the opportunity to capture CO_2 later on by allowing sufficient space for the extra plant and by providing suitable places to extract steam and other gases. Such preparation is most easily achieved in gasification-based power stations where the modification needed to capture CO_2 would be relatively small, if this is planned at the design stage. Plans have been announced for such power stations in the Netherlands and Germany and for several in the UK.

Post-combustion capture may be fitted to new pulverized coal power stations in the UK and Germany and during the refurbishment of an existing power station in the UK. Plans have also been reported to build an oxyfuel pilot plant in the Netherlands. Shell's Pernis refinery is preparing to extract concentrated CO_2 for supplying to greenhouses to replace natural gas which is currently burnt to provide CO_2.

In most cases, the storage sites for the CO_2 have not yet been announced.

In Germany, the Swedish-based electricity company Vattenfall has started construction of a 30MW power station using oxyfuel combustion technology. This is seen as the pilot for a full-sized lignite-fuelled power station. The project is located at Schwarze Pumpe near Cottbus and should go into operation in 2008. The captured CO_2 will be compressed for transport but the storage location has not yet been announced.

If all of these projects reach fruition, CO_2 emissions will be about 20 million tonnes per year less than would have been the case if capture and storage had not been used.

Thus, the capture and storage of CO_2 will be able to contribute usefully to energy supply in a world which is becoming more and more serious about tackling climate change. We provide a more detailed description of the technology needed for such projects in the following chapter. The final chapter will consider some of the factors determining the extent to which the capture and storage of CO_2 might be used in practice.

Suggestions for further reading

IPCC Special Report on Carbon Dioxide Capture and Storage. 2005. Prepared by Working Group III of the Intergovernmental Panel on Climate Change [Metz, B., O. Davidson, H. C. de Coninck, M. Loos, and L. A. Meyer (eds.)]. Cambridge University Press, Cambridge, United Kingdom and New York, NY, USA, 442 pp.

Carbon Capture and its Storage. An integrated assessment. 2006. S. Shackley, C. Gough (Eds.). Ashgate Publishing Ltd, Aldershot, UK

Endnotes

1   Some oil is left behind following the extraction process, perhaps because it is not in the pathway swept by the injected fluid, or because it is trapped by surface tension in pores and small spaces in the reservoir rock.

2   See p. 29 in "Resources to Reserves", 2005, OECD-IEA, Paris.

3   IPCC special report on CO_2 capture and storage, 2005, published by Cambridge University Press.

4   Ibid.

5   Ibid.

6   Hydrogen storage might be underground, as is carried out today in industrial processes.

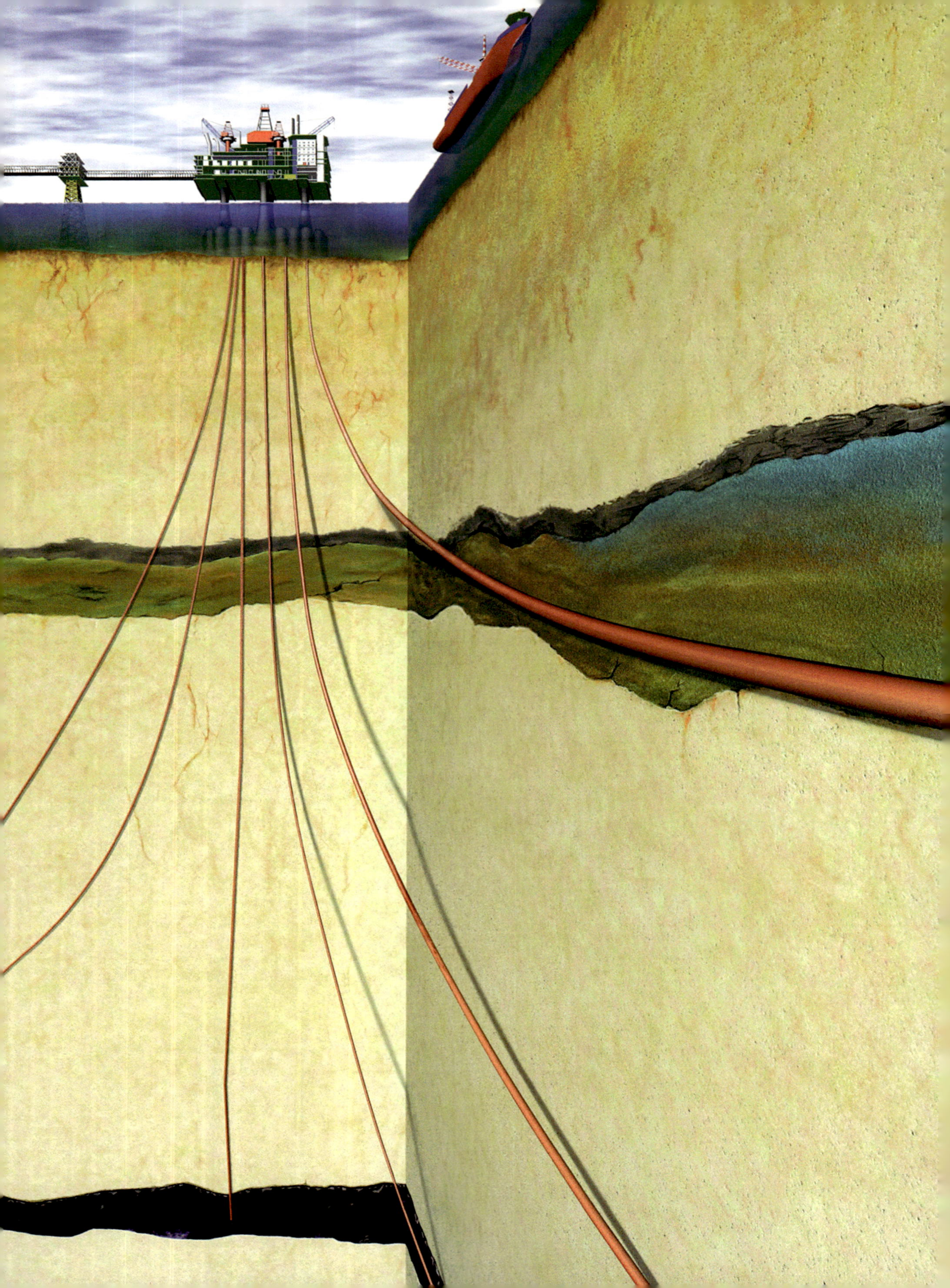

Behind the headlines

What will the capture and storage of CO_2 cost? Are there any risks involved in using it? How will its application be managed? As with any new technology, these and other questions will be raised about it. In order to provide some answers, we must first explain some of the practical details of the technology. The main examples will be based on power generation, but other uses will also be addressed briefly.

Fig. 6.1 Sleipner CO_2 injection.

Capturing CO_2 in power generation

Capturing CO_2 in a power station is most easily illustrated by considering the post-combustion mode. This is applicable to any design of power station that is fuelled by coal or gas.

After the fuel has been combusted, the exhaust gas stream consists mainly of nitrogen, with smaller amounts of other gases, including CO_2. Solid particles, nitrogen oxides and sulphur dioxide (in the case of coal-firing) are normally removed first. To capture the CO_2, the exhaust gases are washed using a chemical solvent which dissolves the CO_2 preferentially. This washing is done in a tall tower, where the solvent falls downwards whilst the gases rise upwards, causing the two to mix well.

The amount of CO_2 left in the gases after washing is determined by the size of the tower, and the type and quantity of the solvent – in other words, it is a matter of economics. Based on current practice, 85% to 90% of the CO_2 would be

Post-combustion capture of CO_2 at a power station

Power stations built today mostly use either pulverised coal or natural gas. Both types could be fitted with equipment to separate the CO_2 after combustion from the other gases in the exhaust, especially nitrogen and oxygen. This could be done using water to wash the gases but certain chemicals have a greater affinity with CO_2 – for example, various amines. By adding these to the water, the system can be made more compact. The extra cost is more than justified by the improved effectiveness of capture. However, amines suffer from oxidation when used in this way so some additives are needed to avoid degradation but, even so, a small amount of solid waste is produced.

Any SO_2 (which is produced from the coal) would also be removed by an amine solvent, so it must be extracted before the CO_2 separation stage.

The process is carried out in tall towers. In the first, the amine solvent washes the CO_2 out of the gases, dissolving CO_2. After this, the solution is heated in the second tower in order to release the CO_2, which is compressed for transport. The cleaned solvent is passed back to the first tower to extract more CO_2. Heat for this process is provided by low pressure steam from the power station – steam used in this way is not available for generating electricity, so adding post-combustion capture to a power station design reduces the useful output, by about 18% in a natural gas fired combined cycle power station, and by 28% in a pulverised coal station. This is a significant issue when considering the use of CO_2 capture. The lower penalty for the gas-fired power station arises from the lower carbon content of the fuel and the higher efficiency of the combined cycle power station (approximately 60% versus approximately 45% for the pulverised coal station).

Chapter 6 | Behind the headlines

removed in this way. The remaining gases go to the chimney and are vented to atmosphere.

The solvent, laden with CO_2, is passed to a second tower where heat is applied which releases the CO_2. The cleansed solvent is then returned to the first tower whilst the CO_2 is compressed for transportation to the storage site. The cost of the extra equipment, as well as the heat needed for treating the solvent, adds substantially to the cost of the electricity generated by the station.

Several power stations have already been fitted with this equipment, although not in order to protect the climate. Instead, they supply the CO_2 for carbonated drinks. In each of these stations, only about 50,000 to 100,000 tonnes of CO_2 per year are captured, which is much less than will be required to protect the climate. Nevertheless, this does demonstrate that the technology works and that its products are so clean that they can even be used in drinks. Such experience also provides a measure of the cost of the equipment, admittedly for a much smaller unit, one where there is less emphasis on its energy consumption.

Fig. 6.2 Post-combustion CO_2-capture using coal fuel. A similar process is used for natural-gas-fired power stations but without the need to remove fly-ash or sulphur (Illustration: Vattenfall).

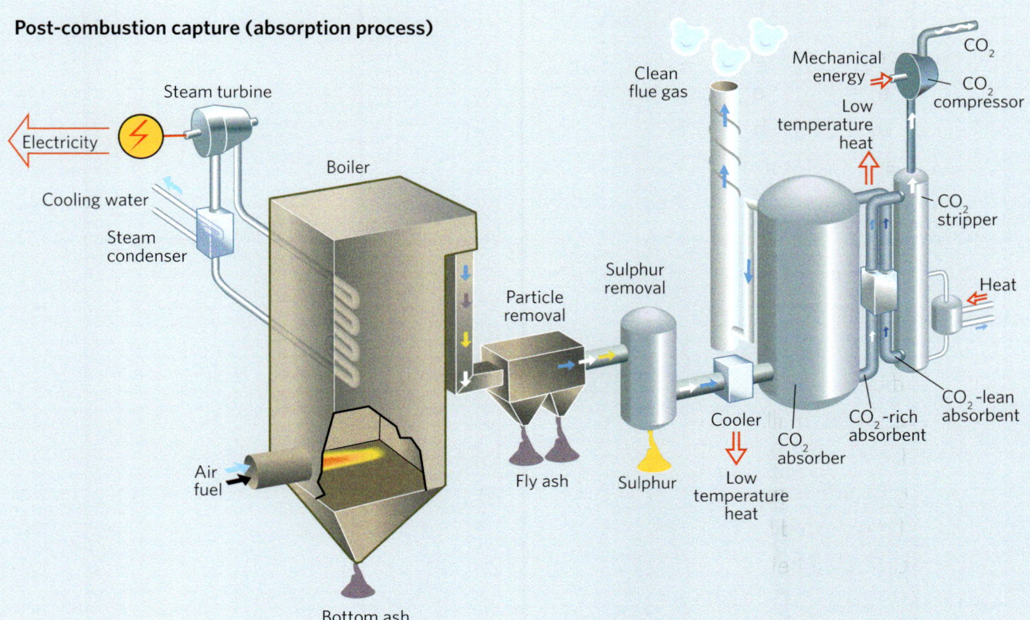

Fig. 6.3 Example of power station equipped with CO_2 capture showing the uses of the various columns and exchangers.

The removal of CO_2 from flue gases is quite similar, in principle, to the removal of sulphur dioxide (SO_2), something which is widely practised in coal-fired power stations. A key difference is that the quantity of CO_2 is over a hundred times as much as the quantity of SO_2. The extraction, compression and transportation of the CO_2 would thus require much greater investment.

An alternative approach, pre-combustion capture, involves converting the fossil fuel into a gas consisting of hydrogen (H_2) and CO_2 prior to combustion. Coal would first be turned into a gas by heating it under pressure in pure oxygen. This avoids introducing nitrogen into the fuel gas stream so that it does not have to be separated out later. The CO_2 is captured using a solvent, one which physically absorbs CO_2. This method can take advantage of the elevated pressure in such a system – for example, the CO_2 can be released from the solvent by simply reducing the pressure. Capturing CO_2 in this way has advantages in terms of the reduced size of the equipment, as well as the relatively low need for energy, so there is only a small increase in the cost of the electricity. After the CO_2 has been separated out,

Pre-combustion capture of CO$_2$

The pre-combustion approach is slightly different for each of the two main fuels, coal and natural gas, but the same principles apply – the fuel is first converted into a mixture of hydrogen (H$_2$) and CO$_2$ which can then be separated relatively easily.

In the case of coal, the fuel is heated under pressure in pure oxygen which gasifies it, producing a mixture of H$_2$, carbon monoxide (CO) and several impurities which can be removed relatively easily from the gas stream. Solid wastes are extracted from the gasifier. The CO in the fuel gas is changed into CO$_2$ in a shift reactor which, using extra steam, converts CO to H$_2$ and CO$_2$. The resultant gas stream is passed to a separation stage, where a physical solvent absorbs CO$_2$. The concentrated CO$_2$ is released by reducing the pressure on the solvent.

One of the advantages of this approach, compared with post-combustion capture, is the high pressure of the gasifier, which means that the equipment is smaller and less energy is needed to compress the CO$_2$ for transportation. In addition, the solvent needs little or no heating to recover the CO$_2$, which avoids penalising the efficiency of the power station.

The fuel gas remaining, after the CO$_2$ has been removed, is nearly pure H$_2$. This is not something which can be burnt in existing gas turbines so it must be diluted with nitrogen (or other inert gases), although this reduces the efficiency of the gas turbine. Several development projects are underway which aim to modify gas turbine designs so that they can burn almost pure H$_2$.

An IGCC-based power station is more expensive to build than a conventional pulverised coal station, but removing CO$_2$ can be done with less penalty so, overall, the cost of electricity generation in an IGCC with capture is similar to that of a pulverised coal station with capture.

For natural gas, a similar process based on reforming the gas can be used to make a mixture of H$_2$ and CO, which can be treated in the same way as described above. However, the advantages are less marked than in the case of coal because of the lower proportion of carbon in the fuel. This means that the cost of the extra gas production equipment is more difficult to justify than in the case of a coal-fuelled station.

Fig. 6.4 Pre-combustion CO$_2$-capture with coal fuel in an IGCC power station. (Illustration: Vattenfall).

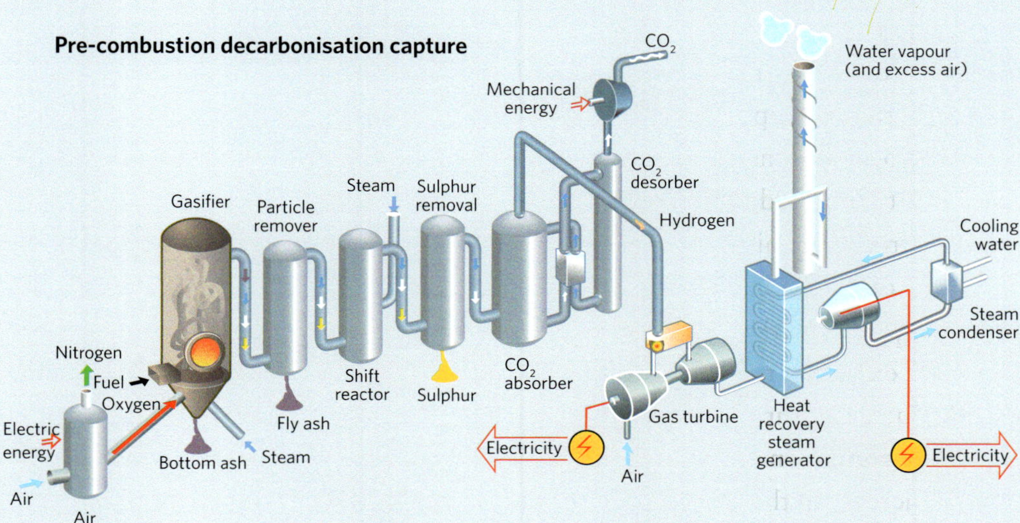

Fig. 6.5 An IGCC power station without CO_2 capture. The Buggenum coal gasification power station in the Netherlands.

the H_2 is mixed with nitrogen and burnt in a gas turbine to generate electricity (a steam turbine captures waste heat from the gas turbine and generates even more electricity).

This approach is a modest alteration to the design of a new type of power station – the Integrated Gasification Combined Cycle (IGCC) station. Several full-scale examples of this type of power station have been built to demonstrate the technology (without CO_2 capture). However, as yet, it has not been accepted as commercially competitive vis-à-vis conventional coal-fired power stations. The core component, the gasifier, is already used for other purposes, e.g. making fertilisers or hydrogen from coal or heavy oil.

A similar approach can be taken with natural gas. Here, too, the fuel would be converted into a mixture of H_2 and CO_2, making it easy to remove the CO_2.

Following separation, the CO_2 is compressed for transportation as in the case of post-combustion capture.

Both the post- and pre-combustion methods of capture involve modifying established power station designs. All of the components needed are available and

Chapter 6 | Behind the headlines

proven, which limits, but does not fully remove, the technical risk. In contrast, the third approach, i.e. oxyfuel combustion, would involve changing the combustion conditions so as to avoid mixing nitrogen with the CO_2. This idea has never been demonstrated in a power station, but several prototypes are now under construction in order to find out how it compares with the other methods.

In a station like this, nitrogen is kept out of the combustion chamber by separating the oxygen needed for combustion from the air. However, burning fossil fuel in pure oxygen produces very high temperatures which would require the use of unconventional, or even yet-to-be-developed, materials. Instead, in order to moderate the temperatures to levels more typical of conventional boilers, some of the exhaust gases are re-circulated to the combustion chamber. Because nitrogen has been kept out of the system, the exhaust gases are mainly CO_2 and steam, which can be separated quite easily by condensing water.

In an oxyfuel coal-burning power station, there would be other contaminants, especially sulphur, in the exhaust which must also be removed before the relatively pure CO_2 is prepared for storage.

In principle, the same thing could be done with natural gas but this may be less attractive because of the molecular nature of the main component of natural gas – i.e. methane. The methane molecule consists of one atom of carbon and four atoms of hydrogen so, for combustion in pure oxygen, much more of the (expen-

Fig. 6.6 Pre-combustion CO_2 capture with natural gas fuel. The Peterhead project was to have used gas reforming to create a mixture of H_2 and CO_2 – the CO_2 would then have been separated and the H_2 used as fuel for power generation and other purposes (Illustration courtesy BP).

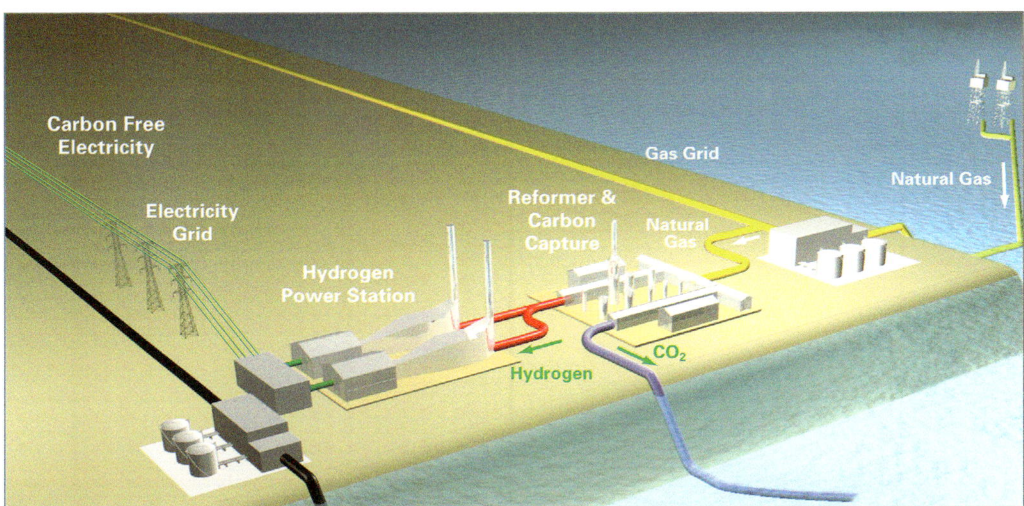

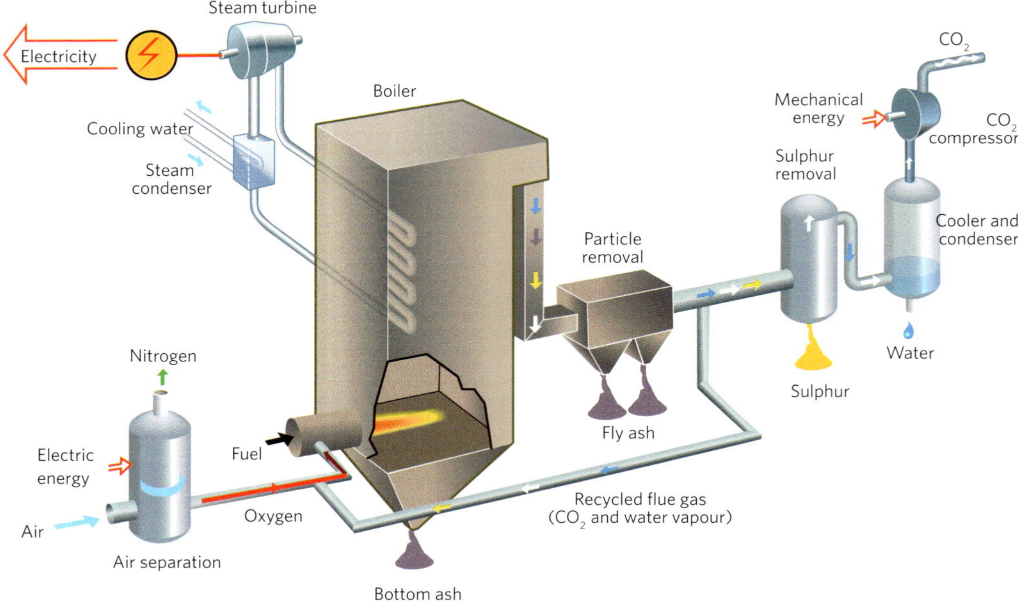

Fig. 6.7 An oxyfuel power station for CO$_2$ capture using coal fuel (Illustration: Vattenfall).

sive) oxygen must be produced in order to oxidise the hydrogen than is the case using coal. This suggests that a more fruitful application of oxyfuel technology may be using it with coal or possibly heavy oil.

Novel approach to combustion of clean gases with oxygen.

In contrast to the oxyfuel approach, where exhaust CO$_2$ is used to moderate the combustion temperature, a novel concept is under development which uses steam for this purpose. It has been demonstrated on a practical scale with natural gas but could probably work with any other source of gas, providing it is clean.

The combustion system is based on rocket engine technology which produces a high-temperature, high-pressure gas composed of steam, and CO$_2$. These gases drive a multi-stage turbine to run the electricity generator. Water is condensed from the exhaust gases, for recirculation to the combustor, leaving a stream of gaseous CO$_2$ which is processed and compressed for storage. Work is now being conducted to improve the efficiency. The technology is initially being developed in order to supply CO$_2$ to small oilfields for enhanced oil recovery.

 Chapter 6 | Behind the headlines

Other separation methods, such as membranes, are being investigated for the removal of CO_2. However, as yet, none of them has been shown to improve on the established practice of using solvents. The increasing attention being paid to such technologies is arousing the interest of researchers and industrialists, so more promising technologies may yet emerge from the laboratories.

A unique feature of CO_2 capture, when compared with other measures for making sharp reductions in emissions, is that it can be added to existing, modern power stations, or power stations can be designed to incorporate it at a later date. This means that, during the early days of developing responses to climate change, it is only necessary to leave open the option of adding it at a later date. Plans have already been announced to build new coal- and gas-fired power stations which provide for fitting CO_2 capture after construction.

Capturing CO_2 in other sectors

Because of the importance of the electricity sector as a source of emissions, much attention has been paid to capturing CO_2 in power stations. However, the most attractive conditions for capture would be in gas streams with high concentrations of CO_2. Such gas streams are to be found in the chemical processes used to produce ammonia or hydrogen, in blast furnaces and cement kilns, and in the processing of natural gas.

Chemical looping combustion

The conventional way of supplying oxygen is by using cryogenics to separate it from air. This process uses a great deal of electricity. An alternative would be to provide oxygen within the process itself. This can be done by reacting the fuel with a metal oxide, at high temperature. The chemical reaction releases oxygen as well as heat and the fuel is converted into CO_2 and steam (and other impurities). At the same time, the metal oxide is converted into metal which is then removed from the reaction vessel. The metal is re-oxidised in a separate chamber before being returned to the combustion process again.

Such a process might seem attractive, compared with the established technologies, but it has only been demonstrated at laboratory scale, so there is a long way to go before it would be ready for use in a power station. Because of the nature of the small solid particles required for the process, it may be better suited to a gaseous fuel than a solid one which would produce solid ash that might be difficult to separate from the metal particles. A key determinant of the competitiveness of this concept will be the durability of the metal oxide, in particular whether or not it can withstand thousands of cycles before having to be replaced.

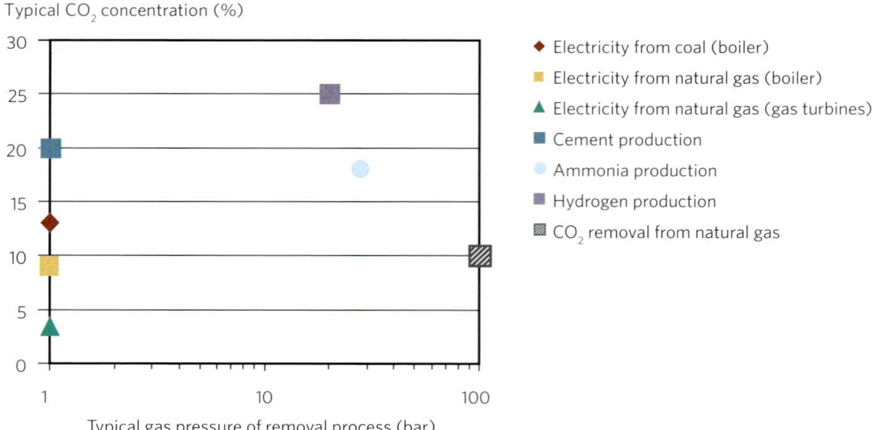

Fig. 6.8 The more attractive conditions for capture are in gas streams with high concentrations of CO_2 and high pressure. These are found in various industrial processes such as ammonia and hydrogen production (based on data from IPCC Special Report on Carbon Dioxide Capture and Storage, 2005).

Some sources of natural gas contain significant amounts of CO_2. This has to be removed before the gas can be supplied to customers. Removal is achieved using chemical solvents or membranes or, where the CO_2 concentration is very high, cryogenic (deep cooling) technologies. Such sources are already providing the CO_2 for several CO_2 storage projects.

Similar reductions could also be achieved by capturing and storing CO_2 from blast furnace gases. This is a form of post-combustion capture – its use in an existing iron and steel works may show advantages, compared with its application in a power station, due to the higher concentration of CO_2 and pressure in the blast furnace gases. A combination of changes to the process and application of CO_2 capture and storage could reduce emissions by 60% by 2050[1] and even more beyond then.

In cement making, an interesting aspect of using CO_2 capture and storage is that it could potentially capture emissions from the raw materials as well as from the fuel, thereby making much sharper reductions than by using any other means. However, the technical obstacles to this are substantial due to the condition of the gases emitted from the cement-making process.

In oil refineries, CO_2 capture could be applied to the principal heaters in the refinery; it could also be used in the on-site power station. Refinery emissions could be cut by 60% through a combination of efficiency improvements, the combined production of heat and power, and CO_2 capture and storage[2]. At the same time, the production of alternative vehicle fuels (made from natural gas or coal) will tend to increase the emissions originating from this industry. It will also be essential to capture the CO_2 from these new processes, so as to avoid adding to the impact on the climate.

Because of its diversity, the chemical industry is less susceptible to generalised remarks about the potential for reducing CO_2 emissions even though, because it uses much the same type of equipment as oil refineries, it is likely that similar levels of emission reductions could be achieved there, too. The exhaust gases from an ammonia plant are almost pure CO_2, making this a relatively inexpensive place for capture. This could be one of the first sources of CO_2 for storage, although in some places, the CO_2 is already being used to make fertiliser.

On the other hand, aluminium refining, if its carbon electrodes can be replaced with inert electrodes, would have no reason to use CO_2 capture (as long as the electricity comes from low-emission sources).

Due to the small scale of the emissions from individual buildings, there does not seem to be a sensible case for capturing CO_2 from such sources. Fitting CO_2 capture equipment would be too expensive because of the (dis)economies of scale. The emission reductions possible through the use of local CHP generation would be constrained to no more than 40% to 50% by the extent to which its waste heat could be used. Unlike in large, central power stations, CO_2 capture would not be available to improve on this.

In the transport sector, changing to zero-carbon energy carriers, e.g. hydrogen or electricity, could produce much greater emission reductions at the point of use than any other measure. The cheapest sources of these carriers would be fossil fuels; use of the capture and storage of CO_2 would minimise greenhouse gas emissions during their production.

Transporting captured CO_2

A full-sized power station can produce 3 million tonnes of CO_2 per year or more. At this scale, pipelines are the least expensive way of transporting CO_2 over distances up to several hundred kilometres.

Pipelines are already used for supplying CO_2 to enhanced oil recovery projects in the USA. They have sufficient capacity to move 50 million tonnes of CO_2 per year. After more than 30 years of operation, experience of these pipelines has shown that CO_2 can be transported safely and reliably, providing certain conditions are met. For example, the gas must be dried before it is introduced into the

Fig. 6.9 Laying the OCAP CO$_2$ pipeline in the Netherlands, to carry CO$_2$ from the Pernis refinery to greenhouses.

pipeline, so as to avoid corrosion of the steel; the amount of sulphur (in the form of hydrogen sulphide (H_2S) in the gas must be kept low in case of leakage, especially if the pipeline passes through inhabited areas; pipelines must be equipped with automatic shut-off valves to limit the amount of CO$_2$ released in the event of a leak.

Before the CO$_2$ goes into the pipeline, it is compressed to such a degree that it is in the dense phase. The largest compressor currently in use with CO$_2$ is at the Dakota Gasification plant (USA), supplying about 1.2 million tonnes of CO$_2$ per year to a 320km pipeline to the Weyburn oilfield in Canada.

Fig. 6.10 Compressor for CO$_2$ at the Sleipner T platform.

Chapter 6 | Behind the headlines

Ships as an alternative means of transporting CO$_2$

The preferred method of transporting carbon dioxide, in most cases, is through pipelines. Since CO$_2$ is as dense as water at high pressure and has a low viscosity, pipelines of moderate size can carry large volumes. Sometimes, however, transporting CO$_2$ by ships is more economical. This situation occurs when the volume to be transported is low relative to the distance to be covered. Today, there are five small ships that carry liquid CO$_2$ (cooled and pressurised) between ports in Northern Europe. The CO$_2$ is food-grade; each vessel carries between 1,000 and 2,000 m^3 of it.

The CO$_2$ is gathered from various industrial sources, then cooled, compressed and liquefied before being loaded onto the ship. Storage tanks are installed at all ports to hold stocks in between visits by these ships. A transportation chain like this is similar to that used for propane, butane, and ammonia, but is quite costly due to the small amounts shipped. Japanese and Norwegian groups have studied the transportation of larger amounts of CO$_2$ by ship for use in CO$_2$ storage projects. The results of these studies showed that larger ships were substantially cheaper (per tonne of CO$_2$). However, so far, no opportunity has been found to use this form of transportation.

Fig. 6.11 The "Coral Carbonic" carries CO$_2$ across the North Sea and the Baltic; it has a capacity of 1250 m^3; the CO$_2$ is at –40°C and 18 bar pressure.

Storing captured CO$_2$ underground

Having captured and transported the CO$_2$, the final step is to store it safely and securely. This requires finding geological formations with sufficient capacity, having a means of introducing it into these formations, and being able to monitor and deal with it if something goes wrong. All of these factors affect the choice of storage reservoir.

Contrary to the popular notion of underground caves being filled with oil, geological reservoirs hold fluids (such as oil, gas or water) in the multitude of small spaces between the grains of rock. These small spaces are connected to each other, in a random fashion, thus allowing the fluids to move through the formation[3]. Examples of such rocks are sandstone, limestone and chalk – quite similar to some building materials.

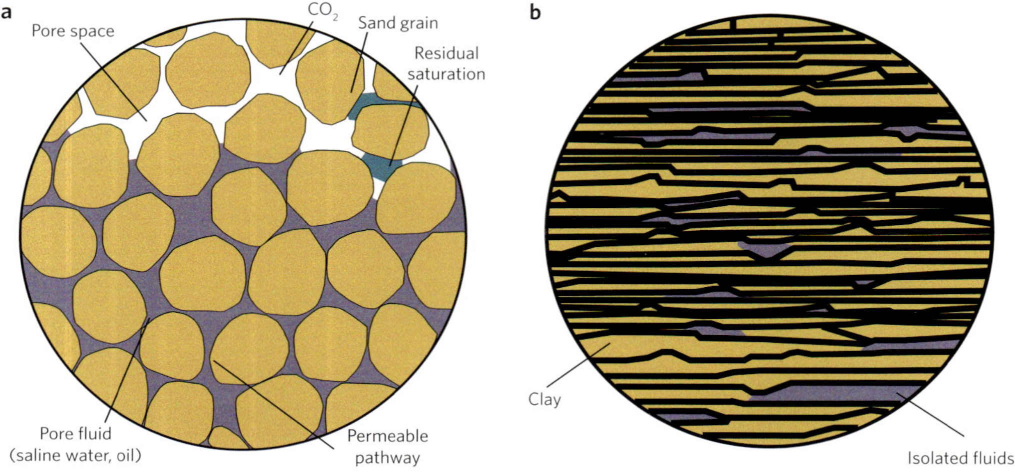

Fig. 6.12 What geology would look like through a magnifying glass. (a) the pore spaces in the reservoir rock are filled by saline water, oil or natural gas; this can be partially forced out by injecting CO_2. (b) the cap-rock contains many clay particles (in yellow); the very small amount of space *between* these particles makes the cap-rock impermeable.

In contrast, other types of rock have little or no space between their grains, or the spaces are not connected, so that fluids can only move through them very slowly. Examples include salt layers, shales and mudstones. Such impermeable layers are important for trapping oil or gas, and are also essential if a geological formation is to be able to store CO_2.

So, to find potential storage for CO_2, we first look at oil and gas fields as these should have good seals, providing they have not been damaged by the extraction process. Once the hydrocarbons have been extracted, CO_2 would be injected, filling the spaces that once held hydrocarbons. In some cases, water may have already entered the pores – either naturally or because it was injected into the field to enhance the production of oil. In such circumstances, the CO_2 would have to push the water out again. Thus CO_2 would have to be injected at sufficient pressure so as to be in the dense phase and able to displace the fluids in the formation. Providing the formation is more than 800m below the surface, the pressure of the overlying strata and water will be sufficient to keep the CO_2 in the dense phase.

Other geological formations may just hold saltwater. It is likely that there are many more of these saline aquifers than oil and gas reservoirs but, because they have no commercial value, there has been less exploration of them. Nevertheless, where they have a suitable sealing layer, these could also be used to store CO_2, if they are deep enough for the CO_2 to be in the dense phase.

Having found a suitable storage formation, the CO_2 will be introduced into it using oil industry technology for drilling wells and injecting fluids. Indeed, these very techniques are already in use for injecting CO_2 in order to enhance oil recovery. The amount of CO_2 would be measured as it is injected.

Enhanced recovery of oil, gas and coal bed methane

Enhancing oil recovery using CO_2 is illustrated in Figure 6.13 where CO_2 and water are alternately injected in order to dissolve in the oil and then sweep it to the production well. Any CO_2 left in the field at the end of production is considered to be stored.

The same cannot be done with gas fields where the solvent properties of supercritical CO_2 are irrelevant, but the injection of CO_2 early in the life of such a field can be used to maintain the pressure, thus increasing the rate of production.

A further opportunity to increase the production of hydrocarbons is provided by coal-bed methane. The extraction of this gas is carried out in various places (e.g. the Western USA and Canada). It has been found that production can be improved through the injection of nitrogen or CO_2. The CO_2 preferentially displaces methane from the coal and is adsorbed into the coal. This has stimulated interest in using coal to store CO_2, with the additional benefit of increasing the production of coal-bed methane. A primary requirement for CO_2 storage would be that the coal is never disturbed afterwards. It would be virtually impossible to guarantee this, unless the coal is unminable for practical reasons, perhaps because it is very deep or under the sea. If suitable coals can be found, they would still need to meet the requirements of other geological storage formations, e.g. capacity and permeability. Unfortunately, relatively few coals in Europe are sufficiently permeable to allow gas to pass through them easily, although there may be suitable coals in some other parts of the world.

Fig. 6.13 CO_2 can be used for enhancing oil recovery from old or new oil fields. CO_2 is typically injected for a month, followed by water for a month in a repeating cycle. The graph shows the history of oil production from the Weyburn oilfield with a forecast for the extra production from injection of CO_2 up to 2025.

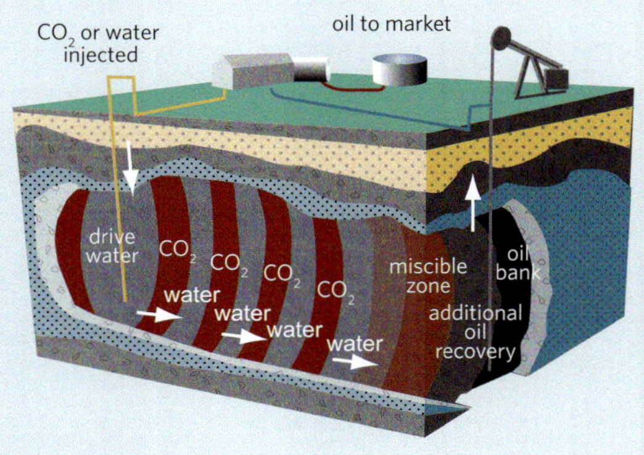

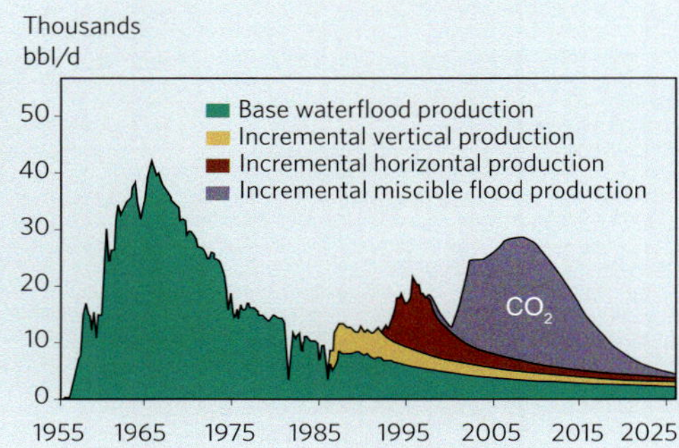

Fig. 6.14 Schematic diagram showing the horizontal CO_2 injection well at the Sleipner project. Also shown is one of the deeper wells used to extract natural gas.

The well could be drilled vertically from the surface but modern techniques allow wells to follow a curved path until, at the extreme, they become horizontal inside the target formation. The ability to control the direction of a well is very useful when placing the CO_2 exactly where it is required. Several wells are drilled from one location, thereby minimising disruption to the neighbourhood (if onshore) or the construction of extra platforms (if offshore). The sizes and numbers of the wells will be determined by the amount of CO_2 to be injected and the permeability of the formation. In some cases, a well might be able to cope with a few hundred thousand tonnes of CO_2 per year but, in the better formations, a single well may be able to handle as much as 2 to 3 million tonnes per year. A commercial-scale storage reservoir might receive 10 million tonnes per year or more (i.e. much more than the systems in operation today).

The well itself contains a metal tube through which the CO_2 passes. In part of the well, at least, the metal has to be resistant to corrosion or be covered with a suitable coating – in either case, this will be more expensive than is normally the case in the oil industry. If CO_2 is injected into an existing oil or gas field, the exis-

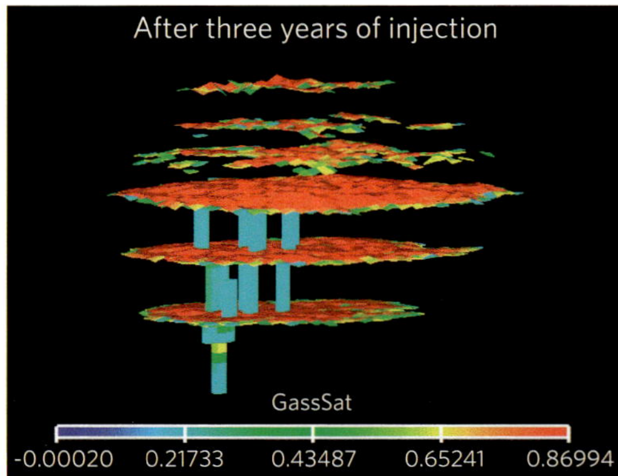

Fig. 6.15 Simulation of the CO_2 in the Utsira formation below the Sleipner platform after three years of injection. The injection from the horizontal well is at the bottom. The largest bubble is 800 metres wide and 200 metres high (Source: Sintef petroleum).

ting production wells are unlikely to have been constructed to this standard, so detailed examination of existing wells would be necessary, followed by replacement of any materials which could deteriorate (and thereby cause leaks).

The pressure of the CO_2 must be sufficient to drive it into the formation, without being so great that damage might be done to the formation rock since this could impede the flow or, even worse, lead to leakage of the CO_2. In the analogous case of natural gas storage, the maximum pressure that can be used is defined by regulations and similar rules will probably be developed for CO_2 storage.

Once CO_2 has been injected into the underground formation, it will initially form a bubble around the injection point. In an oilfield, under suitable conditions, some of the CO_2 will dissolve in the oil. Otherwise the CO_2 bubble will rise to the top of the formation, where it will be trapped under the cap rock. In most cases, but in particular if the CO_2 has been injected through a horizontal well, the CO_2 bubble will be above the point of injection. This separation of the CO_2 from the injector means that the CO_2 cannot escape through the well. Even so, other holes in the cap rock, whether made by nature or by man, could allow the CO_2 to escape. Even if a fault like this does not itself reach the surface directly, it may still allow the CO_2 to reach an overlying level. So any such faults must be searched for and located during the initial survey of the site.

Apart from in the presence of oil, the CO_2 will slowly dissolve into the formation water, producing a weak acid. This can dissolve certain minerals in the formation, sometimes within months. Over thousands of years, such a reaction can lead to the precipitation of minerals which will then be deposited in the forma-

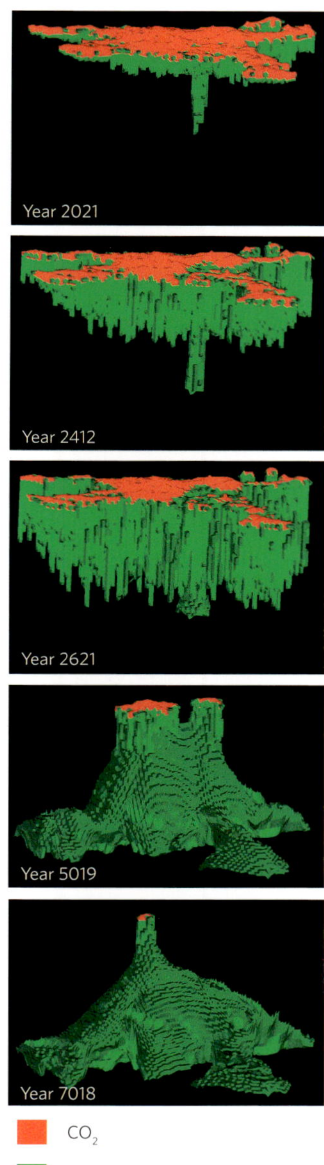

Fig. 6.16 Modelling shows the future dissolution of CO_2 in salt water in the Utsira formation. Because the brine containing dissolved CO_2 is denser than ordinary brine, it will sink to the bottom of the formation (By permission of Erik Lindeberg, Sintef Petroleum).

Many other ideas have been proposed for storing captured CO$_2$. These include making artificial containers to hold it on land, injecting it into the deep ocean, or converting it into a solid material which can lock-in the CO$_2$ for ever.

The first proposal for storing CO$_2$ involved injecting captured CO$_2$ into ocean currents which could carry it into deep water. As there is a relatively slow circulation between shallow and deep water[4] in the oceans, putting the CO$_2$ into deep water would keep much of it isolated for hundreds of years. However, if the CO$_2$ were to reach shallow depths, where there is a rapid exchange with the atmosphere, it would rapidly escape again.

CO$_2$ placed very deep, below 3,000 m, would be denser than the water around it and so would sink to the bottom. A lake of CO$_2$ might be formed on the seabed. However, this would have a severe impact on the environment, killing any life on the seabed (although fish could swim away). An alternative would be to mix the CO$_2$ with seawater and disperse it, thereby avoiding any significant impact on the marine environment (except close to the injection point). However, such schemes would be practicable only at intermediate depths (say 1,500 m) and so the CO$_2$ would not be isolated for as long as in the deep lake scheme. For all these reasons, and because this would be contrary to international conventions protecting the marine environment, the use of the oceans for CO$_2$ storage is unlikely in the foreseeable future.

The construction of an artificial repository on land has been considered. This would have to be refrigerated and might have to be pressurised. The cost of such an installation, not to mention its size, would be such that this approach would not be able to compete with the geological storage of CO$_2$.

Carbonate rocks are found in many parts of the world. Making an artificial carbonate from CO$_2$ could be one way of permanently locking it into a solid. However, CO$_2$ is a relatively stable material, so energy would be needed to convert it into a carbonate; using energy would produce more emissions of CO$_2$. Various schemes have been considered for combining CO$_2$ with natural minerals, such as serpentinite, but the overall cost, energy requirements, and the space needed to dispose of the solid carbonate, make it unlikely that this would be worthwhile if geological formations are available to store CO$_2$.

tion, essentially locking in the CO$_2$ for ever. At the same time, a significant proportion of the CO$_2$ becomes trapped in the pore spaces between the rock grains and by adsorption onto the surface of the rock grains. This will also be locked in.

At the end of injection, the well will be sealed to prevent the escape of fluids. Sealing might involve the removal of the well tubing and the insertion of plugs made from CO$_2$-resistant cement.

Monitoring the injected CO$_2$

Injecting CO$_2$ into the ground is not the end of the matter. It is necessary to know that it is staying put, so that credit can be claimed for avoiding emissions to at-

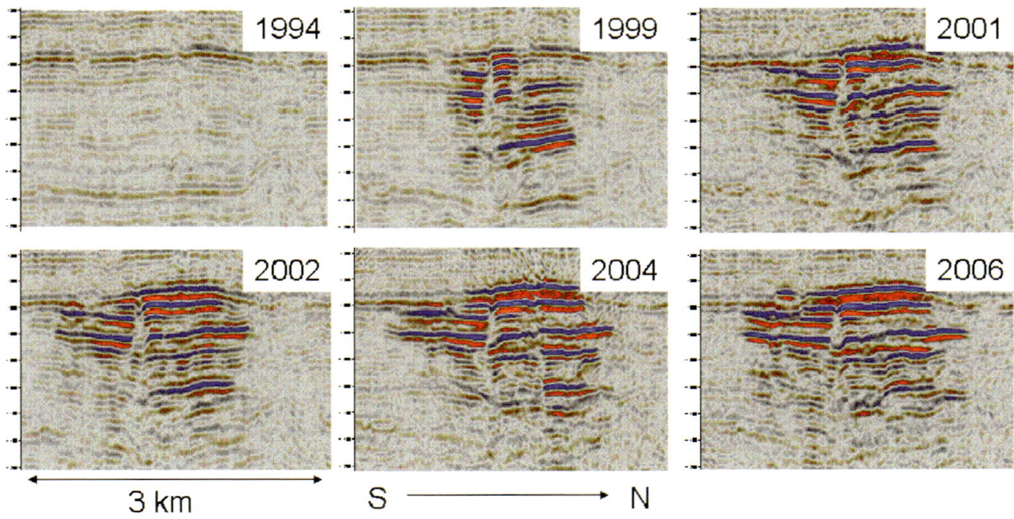

Fig. 6.17 Seismic survey results over several years show the progression of CO_2 in the Utsira formation (Source: StatoilHydro).

mosphere and to be sure there are no hazards arising from storing the CO_2 underground. The surface area around the storage site will be monitored, primarily for safety reasons, in case of an accidental release of CO_2. The most likely source of a leak is a well passing through the storage formation, so all such wells must be identified and checked. Other possible escape paths might open up with time, so it will be standard practice in such projects to monitor underground water layers above the storage level (especially onshore sites), as well as the air above ground level. Other techniques for monitoring offshore storage are being investigated because of the high cost of drilling wells in such places.

These measurements will provide assurance that the CO_2 has not leaked out of the reservoir. However, they will not provide positive proof of the quantity of CO_2 in the formation. Direct measurement of the CO_2 underground is not easy. In some circumstances, if wells have been drilled into the formation, samples can be taken which will show how much CO_2 has dissolved and how much has reacted with the formation rock. However, introducing more wells into the formation increases the risk of leakage, so it may be better to make remote observations.

One established method of remotely observing fluids underground is by doing a seismic survey, where sound waves are passed through the ground; the reflections then show the extent of the CO_2. Through a complex process of analysis, a detailed picture can be built up of the location of the various fluids beneath the surface. This can be repeated at intervals in order to check how the CO_2 is expanding and

Gaining experience from the Sleipner storage project

An international collaborative research programme was started in 1997 to take advantage of the unique opportunity presented by the Sleipner project to monitor the behaviour of CO_2 underground. Due to its offshore location, the range of monitoring techniques that could be deployed was limited. An observation well has not been used because in this case there was some concern about the risk of leakage from such a well placed within the CO_2 bubble, and because more than one well would have been necessary to gain sufficient spatial information. Instead, several seismic surveys have been conducted – an initial, baseline survey in 1994 and 5 further surveys during injection (in 1999, 2001, 2002, 2004 and 2006); the results of these measurements have been used to estimate the position of the CO_2 and to test geophysical models. Subsequently, other techniques for monitoring the CO_2 have also been used (see fig. 5.22 and 6.15).

An extensive analysis of the results has been carried out – the CO_2 was observed to have risen vertically from the injection point but appears to have been delayed by intermediate shale layers. Finally, the CO_2 was seen to be collecting at the upper boundary of the formation under the cap rock in a bubble which is between 500 and 1,000m across. Little geochemical activity was detected during this period. At present, about 80% to 85% of the CO_2 is trapped in the bubble, 15% to 20% dissolved in the water, and less than 1% trapped by reaction with minerals.

Experience gained from the Weyburn monitoring project

The ability of the Weyburn oilfield to store CO_2 is being verified by a collaborative monitoring project which has been running alongside the commercial injection.

The CO_2 is injected into a zone lying at a depth of about 1,450m and consisting of two separate geological intervals. In the study area, there are 19 well patterns, each of which consists of a CO_2 injection well, surrounded by several vertical and (in some cases) horizontal wells through which the oil is removed. In total, there are about 150 wells in an area of approximately 25 km[2] – this allows detailed sampling of the field.

Conducting this work in conjunction with a project taking place in an existing oilfield has a number of advantages, including having access to a large volume[5] of CO_2, multiple sampling points across the field, and detailed information on the sub-surface. However, there are also disadvantages, e.g. the need for coordination with production operations, as well as the complexity of the storage mechanisms, making interpretation of the results more difficult.

The extent of geochemical fluid sampling (made possible by the many wells in this field) provides good insight into the movement of the CO_2. This provides information on three chemical processes – the dissolution of CO_2 into brine, the reaction with carbonate rock, and the mineral dissolution – as well as the CO_2 gas cap (since not all of the CO_2 dissolves, even in this oilfield).

Soil gas sampling at the surface has been carried out three times between July 2001 and October 2003, looking for signs of leakage. All that could be detected was the natural background CO_2 from the soil; there were no signs of any leakage from the reservoir, although there were some anomalously high levels of hydrocarbons that could not be explained.

Chapter 6 | Behind the headlines

to verify the amount of CO_2 underground. Seismic analysis has been deployed to good effect in making measurements of the CO_2 injected into the Utsira formation under the North Sea. However, this technique is only able to detect pure CO_2, and cannot follow it once it dissolves into the formation water. This CO_2-rich water – being heavier than the surrounding water – sinks down to the bottom of the storage formation. Thus, seismic surveys can provide initial confirmation of the presence of CO_2, but in the longer term, they would be insufficient to verify the amount of CO_2 in the formation. Other remote observation techniques are being developed.

Additional problems arise when monitoring CO_2-enhanced oil recovery. CO_2 dissolves faster in oil than in water so the seismic signal is even less useful for confirming the long-term position of the CO_2. Coupled with this, up to two-thirds of the injected CO_2 may return to the surface with the produced oil. There, it is separated from the oil and re-injected but, inevitably, a small amount could be lost. So accounting for the quantity of CO_2 underground involves counting up the amounts injected, recovered, and re-injected. Confirming the amounts underground may be possible by taking samples through wells – this is more likely to be done with an onshore field, which has many wells, than an offshore field, where there will be fewer wells. This is one reason why monitoring the injection of captured CO_2 at the Weyburn oilfield is such a fruitful source of understanding the behaviour of CO_2 underground.

Considering the possibility of leakage

We can feel confident that a properly-designed and professionally-operated storage facility will not leak any appreciable amount of CO_2. However, being confident is not, in itself, sufficient reason for the authorities, or the public, to accept such an approach to dealing with CO_2 emissions. Instead, the risks involved in the geological storage of CO_2 can be analysed systematically. Such risk assessment consists of two separate tasks – first, identifying the processes and pathways which might allow the CO_2 to escape and assessing the chances of this happening; and secondly, estimating the effects of any leakage. The risks involved in storage are then calculated as the product of these two, the likelihood and the consequences.

Because of the novelty of the CO_2 storage concept, there is only a limited amount of information available from the CO_2 injections carried out to date which would allow an assessment to be made of the likelihood of leakage. Instead, the likelihood can be estimated using information from other, analogous systems[6]:

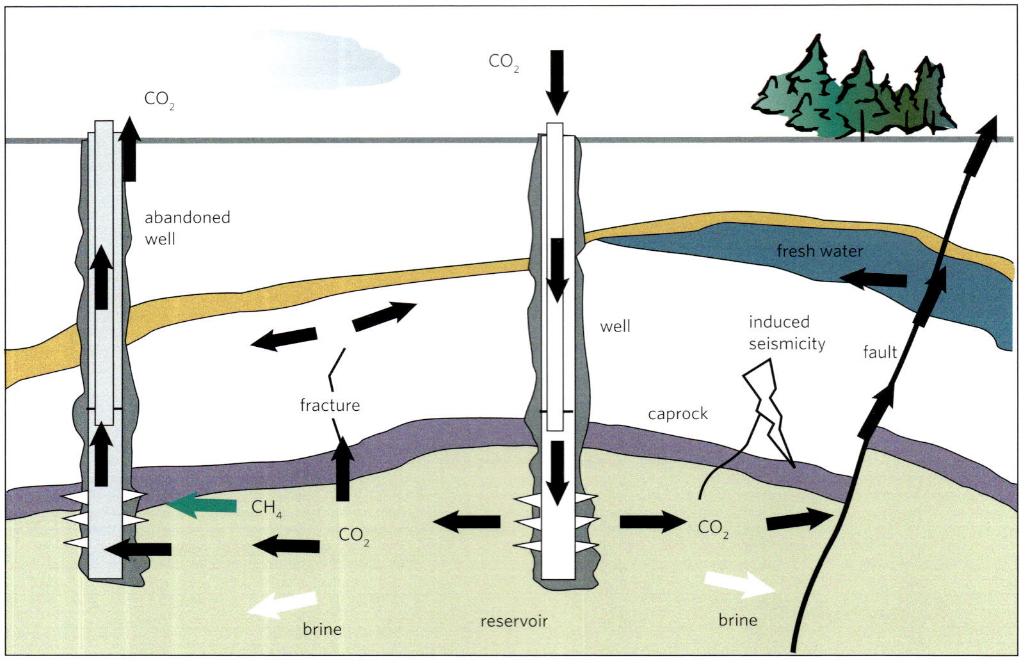

Fig. 6.18 Illustration of the type of paths that CO$_2$ might follow to escape from underground storage (after Damen et al 2003).

- Natural formations, which trap CO$_2$ or other gases or oil – these demonstrate that such fluids have been held underground for millions of years.
- Engineered systems, such as natural gas storage, show that major failures in the injection wells occur about once every 20,000 to 50,000 years. CO$_2$-enhanced oil recovery also provides relevant experience from over a hundred oilfields during the last 35 to 40 years.
- Laboratory data on the physical, chemical and mechanical nature of the formation rock.
- Numerical models of CO$_2$ trapping and transport underground show that storage should become more secure with the passing of time, becoming highly secure within 100 to 1,000 years of injection, depending on the type of reservoir.

To estimate the consequences of leakage, we can recognise various potential effects:

- Hazards to human health or safety
- Effects on groundwater and ecosystems
- Effects on climate

A hazard to human health would arise from concentrations of CO_2 of more than 1% to 2% which might occur if the escaping gas was somehow confined to a restricted space. Such a threat, whilst improbable, might occur if someone drilled into the formation whilst the CO_2 was still undissolved. This could be avoided by ensuring appropriate licensing of the area of the storage site.

Groundwater might be affected if toxic metals were leached by acidic water containing dissolved CO_2; the worst outcome would be if this affected drinking water. Experience of injecting other fluids underground indicates such outcomes are rare. Nevertheless, if the CO_2 contained impurities such as sulphur, the consequences would be even more severe than with pure CO_2, suggesting that storage will have to be restricted to relatively pure CO_2. The leakage of CO_2 from natural sources (such as in volcanic areas) has been observed to affect ecosystems, such as microbes, plants and animals. However, in order to do damage, the flux of CO_2 has to be at a level which is much greater than would be acceptable from manmade CO_2 storage. If the leakage was sub-sea, rather than subterranean, the likely effects would be limited because some of the CO_2 would dissolve into the water and then be dispersed.

Probably the most important issue is what effect the leakage of CO_2 from storage would have on the climate. In other words, would it add significantly to the amount of CO_2 in the atmosphere? Without having precise figures on the likelihood of leakage, we cannot make a conclusive statement about this. But we can ask whether there is a threshold below which there would essentially be no harmful effects on the climate? This can be assessed using simulations similar to those developed for modelling climate change. These suggest that, if 99% of the CO_2 can be stored for a period of a thousand years, then such a minor amount of leakage would not interfere significantly with the contribution this technique can make towards stabilising the amount of CO_2 in the atmosphere. Our understanding of geological storage gives confidence that this can be achieved. Leakage at such low levels would have no effect on surface ecosystems.

What if something were to go wrong?

When preparing to store CO_2, it is prudent to consider what might happen in the unlikely event of a leakage of CO_2. Then, the relevant questions would be whether or not to do something about it, and if so what? The need to take action would depend on the scale of the leak and the threat that it posed to health, ecosystems and the climate.

The most likely source of leakage is the injection well, or another well penetrating the cap rock. The CO_2 could not escape faster through a well than the rate at which it was injected in the first place, so the scale of any such release would be manageable. The oil industry has experience of dealing with problem wells, so there are techniques available for repairing them or, in the worst case, sealing them for good.

The escape of CO_2 through a fracture in the rock could be dealt with, in principle, by reducing the pressure in the reservoir (i.e. reducing the force driving the leak). Alternatively, action could be taken to isolate the area in the reservoir which was feeding the leak. In the worst case, any free CO_2 could be removed from the reservoir – some of it would already be so tightly locked in that it could not be removed, but then this would not present any danger of leakage.

For minor leakages, the main concern would not be the potential threat to the climate, but to human health. In such cases, measures would be implemented to avoid the build-up of CO_2 in confined spaces and to deal with any acidification of groundwater.

Legal and regulatory aspects

For such a new technology, which has been developed for a new purpose (i.e. protecting the climate), it is not surprising, perhaps, that issues have arisen which are not specifically covered by existing regulations. This is particularly the case offshore, where the international legal framework for protecting the oceans has been developed over decades without recognising the nature of the climate problem. Onshore, regulations are typically under national control so they cannot be generalised in a simple way. However, several countries already permit the injection of gases underground, so it seems likely that national rules already exist that could be adapted to handle CO_2 storage.

The protection of the marine environment is entrusted to the London Convention which was first agreed in 1972 and was later supplemented by the London Protocol. The Oslo-Paris Convention (OSPAR) is a related convention for the North East Atlantic; similar conventions cover other regions. As ratified, the London Protocol was seen to prohibit certain applications of CO_2 capture and storage, especially if the CO_2 had been captured onshore for storage sub-sea, something which is of interest in Europe. Recognising the potential role of the capture and storage of CO_2 as a means of addressing climate change, the London Convention is now

Chapter 6 | Behind the headlines

developing guidelines for the sub-sea bed storage of CO_2. The OSPAR Convention has recently been amended to allow CO_2 storage under the seabed.

Is there enough capacity to store CO_2 underground?

The amount of CO_2 which could be stored is one of the key pieces of information that will determine whether or not underground storage can make a useful contribution towards combating climate change.

Oil and gas fields are probably the best understood potential stores. Based on known fields, it is estimated that there is capacity for between 675 and 900 billion tonnes of CO_2 worldwide. For deep saline aquifers, global estimates are more uncertain, ranging from 1,000 billion tonnes to possibly as much as 10,000 billion tonnes[7].

To put these figures into some perspective, global emissions of CO_2 from fossil fuel combustion are currently about 26 billion tonnes per year, indicating that there could be hundreds of years of capacity at current emission rates.

How much would it cost?

Even if it is feasible to capture CO_2, and if there is sufficient capacity to store it, and it is safe and legal to do so, we will still need to know whether this can be done at a competitive cost.

In a new power station, the additional equipment needed for capturing CO_2 would incur substantial capital expenditure, as well as increase running costs. The compression of CO_2 for transportation would also present a significant extra cost. Also, the energy used in capturing the CO_2, especially for post-combustion capture, would reduce the amount of electricity being despatched by the power station, further increasing the cost of generating electricity.

In an existing power station, it is more difficult to generalise about the cost of capture and compression because of the differences between actual power stations. Capture would most

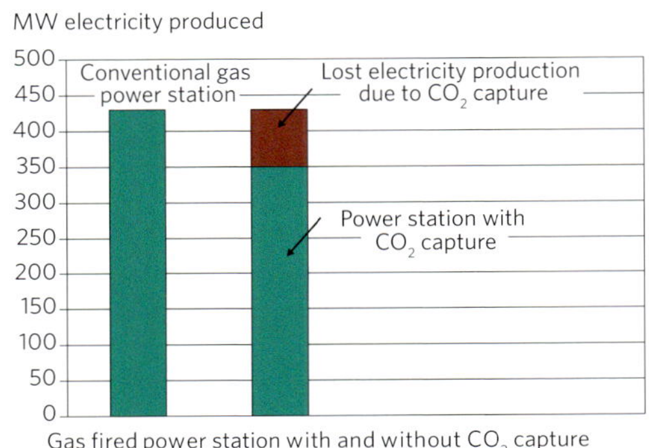

Fig. 6.19 Less electricity is generated when capturing and storing CO_2 from a power station.

likely be carried out using post-combustion technology, but this imposes the largest energy penalty; as older stations tend to have a lower efficiency than modern ones, adding an extra energy load in such circumstances could make the whole plant very inefficient and thus uncompetitive. In addition, the remaining service life of existing stations will be less than that of new stations, so the investment would have to be paid back relatively quickly, further increasing the cost of electricity generation. For both these reasons, the retrofitting of capture to existing power stations is unlikely to be attractive. However, if the station were to be refurbished with new boilers and turbines, the new system would have a higher efficiency than the old one, so the cost of fitting capture would be less prohibitive.

Transport by pipeline also requires capital investment (booster stations may also be needed to increase the pressure, which will thus use power). The storage installation involves the expense of drilling wells and some equipment on the surface; there will also be an ongoing requirement for monitoring to ensure the CO_2 stays put. In case of unexpected problems, remediation will be an extra cost.

In order to understand the costs and benefits of the capture and storage of CO_2, we need to establish some common assumptions representing typical situations where this technology might be used. Important factors include the cost of fuel, materials, labour, and capital. The first stations of this type will incur extra costs, as does every new type, because the constructors and the operators will have to amass experience, and because unexpected things sometimes happen. As more stations are built, experience will help to improve the technology and costs will be reduced, as has been the case in other energy technologies.

Looking ahead, when multiple examples are built, the cost of generating electricity will be increased by between 50% and 100%[10], compared with an existing coal- or gas-fired power station. This incremental cost, however, is quite dependent on the cost of fuel, in particular the cost of natural gas as this tends to be greater than the cost of coal. Illustrative values[11] of the cost of avoiding CO_2 emissions by capture, together with compression for transport, are USD 34 per tonne of CO_2 for post-combustion capture using coal (at a coal cost of USD 2.2/GJ) and USD 58 per tonne using gas (at a gas cost of USD 7.8/GJ)

In addition, the large scale transportation of CO_2 would add a small amount, depending on the distance and the number of power stations feeding into the pipeline network. The first such stations will not able to achieve such low costs for transportation unless special opportunities arise, for example the re-use of existing pipelines as has been proposed in the UK and the Netherlands.

Chapter 6 | Behind the headlines

Experience matters

The cost of technology will change with time. Over many decades, the evolution of technologies has been observed to result in reductions in unit cost. Factors such as improvements in process design, materials, product standardisation, integration, the reduction in raw material costs and economies of scale all contribute to reducing costs. Many of these reflect the fact that, as the manufacturers and users learn more about the technology through building and using it, they find ways of improving it, leading to reductions in cost. These reductions can be analysed and portrayed as cost reduction curves (for example, Fig. 6.20). Such curves have been produced for several technologies that are relevant to CO_2 capture and storage, including flue gas desulphurisation (FGD) in power stations, selective catalytic reduction (SCR) for NO_x reduction in power stations, pulverised coal boilers, and gas turbine combined cycle stations. Analysis[8] of various process technologies indicates that, in most cases, capital costs have been reduced by between 10% and 15% for each doubling of the installed capacity. The corresponding reduction in operating and maintenance costs is between 5% and 30%.

The *learning rate* represents the fractional reduction in cost associated with each doubling of the installed capacity. Based on data from analogous process technologies, the cost of electricity from power stations with CO_2 capture is predicted to fall by between 10% and 18%, once 100 GW_e of capacity has been installed.

Much of the extra costs of a power station using CO_2 capture is for equipment which is already widely used, e.g. pulverised coal boilers and gas turbine combined cycles. Reductions in the incremental costs of capturing CO_2 are predicted to be between 13% and 40%, i.e. greater than the expected reductions in the cost of electricity.

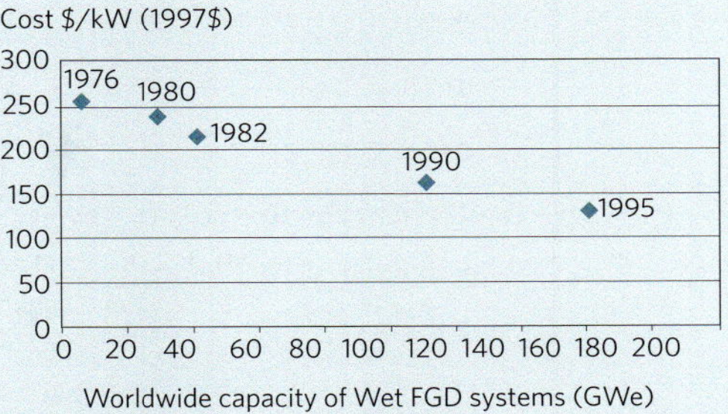

Figure 6.20   The reduction in capital cost of flue gas desulphurisation systems from the earliest use in 1976. Capital cost was reduced by 11% for each doubling of installed capacity. The costs of operation and maintenance were reduced by twice as much as this during the same period (Graph redrawn from Rubin, Taylor, Yehand Hounshell at the EXCETP-6 Workshop in Paris, France in January 2003)[9].

A notable feature of geological storage is the large potential capacity for storage known to exist. The cost of the storage itself is in the range USD 0.5 to 8 per tonne of CO_2[12]. Long-term monitoring and remediation (if needed) are not expected to add much to this. Such costs are relatively small compared with the cost of capturing the CO_2 in the first place. Overall, the extra cost of CO_2 capture and storage can be regarded as a fixed amount per kWh of electricity for a particular region at a given fuel price.

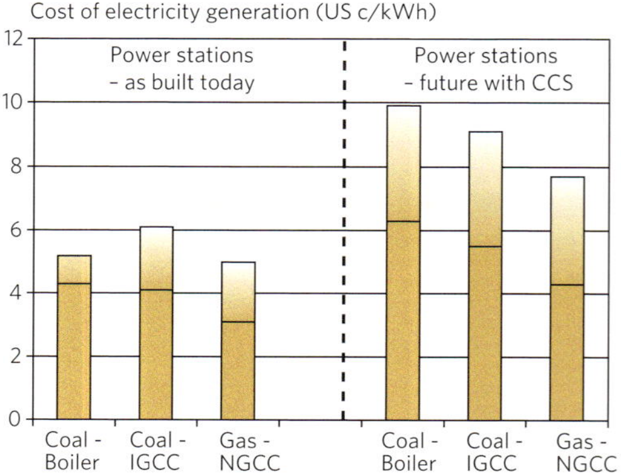

Fig. 6.21 Extra cost of electricity generation due to capture and storage of CO_2 (CCS) for gas and coal fired power stations (source: IPCC Special report on CO_2 capture and storage, 2005).

In the case of using CO_2 for enhanced oil recovery, extra costs would be incurred for separating CO_2 from the produced oil and re-injecting it. On the other hand, there will be some extra income which should help to offset some of the cost of supplying the CO_2. Similarly, if CO_2 is used to enhance coal bed methane production, then income might be generated. For enhanced gas recovery, if done properly, extra equipment should not be needed to separate CO_2 from the produced gas, at least in the short term. At the same time, the extra gas production may be more difficult to quantify, especially if this is done in a new gas field. The value of CO_2 for onshore oilfield operators ranges from USD 12 per tonne at an oil price of USD 18/barrel of oil, to USD 33 per tonne at USD 50/barrel[13]. In fact, up to 3 times as much CO_2 could be injected for storage as would be used in conventional enhanced oil recovery, but the extra CO_2 would generate no more oil, so it would not have the same value for the oilfield operator.

Producing more oil could raise public concerns because it would seem to suggest more CO_2 emissions. However, the situation is not that clear – for example, oil demand will not change in the short term as a result of an enhanced oil recovery project, so the oil produced in this way would largely displace oil from another source rather than add to global emissions. In addition, even if CO_2 were not used for enhanced recovery, other fluids might be used, so, in the long term, not all of the CO_2 released by burning this oil would be additional to what would otherwise have been released. So the effect on emissions of using CO_2 for enhanced oil recovery is not open to simple analysis.

The cost of capturing CO_2 in energy-intensive industries (such as oil refining, cement production, chemicals, and iron and steel) varies considerably – from producing ammonia, where there would be very little extra cost for capturing much of the CO_2, to oil refining where the extra cost might be as high as in power generation.

Chapter 6 | Behind the headlines

Changing to zero-carbon energy carriers, such as hydrogen or electricity, could produce much greater emission reductions at the point of use than any other measure in the transport sector. The lowest cost sources of these carriers are fossil fuels (even if using capture and storage of CO_2). The cost of purchasing and operating vehicles designed for zero-carbon energy carriers would be substantially greater than for current vehicles so, as a means of avoiding CO_2 emissions, these substitutions would be considerably more expensive (per tonne of CO_2 avoided) than CO_2 capture in power stations.

Fig. 6.22   The Weyburn field uses CO_2 for increasing oil recovery – the CO_2 will be stored in the field at the end of oil production.

How can CO_2 capture and storage contribute towards reducing greenhouse gas emissions?

In places where there are accessible geological storage formations, capturing CO_2 from power stations could reduce emissions by more than 80%. This would have best effect in base-load power stations, but it could also be used in stations operating more sporadically if hydrogen is produced for short-term storage and subsequent reuse. Similar reductions could be achieved with other major sources of CO_2 emissions. The opportunity to produce zero-carbon energy carriers for use in vehicles opens up a practical method of supplying the transport market, although many other changes will be needed to distribution systems and vehicles in order to bring these carriers into widespread use.

The cost of avoiding emissions through the use of this technology in base-load power stations will be more or less a fixed amount per tonne of CO_2, independent of capacity, a feature which is similar to nuclear power. This contrasts with some of the renewable energy sources for which the cost increases significantly as the number of installations rises in a particular area.

So, the capture and storage of CO_2 is potentially attractive as a way of reducing emissions from large, central sources. In the final chapter of this book,

Vehicles fuelled by zero-carbon energy carriers

The two carriers of interest in this respect are electricity and hydrogen; the production of electricity is dealt with elsewhere in this chapter; the cost of producing hydrogen from fossil fuels using CO_2 capture and storage would be about USD 8/GJ[14] from coal (priced at USD 1.2/GJ) or USD 13/GJ from natural gas (priced at USD 5/GJ). This is less than the cost of producing this energy carrier from renewable energy sources via the electrolysis of water, which is an energy inefficient process. Given the constraints on the capacity to supply renewable electricity in many countries, it seems more likely that renewable sources would be used directly as sources of electricity than to make hydrogen.

The cost of generating electricity is about USD 21/GJ (compared with USD 13/GJ without capture), using coal at a cost of USD 1.2/GJ; for gas, the cost of electricity would be raised from USD 12/GJ to USD 16/GJ by use of capture and storage at a cost of gas of USD 4.4/GJ. The increase in the generating cost is relatively small in comparison with the retail price of electricity to small users (in the UK, this is about USD 40/GJ at present).

In comparison, the current cost of petrol (wholesale) is about USD 12/GJ, without considering distribution costs and changes in tax. The efficiency of using the different fuels would be quite different, so considering fuel costs alone tends to undervalue the advantages of the new energy carrier.

In a study for the IEA Greenhouse Gas R&D Programme, from which these figures are derived, the cost of car ownership, using various fuels, was estimated for a Western European family-sized car meeting the Euro IV standards. Cases examined included vehicles with internal-combustion engines running on compressed natural gas (CNG) or hydrogen, a fuel cell vehicle running on hydrogen, and an electric vehicle.

The degree of emission reductions when using CO_2 capture and storage to make hydrogen is nearly as high as when used for electricity generation, but the cost of avoiding emissions is much higher because of the capital investment needed in the vehicles for the electric drive-train and the storage system. Precise numbers vary considerably between different sources of information and scenarios. These vehicles have a similar range, except for the electric vehicle which could not hold a large enough battery, so these figures present an optimistic picture for the electric vehicle; the fuel cell costs are speculative, too.

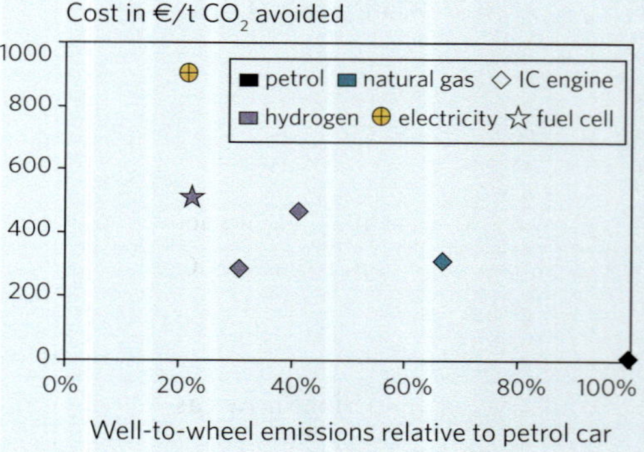

Fig. 6.23 Cost of emission reduction by using various energy carriers in possible future European cars.

we will examine how capture and storage of CO_2 might be brought into use. In particular, we will consider the decisions which will need to be taken at national and international level before this technology can make a useful contribution to addressing the problem of climate change.

Suggestions for further reading

Carbon Capture and its Storage: an integrated assessment. 2006. S. Shackley and C. Gough (eds). Ashgate Publishing Ltd, Aldershot, Hampshire.

Carbon dioxide capture for storage in deep geologic formations – results from the CO_2 capture project; vol. 1 – capture and separation of carbon dioxide from combustion, vol. 2 – geologic storage of carbon dioxide with monitoring and verification. D. Thomas, S. Benson (eds.) Elsevier. 2006.

IEA GHG Weyburn CO_2 Monitoring and Storage Project Summary Report 2000–2004. By Wilson, M., and Monea, M. (eds.), 2004, Petroleum Technology Research Centre, Regina.

IPCC Special Report on Carbon Dioxide Capture and Storage. Prepared by Working Group III of the Intergovernmental Panel on Climate Change [Metz, B., O. Davidson, H. C. de Coninck, M. Loos, and L. A. Meyer (eds.)]. Cambridge University Press, Cambridge, United Kingdom and New York, NY, USA, 442 pp.

Endnotes

1   Published data is limited by commercial confidentiality but information published by the CO_2 Capture Project and other sources suggests capture of several million tonnes of CO_2 would be feasible at a large refinery.

2   ULCOS: Ultra Low CO_2 Steelmaking Project.

3   This relates to an important property called permeability, which describes how easily fluids can move through the reservoir rock.

4   There is no hard and fast rule distinguishing between shallow and deep water but, for CO_2 storage, a depth of more than 1,000m is likely to be needed to ensure the CO_2 remains out of the atmosphere for hundreds of years.

5   Having access to fields containing commercial quantities of CO_2 is no small benefit for a monitoring project because the cost of purchasing similar amounts of CO_2 (hundreds of millions of USD) would otherwise be outside the means of a research project.

6   For further information, see the IPCC special report on CO_2 capture and storage, 2005, published by Cambridge University Press.

7   IPCC special report on CO_2 capture and storage, 2005, published by Cambridge University Press.

8   "Estimating future trends in cost of CO_2 capture technologies." 2006. IEA Greenhouse Gas R&D Programme.

9   "Learning curves for environmental technology and their importance for climate policy analysis." Rubin, E.S., Taylor, M.R., Yeh, S, Hounshell, DA. Energy 29 (2004) 1551–1559.

10 IPCC special report on CO_2 capture and storage, 2005, published by Cambridge University Press, Chapter 3.

11 "CO_2 capture as a factor in power station investment decisions." IEA Greenhouse Gas R&D Programme report 2006.

12 See the IPCC special report on CO_2 capture and storage, 2005, published by Cambridge University Press; these costs relate to large-scale storage, with at least tens of millions of tonnes of CO_2 stored in a reservoir.

13 IPCC special report on CO_2 capture and storage, 2005, published by Cambridge University Press, Chapter 5.

14 IPCC Special Report on Carbon Dioxide Capture and Storage, Cambridge University Press, 2005

IT'S GLOBAL W
M11 TOS

Making it happen

Climate change presents a real threat to the way we live our lives. As each day passes, there is growing recognition of the danger. But the major challenge facing the world is not recognising the problem, but taking action by reducing emissions far enough and fast enough to stabilise the amount of greenhouse gases in the atmosphere. An unprecedented rate of reduction in emissions is required, carried out consistently over decades, if stabilisation is to be achieved by the end of this century.

Fig. 7.1 Commentary on climate change in a public place.

The Fragile Atmosphere

Astronauts, when asked what impressed them most on their journeys into space, have remarked on the thin and flimsy appearance of the atmosphere. The atmosphere is being altered by extra greenhouse gases produced by human activities. These changes are affecting the climate now, something which will get worse in future. The main sources of these emissions are fossil fuels, being used to provide energy, as well as deforestation. Reliable supplies of energy are critical to an industrial society and to enable developing countries to expand their economies.

The world's consumers have become accustomed to energy that is supplied by fossil fuels; they should not expect any other source of energy to be as reliable or

Fig. 7.2   The insubstantial atmosphere: the blackness of space contrasts sharply with the whiteness of the clouds and the ice and snow on the southern tip of Greenland.

    Chapter 7 | Making it happen

Fig. 7.3 International negotiations can take various forms.

International negotiations

International action on climate change (and on other environmental and developmental problems) was first inspired by the 1987 Brundtland Report "Our Common Future"[2]. This led to the Rio Earth Summit in 1992, which produced the United Nations Framework Convention on Climate Change[3]. From that, came the Kyoto Protocol[4] in 1997, which was an agreement between the developed countries to reduce their emissions of a number of greenhouse gases by 5.2% by the first commitment period, which will be completed in 2012.

At the time, there was some optimism that these agreements were building on the previous success of the Montreal Protocol, which reduced emissions of chlorofluorocarbon gases. It seemed that global warming could be tackled in a similar way. However, it has since turned out that protecting the climate is a much more complex problem than protecting the ozone layer. The solutions affect many more countries and have much wider commercial implications. Many countries have enough to do just tackling the problems of today – obtaining clean water and sufficient food, creating effective sanitation, tackling over-population, or even surviving war. Consequently, it has taken eight years for the Kyoto Protocol to come into force and not all of the countries that agreed on targets in the Protocol have ever ratified it – notable exceptions being the USA and Australia, which are responsible for a large part of the emissions covered by the Protocol.

Thus, the international process started with a show of statesmanship, but since then progress has steadily slowed down.

as cheap. Rising oil prices have prompted fears of a shortage of fossil fuels, but these concerns are misplaced because high oil prices encourage the development of new supplies. Natural gas, in particular, could still make a major contribution to meeting growth in world energy demand. Coal is available in many countries, giving it a key role in ensuring long-term energy supplies. The conversion of coal and gas into transportation fuels will improve the security of supply for some countries, but cause even more CO_2 emissions.

In view of the threat of climate change, is it wise to rely so much on fossil fuels? Without the technology to capture and store CO_2, the answer to this question would undoubtedly be no. Eventually, the use of this and other technologies will allow the world to largely decouple greenhouse gas emissions from energy use. But there is much inertia in the system, not least due to the amount of capital which has been invested in the existing stock of power stations, refineries, buildings, etc. So how much change is practicable, and how fast? This is influenced by many factors. First, let us consider what is being done internationally to limit emissions.

International action on climate change needs to have more impact

Climate science, reinforced by the evidence for climate change seen in nature, indicates that prompt action is needed. Despite 15 years of international negotiation, very little reduction in emissions has been achieved and the world is, today, emitting 10% more CO_2 than it was in the 1990s[1]. Where reductions in emissions have been made, this has been due as much to the closure of uneconomic coal mines and other such events as to actions directed at tackling climate change.

This does not bode well for the future. More vision is needed. Some countries, organisations and individuals must be willing to set an example, to move beyond treating the atmosphere as a dumping ground, as we do today. As Sir Winston Churchill said: "People trying to build the present merely in the image of the past will miss out entirely on the challenges of the future."

In view of the lack of any substantive progress from 15 years of international negotiations, it might reasonable to ask whether the world should continue along the same path. Can 193 nations agree on more than minor changes in the way they use energy, a commodity which is at the heart of all their economies?

Chapter 7 | Making it happen

The threat of climate change suggests we need to take bold and forward-looking action to limit emissions. This may have to take place without full international agreement, if we are to make substantial inroads into emissions fast enough.

A more practicable approach may be to limit the number of countries involved in negotiations, since a smaller group is more likely to be able to resolve its differences than a very large one. Fortunately, a mere 10 nations produce 65% of global CO_2 emissions; and only 10% of all the countries in the world are responsible for 80% of global CO_2 emissions. So, in practical terms, 15 negotiators could formulate an agreement concerning the bulk of the world's greenhouse gas emissions. Such a focused group may have a better chance of making progress than the current fully-international approach.

The targets that these "early adopters" set themselves will have to relate directly to the problem to be tackled, the burden on the climate. In contrast, the Kyoto Protocol was based on an agreement regarding percentage emission reductions; this was complicated by setting different targets for different countries. Such an approach does not provide a clear basis for setting targets for other countries that might join later. Indeed, setting targets based on reductions (rather than emission levels) provides the opportunity for confusion, whether accidental or deliberate. It would be far better to focus on the actual level of emissions since these determine the burden placed on the atmosphere. Such targets would fit better with caps on emissions such as those needed in the emission trading schemes now being used in Europe and under consideration elsewhere.

So, a more logical and straightforward basis for international agreement would be to agree on:

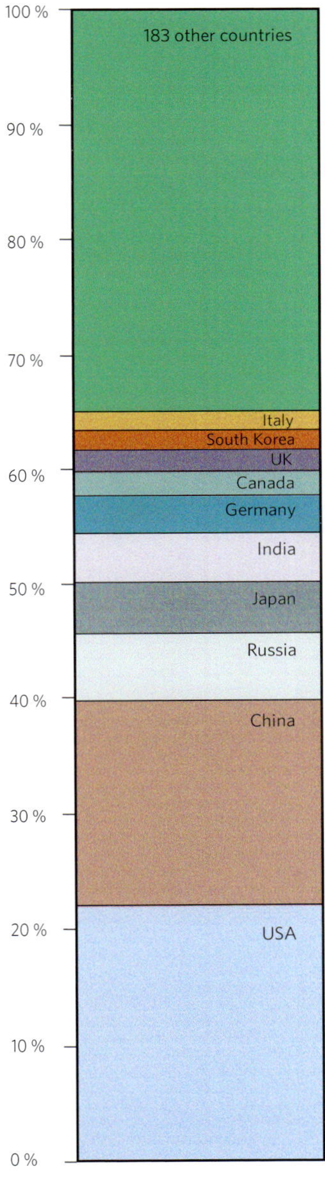

Fig. 7.4 Ten nations are responsible for 65% of the world's CO_2 emissions from use of fossil fuels.

Whether or not CO_2 capture and storage could make a worthwhile difference to how the climate changes this century will depend on how much CO_2 would be in the atmosphere in a hundred years' time, and on how the world would look if nothing were done in the meantime.

For all their faults, mathematical models integrating energy and economic factors are the only way of attempting to see what might happen ahead of time. In these models, the amount of CO_2 in the atmosphere is represented by the CO_2 concentration, measured in parts per million by volume (ppmv). Currently, there are about 380 ppmv of CO_2 in the atmosphere, having risen from about 270 ppmv before the industrial revolution.

Target levels for the end of the century have been considered to be: 450, 550, 650 or 750 ppmv. These represent a range of outcomes from hardly any further change in the amount of CO_2 (450 ppmv) to one where we add 175% of the natural amount of greenhouse gases (750 ppmv), something which is expected to have severe consequences.

The models use a base case (or reference scenario) which presents a picture of the world in the absence of climate change. There is a great deal of variation between possible reference cases ranging, at one extreme, from the world economy growing like it is today to, at the other extreme, a world which has changed its pattern of development and energy use so that there is very little growth in CO_2 emissions.

(a) an explicit goal for limiting global emissions in order to achieve stabilisation[5] – the eventual goal would be a fixed level of about 8 billion tonnes/year of CO_2 emissions;

(b) a clear timetable regarding how to achieve stabilisation by the end of the century – this would translate into a practical ceiling on emissions which would be reduced annually;

(c) a system of sharing the allowable emissions between the countries – the most equitable system would be to divide up the allowed emissions equally amongst all of the people on the planet, with trading used to match needs and rights.

The new strategy would begin once the first Kyoto commitment period has been completed in 2012. It would involve reducing emissions by 3% every year for the first 40 years. It is worth noting that such a path would be broadly in line with the 60% reduction by 2050 proposed by the UK's Royal Commission on Environmental Pollution, and by other organisations. After 2050, the rate of reduction would necessarily slow down because, by then, the relatively easy steps would have been taken. Even so, this approach should still achieve the goal (stabilisation) by 2100. Many scenarios have been proposed for achieving the same end, but this one illustrates what needs to be done. Let us use it to explore the steps the world should take in order to achieve stabilisation by the end of the century.

What would the early adopters do?

As we have seen in the previous chapters, there are many ways of reducing emissions. Some of these measures can only achieve modest reductions, a few could make sharp reductions; some will cost more than others; there are different environmental impacts between the various measures. Together, they can be thought of as a toolbox of measures, from which users can choose the best selection for their circumstances.

Fig. 7.5 The toolbox of measures for mitigating climate change[6].

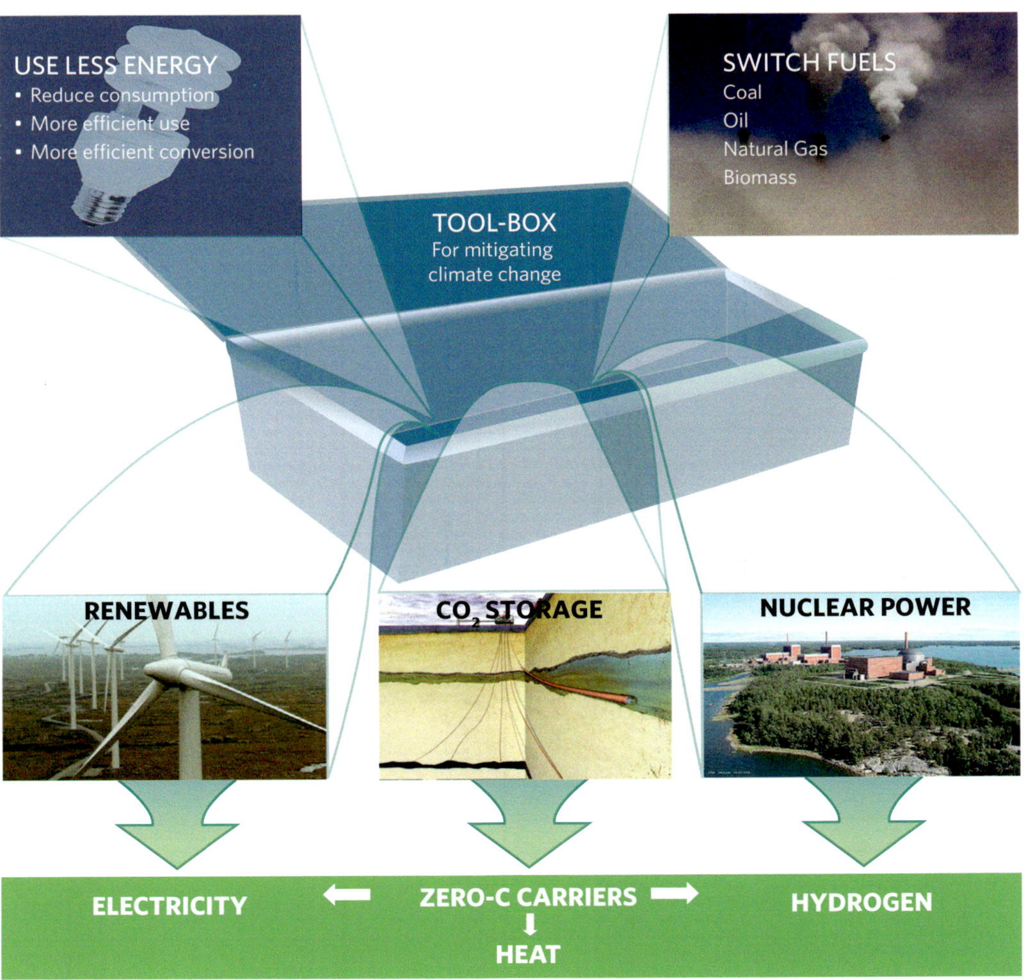

Do we know how much each measure will be used? Can we pick the winners? The simple answer is no, we do not have enough information to predict with any confidence how extensively each measure will be used. The climate change problem is so large that we cannot allow ourselves to have favourites amongst these measures. Not all countries will choose the same combination of tools.

One way of estimating how much each of the measures would be used is by looking at the way of achieving the required emission reductions which has the lowest cost. This type of analysis is typically based on energy-economic models, as used when developing energy policy. But all models contain uncertainties. As we noted earlier, climate models contain considerable uncertainties, although these are, at least, based on physical and chemical phenomena, some of which can be subjected to measurement. Energy-economic models contain even greater uncertainties; using them to look 50 to 100 years into the future requires heroic assumptions regarding how the world will be then. In practice, such models tend to assume that tomorrow's world will be much like today's, but altered in a number of more or less predictable ways – e.g. the world population will be a little larger than it is today and most people will be better off than they are today; less predictable events may not be represented at all; few of the assumptions can be tested, except in retrospect.

So, looking 100 years ahead using energy/economic models would be an activity of questionable usefulness. Even looking 30 or 40 years ahead involves making guesses about a world which will, undoubtedly, be quite different from that of today, with increased numbers of people living in urban areas, radically different use of information technology, major changes in healthcare, etc.

Nevertheless, several important features of the supply of energy and its use are unlikely to change dramatically in 30 or 40 years – power stations being built today are expected to have a service life of at least 40 years, so they may still be operating in 2050 (after appropriate refurbishments). Most of today's buildings will still be in use in 2050 – in the developed countries, housing built between now and then will only account, perhaps, for a quarter of the total stock. The layouts of cities and transport infrastructures of the developed countries will change only to a moderate degree because of the long lead times of such projects. We must consider what plans the energy industries should make to ensure their capital investments are best prepared for protecting the climate.

On the other hand, energy-using appliances, especially vehicles, have much shorter service lives and thus are likely to change substantially in 40 years. Plans

Chapter 7 | Making it happen

What does the IPCC deduce from energy/economic models regarding CO$_2$ capture and storage?

An IPCC Special Report[7] reviewed the potential for CO$_2$ capture and storage based on the results of a number of energy/economic models. The future deployment of this technology was considered in the context of scenarios that achieved economically efficient ways of stabilising the amount of CO$_2$ in the atmosphere. From this, the extra cost of using this approach could be calculated. The report recognised that there are significant uncertainties in the quantitative results of such models.

All of the models indicated that CO$_2$ capture and storage systems are unlikely to be deployed on a large scale in the absence of an explicit policy that substantially restricts greenhouse gas emissions. On the other hand, many of these models show that, when controls are imposed on greenhouse gas emissions, the large-scale deployment of CO$_2$ capture and storage would take place within a few decades.

These models also indicate that CO$_2$ capture and storage is only likely to contribute significantly to tackling climate change if it is deployed extensively in electricity generation. For this to happen, the price of an allowance[8] to emit one tonne of CO$_2$ will have to exceed USD 25 to 30.

In this range of scenarios, cumulative global CO$_2$ emissions over a period of 100 years range from around 3,000 billion tonnes of CO$_2$ (in the scenarios with the lowest emissions) to more than 6,600 billion tonnes if the world continues to operate as it does today. The use of CO$_2$ storage during this period, according to

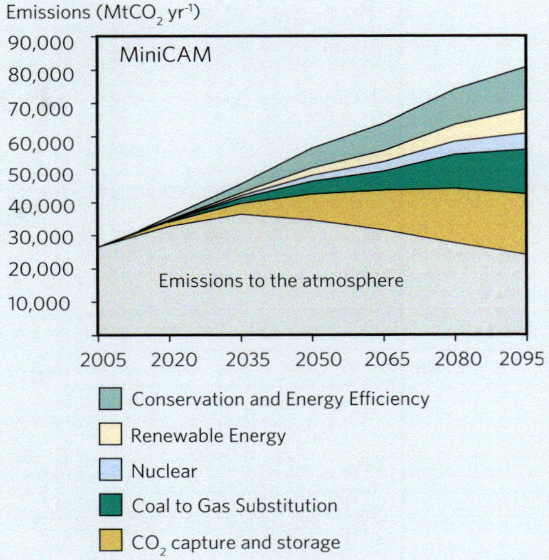

Fig. 7.6 An example of results from one economic model illustrating how the various measures could contribute to reducing emissions.

the models, could be as little as 380 billion tonnes of CO$_2$ (averaged over the 750 ppmv cases) or as much as 2,160 billion tonnes (in the 450 ppmv cases)[9]; capture and storage would contribute between 15% and 54% of total emission reductions. This amount of storage is consistent with what is thought might be available using depleted oil and gas fields and deep saline aquifers worldwide.

If CO$_2$ capture and storage were not used, the extra global cost of meeting the climate targets would be huge – estimated at between tens of billions and trillions of US dollars. Although such numbers are incomprehensibly large, what they do indicate is that it would be significantly cheaper to meet climate goals by including CO$_2$ capture and storage in the toolbox than by excluding it.

for developing their replacements must be equally concerned with protecting the climate.

Action on climate change is already starting to be taken by individuals and companies[12] as well as by governments. Their goals may vary and none have, as yet, adopted firm targets for anything more than minor reductions in emissions. If it does not make commercial sense to act, there is only so much that even the most far-sighted chief executive will be prepared to do. Developing, purchasing, and using equipment to reduce emissions tends to increase costs. The absence of a commercial rationale for reducing emissions will be a major barrier to companies taking substantial action on their own. Without the lead of government, it is hard to see that any of the other players will implement any substantial changes.

Yet, perversely, commercial organisations may be the best hope for action since, given appropriate incentives, the necessary decisions would be in the hands

Predicting the use of CO_2 capture and storage in the period up to 2030 or 2050

Of necessity, each energy/economic model has its own unique characteristics that may affect the results and conclusions, which is why the IPCC brought together the results of a number of models in its work. However, in order to examine the results in detail, it will be necessary to look at individual models, so we shall examine what the IEA's Energy Technology Perspectives (ETP) model tells us could turn out to be the future use for CO_2 capture and storage[10]. As with any model, ETP is a highly stylized representation of the world's energy supply and demand, based on a dataset that starts with a close approximation of the world of today.

The range of contributions that CO_2 capture and storage could make is relatively narrow – perhaps only a factor of ten between the upper and lower figures, according to ETP. It also shows that, in 2030, 80% of all CO_2 capture will be taking place in the OECD countries but, by 2050, this share will have declined to 60%, if policies to control CO_2 emissions are introduced worldwide. This would be the consequence of economic growth in the developing world, especially the increased use of electricity, coupled with the global application of policies to reduce greenhouse gas emissions.

The average cost of reducing emissions during the period 2030 to 2050 (as found by ETP) would be cut by about 30% (from about USD 45 to 30 per tonne of CO_2), if CO_2 capture and storage is included, when compared with not using it. This suggests that applying this technology would substantially reduce the cost of emission control.

Using a variety of scenarios[11] can be helpful when considering the implications of climate protection; the results show that known technologies, including the capture and storage of CO_2, should be able to bridge the gap between emissions based on current trends and the levels that would need to be achieved in order to avoid dangerous climate change.

Chapter 7 | Making it happen

of a few (thousand) individuals. Although this will by no means guarantee action, it may be easier to influence this group than to rely on the individual actions of all 6 billion people in the world to achieve global emission reductions.

One thing that we do know will influence everyone's energy-using habits is the cost of energy. Any change in the method of energy supply (to reduce emissions) is likely to increase costs; these will be passed on to the customers, thereby encouraging them to reduce their use of fuel. Although reducing the demand for energy can play a major part in reducing emissions, it is not necessary for the world to regress to lower standards of living in order to protect the climate. Where low

Emission offsets

As an alternative to making all reductions in the home country, it is becoming increasingly popular to purchase emission offsets. In such schemes, the person or company causing the emissions pays someone else to reduce his emissions, or not to increase them as much as he would otherwise do. This is attractive for various reasons, not least the fact that it is consistent with the practice of emissions trading.

Typically, emission offset projects are hosted in developing countries. These may be renewable energy schemes, improvements in energy efficiency, or the planting/management of forests to draw down carbon from the atmosphere and fix it as wood. However, by definition, such schemes have no effect on the emissions of the sponsor or the sponsor's country. Offset schemes merely affect future rises in emissions originating from the host country. As we know that the world is facing a problem due to the current level of emissions, such action will not contribute towards solving this. Indeed, it may aggravate the problem by encouraging the industrialised part of the world to continue with its existing habits of causing high emissions.

Offset projects mainly make use of low-cost opportunities in the developing countries. Recognising that there is a finite capacity for any en-ergy-related activity, if these countries were to participate at a later date in a global agreement for limiting emissions, they might find their best options were not available because they had already been covered by offset contracts. This would mean that the host country would have to make use of more expensive options in order to meet its commitments (although it would have had the use of the income it received when the contract was first agreed).

Forestry-related projects present some of the major difficulties in this respect – forests are not entirely secure places for sequestering carbon; they may be attacked by insects or destroyed by fire in which case the carbon soon returns to the atmosphere. In any case, trees typically have lifetimes of 30 years (in commercial forests) or perhaps 200 years (in non-commercial ones). In the context of climate change, this is not long enough to keep carbon out of the atmosphere. In addition, if the offset project supports new forestry in a region where there are other forests, the effect of this may be just to displace land clearance from one area to another. In terms of value for money, the most effective forest projects involve preventing the destruction of existing forests, but this attracts the criticism that the host country should not have to be paid to preserve its own forests.

emission energy supply technologies are available, their widespread use can deliver a major part of the emission reductions needed. A combination of reduced demand and low-emission supply offers a way of maintaining standards of living whilst taking effective action to combat climate change.

Governments have to set the framework in terms of targets, systems for meeting extra costs, etc. They could require that certain types of energy technology be used, they could impose regulations on levels of emission, they could ration energy, or they could levy "green" taxes on the principal sources of emissions. But currently, the most popular approach is to impose a cap on emissions and allow energy suppliers (and, in future, energy users) to trade with others their rights to emit within that cap. Whichever system is used, it should not favour one measure over another, as that would be wasteful and would increase the overall cost of addressing climate change.

Which measures from the toolbox will be used?

It is immediately clear, when we consider the potential reductions from each of the main sources of emissions, that no single sector of the economy can reduce its emissions enough to meet targets such as those we have proposed. Not even two sectors could do it. Each of the principal sectors has to cut its emissions. The scale of the cuts in each sector may vary, depending on the opportunities for emission reductions in each case, the cost and capacity, but all will have to contribute.

In electricity generation, the growth of renewable sources of energy and the local generation of electricity (with heat recovery) will expand the range and number of sources of electricity. At the same time, industries with a substantial demand for electricity will continue to require reliable supplies at the lowest cost, which will be met mainly by large power stations, including nuclear plants, in industrialised countries. The large-scale interconnection of suppliers and users via national and regional grids will be essential in order for variations in supplies and levels of demand to be balanced.

Controlling the demand for electricity automatically to suit the available supplies will become increasingly acceptable for certain users. Nevertheless, much electricity will still be generated centrally because this offers the lowest cost as well as more reliable supplies than local generation can deliver. Fossil fuels will continue to be used for generating electricity but switching from coal to natural gas, even in accordance with the best modern standards, will produce only limited

Chapter 7 | Making it happen

reductions in emissions. Further reductions will be required. Indeed, as coal is expected to continue to be available as a major fossil fuel, emissions from coal-fired generation will have to be reduced substantially. Improvements in efficiency, whilst necessary, could not achieve this. Meeting such a goal, whilst continuing to use fossil fuels, will only be possible when capturing and storing the CO_2.

Several of the major, energy-using industries can also reduce their emissions substantially. Radical changes to the steel-making process, including the capture and storage of CO_2, could reduce emissions per tonne of steel by 60% by 2050, and even more beyond then. Sharp reductions in emissions would also be possible in cement-making, but this requires addressing the CO_2 arising from the raw materials and from the fuel. With the possible exception of radical changes to the specifications for using cement, CO_2 capture and storage is the only technology that could make such deep reductions.

Emissions from oil refining may be cut by 60% through a combination of efficiency improvements, the combined production of heat and power, and CO_2 capture and storage. The exhaust gases from some chemical processes, such as ammonia and hydrogen production, are almost pure CO_2, allowing the relatively inexpensive capture of CO_2. This could be one of the first places where CO_2 could be captured for storage.

Biofuels require only minor change by the user but are limited only by the agricultural capacity available to make them, as well as the level of emissions arising from the manufacturing processes.

Changing energy carriers for vehicles would involve major changes to fuel storage and may also require different drive-trains, not to mention a radically different fuel distribution system. Zero-carbon energy carriers can be produced from fossil fuels using the capture and storage of CO_2 at a lower cost than when using renewable energy. However, the purchase cost of vehicles designed for these energy carriers will be substantially greater than that of current vehicles. Because most cars are only used from time to time, the substantial capital investment required will mean that the cost of emission reductions will be much greater than in the case of large stationary sources of emissions which are used almost continuously. Changing the energy carriers used in commercial vehicles should spread the extra cost over a much higher degree of usage, thereby keeping down the cost of emission reductions.

Zero-carbon energy carriers could also be used to make sharp reductions in emissions originating from heating appliances in buildings. The practical difficulties of distributing some of these carriers, e.g. heat or hydrogen, should not be under-estimated. Electricity is already widely used for heating buildings in some countries, e.g. Norway, but would probably have to be coupled with heat pumps to ensure a high energy efficiency. In new buildings, high standards of insulation and the effective use of the heat gained from the sun and the occupants should reduce the net heat demand to a small value, making electricity the preferable carrier because it would incur no extra distribution costs.

Are we suggesting that the widespread use of CO_2 capture and storage is the only way forward? Certainly not. There is no magic bullet which can achieve the required deep reductions in greenhouse gas emissions. It is the intensity of the emission reductions together with the breadth of application and the rate at which the measures can be applied that will determine the usefulness of any of these measures. Making sharp reductions will cost more than making mild reductions; some sectors will be more expensive to address than others. Anything which reduces the cost of taking action will be of interest – in the right circumstances, this is what the capture and storage of CO_2 can offer.

The way forward for CO_2 capture and storage

How far and how fast the use of capture and storage expands will depend on both the driving forces behind it and the barriers to its use, several of which we have examined in previous chapters. At the same time, there is a growing interest in this approach from commercial companies faced with finding the best way forward but also faced with a growing number of challenges – national goals for emission reductions; the need to invest in new power stations; the opportunity to develop new business; the desire to use local fuels or not to use nuclear power. These and other factors will influence the extent to which this technology can play a part in reducing global emissions.

At the same time, confidence in the technology will be limited until it has been demonstrated at full-scale in several places. The legality of storage underground, whether onshore or offshore, has to be clarified. Public acceptance must be gained, not least for long-distance pipelines. Such issues require action by government through domestic policy, especially in the developed countries, which is where most of the activity is currently taking place.

Chapter 7 | Making it happen

Capture and storage of CO_2 in the developing countries

It is possible that these projects could be conducted in less developed countries in the future, but the potential for this is restricted, at present, due to problems of funding. Two mechanisms were established under the Kyoto Protocol in order to facilitate action on emission reductions in countries that have not accepted emission reduction targets under the protocol. Where the host country is a signatory to Annex 1 of the Kyoto Protocol[13], the project might be funded via the mechanism known as Joint Implementation. For the developing countries, which tend not to be signatories to Annex 1, the Clean Development Mechanism potentially provides a means for them to obtain emission reduction technology with some of the costs being borne by others who can claim credit for their investment. At present, CO_2 capture and storage is not being accepted for Clean Development Mechanism projects.

Nevertheless, one capture and storage project has already been implemented in a country that is not a signatory to Annex 1 – the In Salah project in Algeria extracts CO_2 from natural gas produced at the site and re-injects it into the same gas field. This project is being monitored in order to demonstrate the potential of CO_2 storage.

Fig. 7.7 The In Salah natural gas project in Algeria involves injection of 1.3 million tonnes per year of CO_2. The project is operated by BP, Sonatrach and StatoilHydro.

Using CO_2 for enhanced oil recovery could be of interest in both the developing countries and the industrialised ones, not least because it would help maintain indigenous oil supplies or avoid job losses as old fields go out of production. A number of developing countries have the potential to host such projects, but the true potential can only be assessed when their underground storage resources have been mapped.

The need for government action – setting domestic policy

In an ideal world, every method of reducing greenhouse gas emissions would receive government support in a comparable way so that users could choose between the options without bias. Unfortunately, real life does not work that way – some emission reduction measures have become known before others, some face public approval whilst others face disapproval, which affects how governments finance them. As a consequence, to take some examples, there are rules setting the

Fig. 7.8 "Putting the world on a low carbon diet." A page from Time Magazine used a picture of the Sleipner platforms as its centrepiece. It is important that projects of this type are used for learning.

efficiency standards for certain types of domestic appliances, and regulations for the construction of new buildings and the refurbishment of existing ones, which determine the level of insulation to be used, whilst there are requirements for the use of renewable sources of electricity, as well as cap and trade systems for some CO_2 sources in some places, and carbon taxes in others.

In Europe, one way of financing projects aimed at protecting the climate is the European Trading Scheme. This is a cap and trade system, so the price to be paid is determined by the level of the cap in relation to the emissions of the companies concerned. Until the price reflects the long-term emission reduction goal, it is unlikely that this system will support CO_2 capture and storage projects, except in individual cases where the cost of capture is low (e.g. capturing CO_2 from concentrated sources). The first large-scale project, the Sleipner project, specifically made use of such a concentrated source, but was not justified by an emissions trading system (Norway was not operating one at that time) but by the avoidance of carbon tax.

Where emission trading takes place, companies may reduce the cost of meeting emission targets by purchasing the right to emit or by selling credits from emission reductions which they have achieved and which lie beyond their own needs. The currently low value of these credits in Europe is a major barrier to investment, coupled with the limited forward period for which they can be obtained[14]. For this system to be able to support major energy projects requiring large investments, it will be necessary that there is a lower cap and a longer forward-view to justify major investment in emission reductions.

In addition to setting the rules for funding and the level of the cap (or the equivalent in other systems), governments are also responsible for reporting the national inventory of emissions each year, as well as environmental protection, health and safety regulations, and many other activities. To avoid a conflict of interests, governments should keep themselves detached from the selection of specific measures for emission reductions, at least once there is enough information available to allow investors to make an informed choice about the portfolio of measures. Governments have recognised the need for support in order to develop technologies to the stage where they are potentially commercial, as has happened with nuclear power, with various renewable sources of energy, and with measures to improve energy efficiency. This ensures that sufficient information is available for commercial users to be able to make informed decisions about whether to use such measures. Such support is necessary in order to demonstrate CO_2 capture and storage in full-scale operation.

The need for government action – establishing a legal framework and a regulatory system

On behalf of society, governments must establish the rules (laws) governing the use of CO_2 capture and storage. Operators of such equipment would be expected to adhere to health, safety and environmental protection rules, as would be the case with any industrial enterprise. Capturing CO_2 would be covered by the regulations governing any major chemical plant. The responsibility for managing the CO_2 in transit would be regulated in the same way as for other pipelines. A key issue concerns the underground storage of CO_2, which is not something that has been done in most countries[15]. National laws will dictate what is to be done in respect of underground storage onshore; few countries have started to review these yet. The development of international conventions on the use of sub-sea formations to store CO_2 was mentioned in chapter 6. The right to use depleted oil or gas fields for storing CO_2, and indeed resolving the competition with other uses of such reservoirs, will also need to be addressed.

It is expected that there will be very little chance of CO_2 escaping from a properly designed and managed storage facility. However, it will be necessary to prepare rules governing damage liability in case some CO_2 does escape. This is likely to continue to be an important issue, at least until sufficient practical experience has been obtained from operating these facilities. Once injection has been completed, the operator of the storage site will continue to be responsible for the ongoing monitoring of the stored CO_2 but, because a commercial company only has a finite lifetime, at some point, it may be necessary for government to take on the responsibility for monitoring the stored CO_2. With the passage of time, storage will become more and more secure but there will still be a need to monitor the condition of wells and to ensure that drilling in the vicinity of the storage site

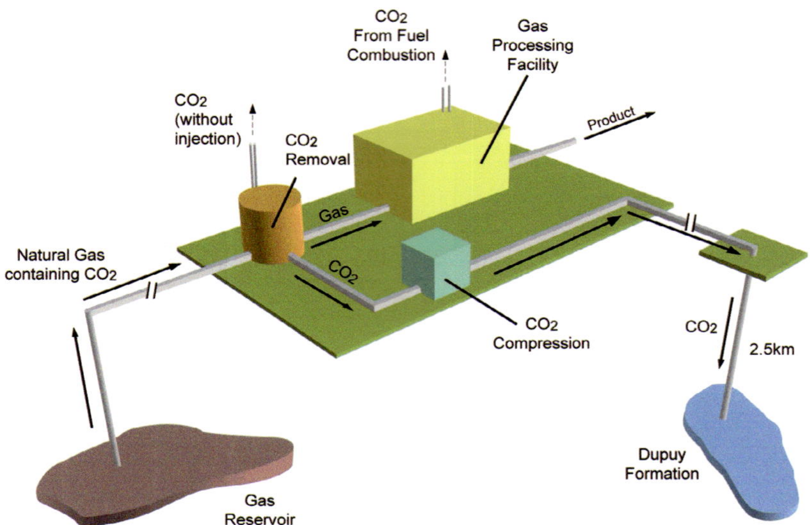

Fig. 7.9 The Gorgon project in Australia: this natural gas production project is at an advanced stage of planning for construction off the northwest coast of Australia. CO_2 occurring in the natural gas will be removed and be injected into a geological formation (Illustration courtesy of the Gorgon Development Project).

is controlled, so governments will need to establish a regulatory agency to supervise these facilities.

An example of how this might develop can be seen in Australia, in connection with the Gorgon project. After CO_2 injection has been completed, the surface facilities will be decommissioned but, it is proposed, monitoring will continue in order to demonstrate site stability[16]. Providing this is satisfactory, and there is no risk to health, safety or the environment, the responsibility for the stored CO_2 will then pass from the operator of the site to the government, as this is the only entity which is likely to persist in the long-term. This plan balances the responsibility of the commercial operator during the operational phase with that of the government during the storage of the CO_2 long after injection has been completed, once storage has been demonstrated to be safe and secure.

It is unclear to what extent the public is familiar with the toolbox of measures for tackling emissions – a few surveys have been carried out with varying results. Awareness of the threat of climate change, as well as the measures which will be necessary, is increasing around the world but to different degrees in different countries. In the Nordic countries, which are on the front line of fighting climate change[17], the public are more motivated to tackle it. Elsewhere, as yet, the new option of capturing and storing CO_2, is not well known, nor is there a clear public attitude towards its use.

Through the medium of this book and other publications, we hope to provide more people with the opportunity to understand the merits of this option.

Given a suitable framework, who will put it into practice?

The first few capture and storage projects have been implemented by oil companies – these are integrated projects involving the capture, transportation, and storage of CO_2. Typically, these store CO_2 extracted from natural gas for commercial reasons. The companies concerned include StatoilHydro, BP, and Gaz de France; Encana in Canada uses CO_2 captured from the gasification of coal to enhance oil recovery.

Oil companies are also involved in several recently announced projects – Statoil-Hydro in Norway, BP in California and Australia, Shell in Australia, Norway and

Fig. 7.10   The Snøhvit project will involve the longest distance transport of CO_2 purely for the purpose of storage. The picture was taken during the laying of the 150 kilometre long CO_2 pipeline, here seen reeled up on the ship. The Melkøya LNG-plant, where the CO_2 is extracted from natural gas, can be seen in the background.

the USA, Chevron in Australia. Some of these projects involve using captured CO_2 to enhance oil recovery, something which is in line with the core business of an oil company. This industry will also be an increasing source of CO_2 emissions in the future as it develops more fields in parts of the world where the gas is particularly susceptible to CO_2 contamination (e.g. in South East Asia). These companies have the knowledge and skills necessary for implementing the capture and storage of CO_2; but does this mean that the oil industry will continue to dominate this field? We shall see.

The downstream, or fuel production, part of the oil industry is currently responsible for substantial emissions from its refineries and other plants, all of which could be fitted with CO_2 capture. Looking to the future, transport fuels may come from different sources, such as via the conversion of gas or coal into liquid fuels, or via the production of hydrogen. As most of these will involve the release of CO_2, these facilities will also have good reason to use CO_2 capture and storage.

Just because the oil industry has the skills needed for CO_2 storage underground, uses CO_2 to enhance oil recovery, and has access to depleted oilfields, this does not necessarily mean that major oil companies will see CO_2 storage as a logical

Fig. 7.11   The "Halten CO_2" project. This feasibility study is being carried out by StatoilHydro and Shell. It will include an 860 MW gas-fired power station with CO_2 capture, transport of CO_2 for underground storage or enhanced oil recovery at Shell's Draugen field, as well as use of the electricity in the gas terminal at Nyhamna and on platforms offshore.

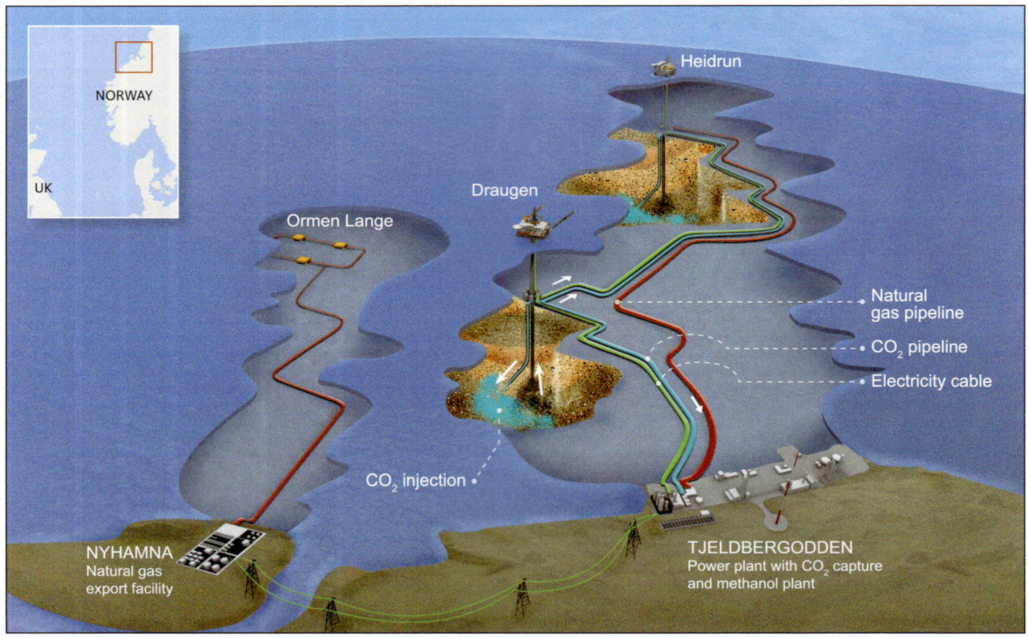

Fig. 7.12   RWE is planning a 450 MW power station based on IGCC technology with CO_2 capture and storage which is intended to be in operation by 2014.

extension of their business model. The history of the oil industry is that smaller companies often take over the management of major oilfields in their later stages from the larger companies who developed them in the first place. A similar evolution is possible in respect of CO_2 storage, with dedicated companies being set up to run such enterprises. These companies would be staffed by geologists and other specialists and would accept the responsibility for injecting and managing the stored CO_2, which might have come from a number of different sources.

Several electricity companies in Europe and elsewhere have announced plans to build power stations, some of which will be fitted with CO_2 capture, whilst others will be similarly fitted if suitable financial arrangements become available to cover the extra cost. Other stations will be refurbished and may also be fitted with CO_2 capture. In view of the large potential for emission reductions, the electricity industry is likely to be one of the prime users of capture equipment.

Responsibility for transporting the captured CO_2 to the storage site is perhaps the most uncertain area to foresee. The CO_2 pipelines in the USA tend to be owned by the users of the CO_2 (which are oil companies), although the pipeline carrying CO_2 to the Weyburn field in Canada is operated by the supplier of the CO_2. For early CO_2 projects, where the pipeline will link one source to one storage site, it might be owned by either the supplier or the user – for example, BP's Peterhead project would have used an existing pipeline already operated by the company, but this was a special case; recent projects announced in Norway rely on the government to fund the pipeline for transporting the captured CO_2 to the oilfields, reflecting the relatively high cost of a pipeline serving a single source of CO_2. Centrica's proposed coal-gasification power station in Northeast England will contract a third party to carry the CO_2. This is an approach likely to be used in other large-scale projects.

As CO_2 storage increases in scale as an activity, it will become possible to couple several sources together, with one major pipeline serving all of them. This will reduce the unit cost of CO_2 transportation and make it more commercial. The variety of organisations involved in the early projects suggests that the final model has not yet been found, especially for transport.

Bottom line

We began this book with the proposition that energy, which is essential for modern society, is being largely ignored because everyone has become accustomed to the reliability and inexpensiveness of current supplies, especially hydrocarbons. We explained how further resources of hydrocarbons, not currently in use, could easily be turned into substitutes for today's transport fuels. The problem is that the continued use of fossil fuels is the main contributor to climate change. Growing recognition of the threat this poses to many people on this planet is causing a re-examination of how the world obtains and uses its energy.

Many options are available which could reduce the demand for energy or could replace fossil fuels, thereby cutting emissions of greenhouse gases. But some are expensive and others do not have the capacity to supply energy in the quantities required today. An additional item is now available in our toolbox – the capture and storage of CO_2. This would provide a means of continuing to use fossil fuels whilst cutting emissions considerably. It is likely that this could contribute substantially to reducing emissions from electricity generation, industry, and transport.

It is still necessary to finalise the legal implications of this new technology, to arrange methods of funding it, and to ensure it will be acceptable to the public. Steps are being taken in countries around the world to handle these issues. There are good prospects that substantial numbers of these systems will be built within the next 20 years. Using the capture and storage of CO_2 will enable the world to buy time whilst it adjusts to the reality of climate change.

We will not run out of fossil fuels anytime soon, but we may be rapidly running out of atmosphere. As Sir Winston Churchill said: "It's no use saying, 'we are doing our best.' You have got to succeed in doing what is necessary."

Suggestions for further reading

Climate Change 2001: Mitigation, 2001. Prepared by Working Group III of the Intergovernmental Panel on Climate Change. Cambridge University Press, Cambridge, United Kingdom and New York, NY, USA.

IPCC Special Report on Carbon Dioxide Capture and Storage. 2005. Prepared by Working Group III of the Intergovernmental Panel on Climate Change [Metz, B., O. Davidson, H. C. de Coninck, M. Loos, and L. A. Meyer (eds.)]. Cambridge University Press, Cambridge, United Kingdom and New York, NY, USA, 442 pp.

Energy – The Changing Climate. 22nd report by The Royal Commission On Environmental Pollution, June 2000. London.

Endnotes

1   "Climate Change 2007: The Physical Science Basis." From the Summary for Policymakers. Contribution of Working Group I to the Fourth Assessment Report of the Intergovernmental Panel on Climate Change, February 2007.

2   The *World Commission on Environment and Development* (WCED) became known by the name of its Chair, Gro Harlem Brundtland. The commission was convened by the United Nations in response to the 1983 General Assembly Resolution A/38/161: "Process of preparation of the Environmental Perspective to the Year 2000 and Beyond."

3   Kyoto Protocol to the UNFCCC, 1998, United Nations, New York.

4   UNFCCC: http://unfccc.int/2860.php

5   Equivalent targets would need to be set for other greenhouse gases.

6   Except for the more exotic measures such as those involving mirrors in space or dusting the atmosphere.

7 IPCC Special report on Carbon Dioxide Capture and Storage, Cambridge University Press, 2005.

8 Often referred to as a carbon price.

9 IPCC Special report on Carbon Dioxide Capture and Storage, Cambridge University Press, 2005, Figure 8.6.

10 "Energy Technology Perspectives" 2006. OECD-IEA, Paris.

11 No scenario is a forecast, since we have no way of knowing how the next 30, 50 or 100 years may develop – each one represents a plausible view of the future, which may or may not happen.

12 The 3C Initiative, a group of 17 companies, is calling for the integration of climate issues into the world of markets and trade facilitated by a global framework from 2013. In another initiative, 10 major US-based companies and four leading environmental organizations have formed the US Climate Action Partnership to call on the US government to enact strong national legislation to achieve significant reduction in greenhouse gas emissions.

13 Parties include the industrialized countries that were members of the OECD (Organisation for Economic Co-operation and Development) in 1992, plus countries with Economies In Transition (the EIT Parties), including the Russian Federation, the Baltic States, and several Central and Eastern European States.

14 The second phase of the European Trading Scheme will coincide with the first commitment period of the Kyoto Protocol 2008–2012.

15 Exceptions are Canada, which for some years has been injecting gases containing CO_2 underground, and the USA which has been using CO_2 to enhance oil recovery for 30 years.

16 As time passes, the CO_2 will become more and more strongly bound to the formation so the risk of escape will be reduced.

17 Such countries, at the highest latitudes, are where increasing temperatures are being felt first.

Chapter 7 | Making it happen

Picture credits

Keywords